Historical Thinking Skills Workbook

A Workbook for World History

John P. Irish

Carroll Senior High School, Southlake, Texas

Barbara S. Brun-Ozuna

Paschal High School, Fort Worth, Texas

W. W. Norton & Company has been independent since its founding in 1923, when William Warder Norton and Mary D. Herter Norton first published lectures delivered at the People's Institute, the adult education division of New York City's Cooper Union. The firm soon expanded their program beyond the Institute, publishing books by celebrated academics from America and abroad. By midcentury, the two major pillars of Norton's publishing program—trade books and college texts—were firmly established. In the 1950s, the Norton family transferred control of the company to its employees, and today—with a staff of four hundred and a comparable number of trade, college, and professional titles published each year—W. W. Norton & Company stands as the largest and oldest publishing house owned wholly by its employees.

Printed in the United States of America

Director of High School Publishing: Jenna Bookin Barry
Project Editor: Melissa Atkin
Editorial Assistant: Aimee Lam
Managing Editor, College: Marian Johnson
Managing Editor, College Digital Media: Kim Yi
Production Manager: Sean Mintus
Composition: Westchester
Manufactured in the United States by LSC Communications

ISBN 978-0-393-602470 (pbk.)

W. W. Norton & Company, Inc., 500 Fifth Avenue, New York, NY 10110-0017 wwnorton.com

W. W. Norton & Company Ltd., Castle House, 75/76 Wells Street, London WIT 3QT

4 5 6 7 8 9 0

John P. Irish received his BA in philosophy and political science, MA in philosophy, and MLS in humanities from Southern Methodist University, and is currently a doctorate student in their humanities program. His research and dissertation topic are on the role that early nineteenth-century American literature had in shaping the American character. John has been teaching for over fifteen years and currently teaches AP® U.S. History, American Studies, and Introduction to Philosophy at Carroll Senior High School in Southlake, Texas.

Barbara S. Brun-Ozuna moved from Switzerland to Fort Worth, Texas, in 1979, and has taught history in the Fort Worth Independent School District since she graduated with a BA in history and Spanish from Texas Christian University in 1990. While teaching, she attended the University of North Texas from where she graduated with an MA in history in 1995. Barbara has taught the AP® World History class since its inception in 2001, first piloting the course for the district and then formally proposing its adoption by the school board. Barbara has also spent time on vertical articulation within the discipline, aligning the pre-AP® World Geography course to the AP® World History course and writing its curriculum for the district. Barbara is currently the dean of instruction and assistant principal at Paschal High School, working to maintain high academic standards for her school while continuing her involvement with AP® World History by teaching one class. She is the mom of two kids—Courtland and Sydney—and the wife of a band director and musician—Rene.

Contents

Causation

Comparison

Defining the Period

Contextualization and Synthesis

Turning Points

Continuity and Change

Argumentation

Interpretation

Chronological Reasoning

Preface

A Workbook for World History is the third in the series of *Historical Thinking Skills* workbooks. The first in the series, *A Workbook for U.S. History*, garnered attention in high school U.S. History classrooms, particularly because of its alignment with the newly redesigned AP® U.S. History course. We hope that this World History edition will empower teachers and engage students of both regular and AP classes as much as the U.S. History edition did, and we are thankful to all the teachers who shared their enthusiasm and feedback with us during the creation of these two workbooks.

These workbooks offer nine types of carefully designed graphic organizers, which can be used in a number of different ways. We encourage you to use these graphic organizers to help students conceptualize the specific historical content under investigation in your class. Allow students time to digest the content independently; have them fill in these graphic organizers as notes during a chapter reading on their own; then as a class, ask students to share their thoughts or conclusions. Collaborate as a class to complete the worksheets, not always but often allowing students to interact with their peers while they discuss the topics with one another. Challenge the class by using Socratic questioning to make students think and rethink their positions. Have students challenge one another to incite debates. In fact, there is only one way that we do not want workbooks to be used, and that is by simply handing them out to students, sitting at your desk, and collecting them at the end of the class. The purpose of these workbooks is to get students critically thinking about the historical content in unique and creative ways.

These graphic organizers have helped tremendously to make our classrooms more student-centered. We are becoming facilitators of learning, using these graphic organizers as springboards to get students writing, which is an important step for students to be successful on the AP exams—as well as in college and life. We use these worksheets to assign follow-up or remediation activities for individual students, asking them to develop their own thesis statements based on their conclusions from the worksheet activities, especially since most of these activities resemble essay prompts from the AP exams. Thus, you can use this workbook as a resource to touch on all three elements of history courses: content, skills, and writing. None of these exist in a vacuum, and none are mutually exclusive. In fact, how would someone teach these historical thinking skills without reinforcing the content? How would someone teach writing without reinforcing the content and the relevant skills?

There are a number of folks to be thanked for all their help and encouragement with these workbooks.

First, Barbara Brun-Ozuna, coauthor of this book, who agreed to join me in publishing this workbook. Her knowledge of world history is impressive, and her enthusiasm for this project is much appreciated.

Second, the staff at W. W. Norton & Company, Jenna Barry, Melissa Atkin, Sean Mintus, Christina Illig, Aimee Lam, and Sumit Poudyal. Jenna showed continued confidence in me when I approached her with the idea for a third workbook. Melissa has been and continues to be an outstanding editor, even with the addition of a new member to her immediate family. Sean, who oversaw the design and production process, was instrumental in helping us meet some tight deadlines. Aimee helped us track down original sources for the Interpretation section. Sumit has been an outstanding proofreader with a passion for world history. Christina spends a tremendous amount of time promoting these books to teachers and school districts across the country. These workbooks would not be here if not for them, their support, hard work, and dedication to bringing the best resources to teachers. They have been great to work with, and they continue to confirm my decision to sign with Norton for publication of the *Historical Thinking Skills* workbooks.

Third, my students who have tested all of these skills over the past two years as AP World History rolled out its redesign. A number of changes from the U.S. History workbook have been implemented in the European and World History workbooks thanks, in part, to them. My students (past, present, and future) always serve as a source of motivation and encouragement to me and always remind me why I do what I do.

Fourth, my father, Johnny Irish, who was so enthusiastic about the publication of the World History Workbook. When things got stressful and I got down, I knew I could always swing by his house and just talk. He always offered me a place to vent, laugh, and cry. His support is essential to anything that I do in life and I cannot thank him enough. He always makes me keep my eye on the big picture, so when things do not go as planned, he is always there to remind me how much my work means to lots of other folks. I care about him more than words can describe.

Fifth, my wife, Elizabeth, and our immediate family. She continues to give valuable feedback on these projects. Without her support and encouragement, this book goes nowhere. Our dog Annie, who constantly reminds me that she exists and needs attention, even when I am really busy, by surprising me by jumping on my lap. Our dog Nellie, who reminds me of how much life can and should be taken in strides and lets me know how much fun our walks are, especially when it's just the two of us. And last but not least, our three cats, Tom, Katy, and Lucy. All three chose us as their family, and I cannot imagine how empty life would be without the three of them. This is my immediate family, and it is the best family a guy could wish for.

To all of these folks I say, thank you!

John P. Irish

Student Instructions: Causation

When we are asked to identify the historical causation of an event, we are asked to identify the events that led up to the historical event under investigation as well as the results of the event. There can be both long-term and short-term causes and effects. Long-term events are those that are further away from the historical event under investigation, and short-term events are those that are more immediate to the historical event under investigation.

The purpose of these Causation activities is to investigate the causes and effects of different events in history. On the surface, it may appear easy to identify different causes and effects; however, upon closer examination, it might be surprising to see certain event having stronger causal connections with one than others. It is also important to practice identifying long-term versus short-term causes and effects, and evaluating the most and least important causes and effects of historical events.

■ NAME: ______________________ ■ Date: __________

Causation: Neolithic Revolution (Example)

CAUSE		EFFECT
Spreading of seeds of desirable plants, probably accidentally at first but then deliberately	→	Growing of wheat, rice, barley
Growing population led to the need for more diverse food supply.	→	Permanent settlement
Domestication, very slowly, of plants and animals	→	Social stratification

Most Important and Why?

Permanent settlement because that is what led to social stratification, development of government, and monumental architecture. The creations of cities and city-states were the building blocks of civilization.

Least Important and Why?

Although we cannot imagine not having a varied diet, diversity of plants was not an important cause for the Neolithic revolution. Rather, it was the fact that a plant or animal could be domesticated. Reliably domesticable plants and animals were critical in allowing humans to rely on agriculture rather than hunting and gathering.

■ NAME: ______________________ ■ Date: ____________

Causation: Neolithic Revolution

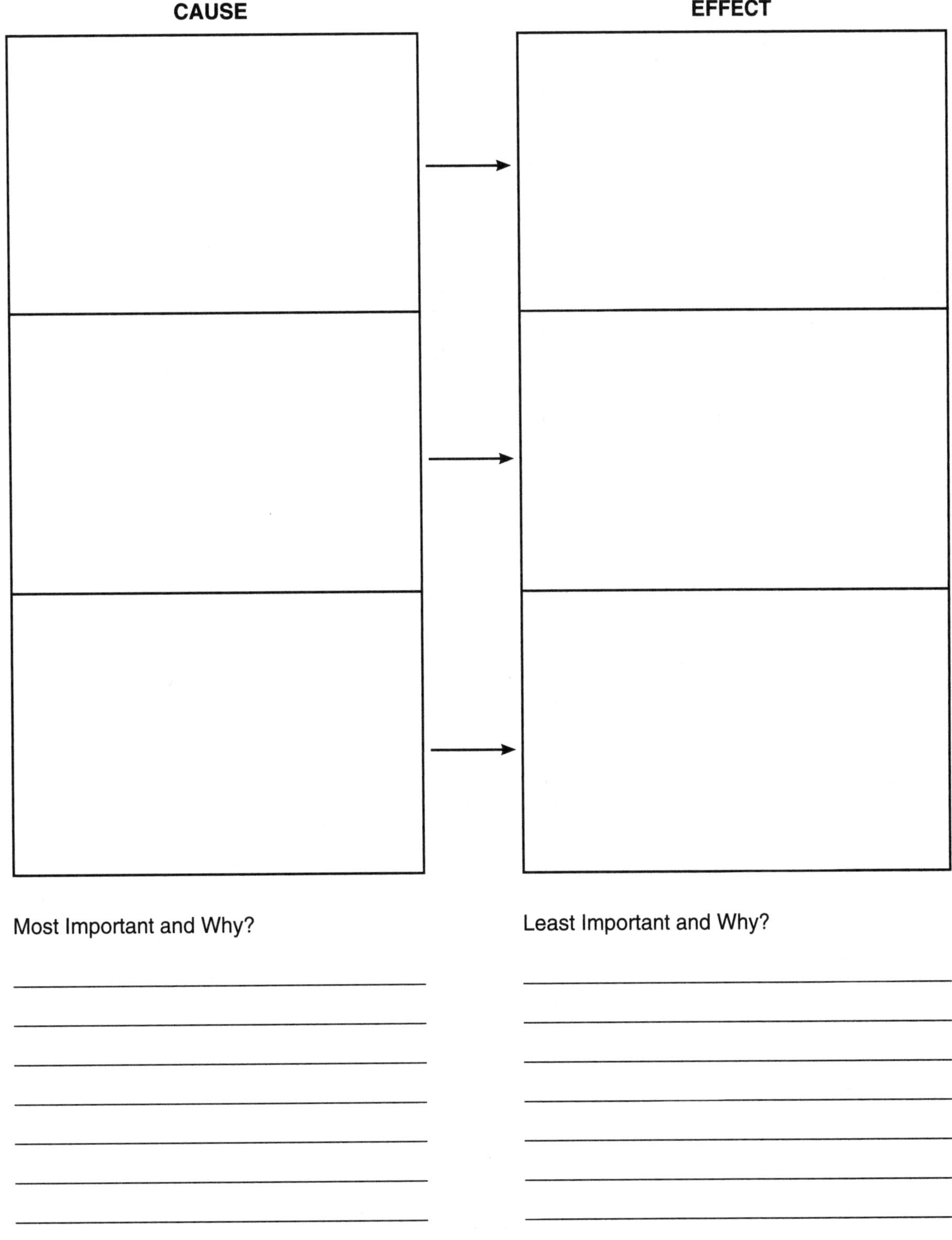

Most Important and Why?

____

Least Important and Why?

____

■ NAME: ____________________ ■ Date: __________

Causation: City-States

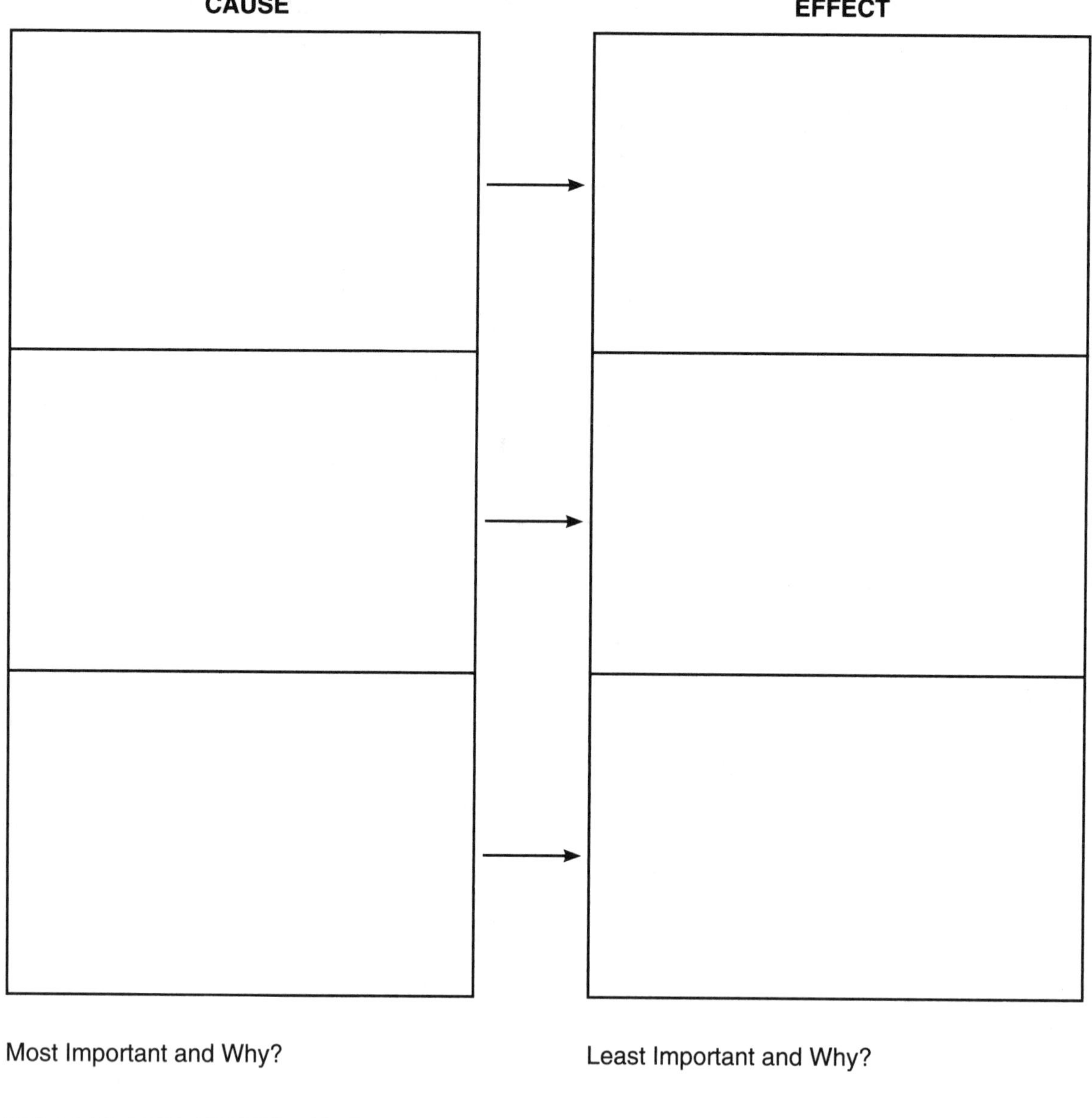

Most Important and Why?

Least Important and Why?

■ NAME: ____________________ ■ Date: __________

Causation: Codification of Religions

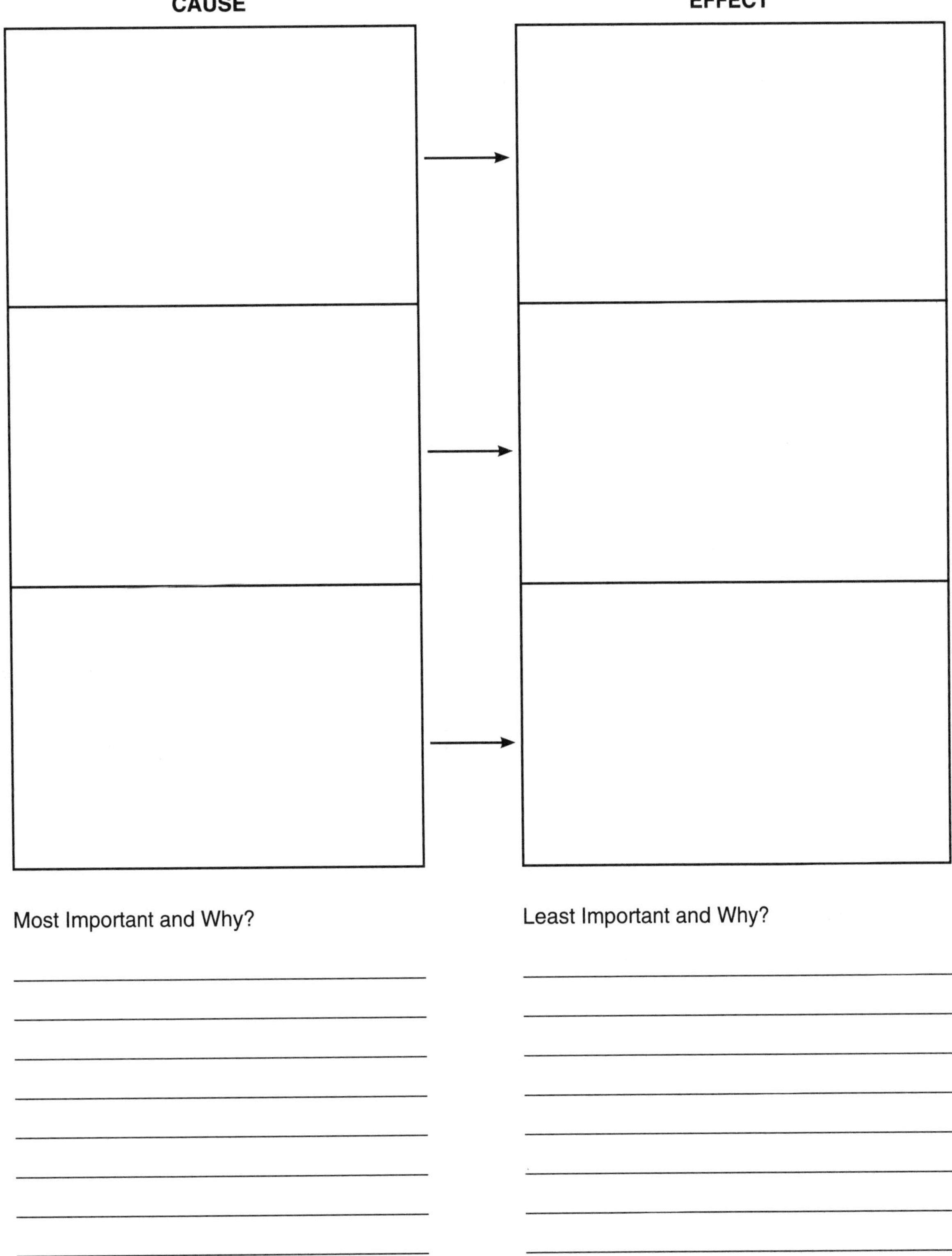

Most Important and Why?

Least Important and Why?

CA4

■ NAME: ______________________________ ■ Date: ____________

Causation: Development of Large Empires

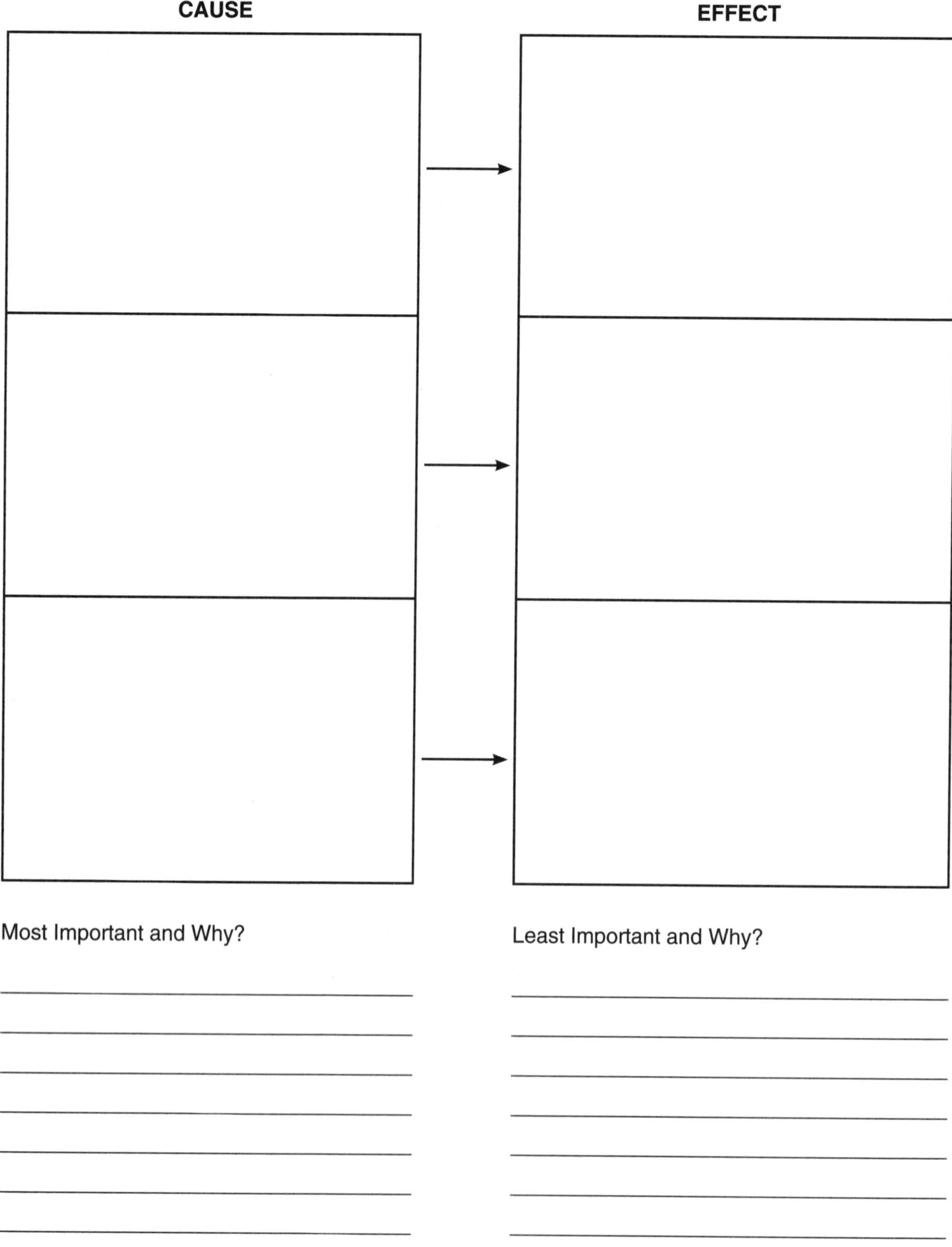

Most Important and Why?

____
____
____
____
____
____
____
____

Least Important and Why?

____
____
____
____
____
____
____
____

■ NAME: ______________________________ ■ Date: ____________

Causation: Patriarchy

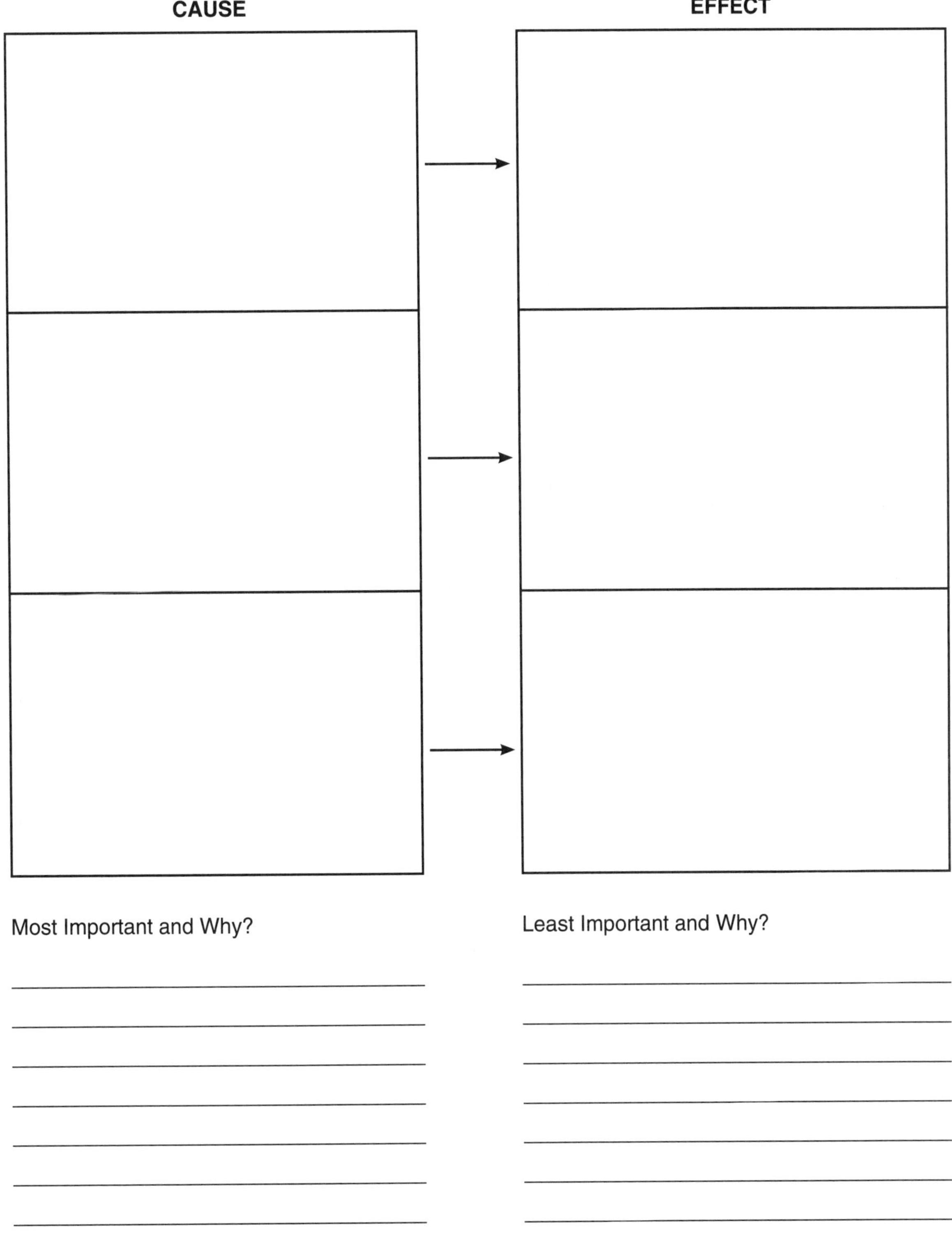

■ NAME: ____________________ ■ Date: __________

Causation: Long-Distance Communication and Exchange

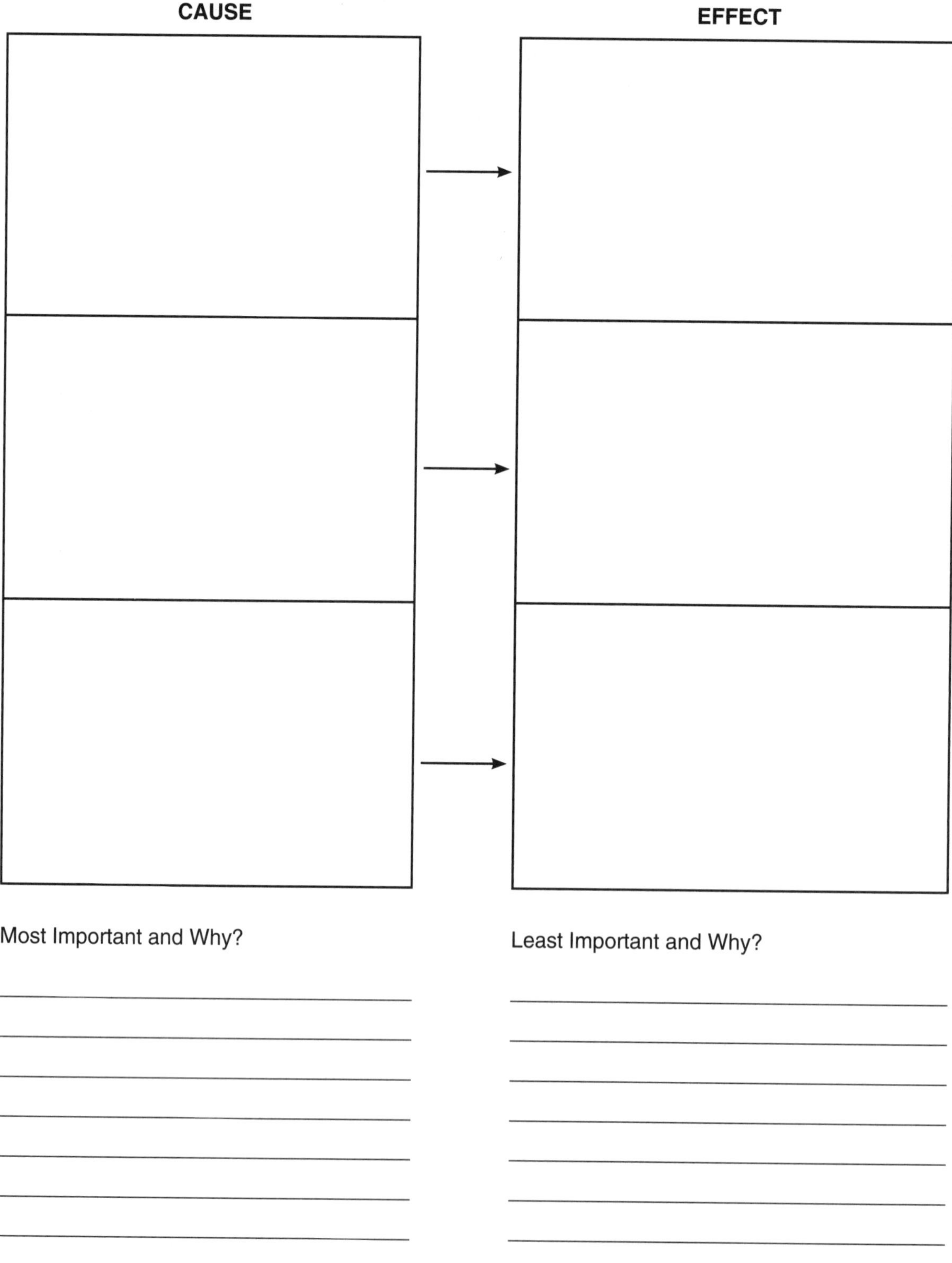

Most Important and Why?

Least Important and Why?

■ NAME: ______________________________ ■ Date: ____________

Causation: Diffusion of Arabic in Afro-Eurasia

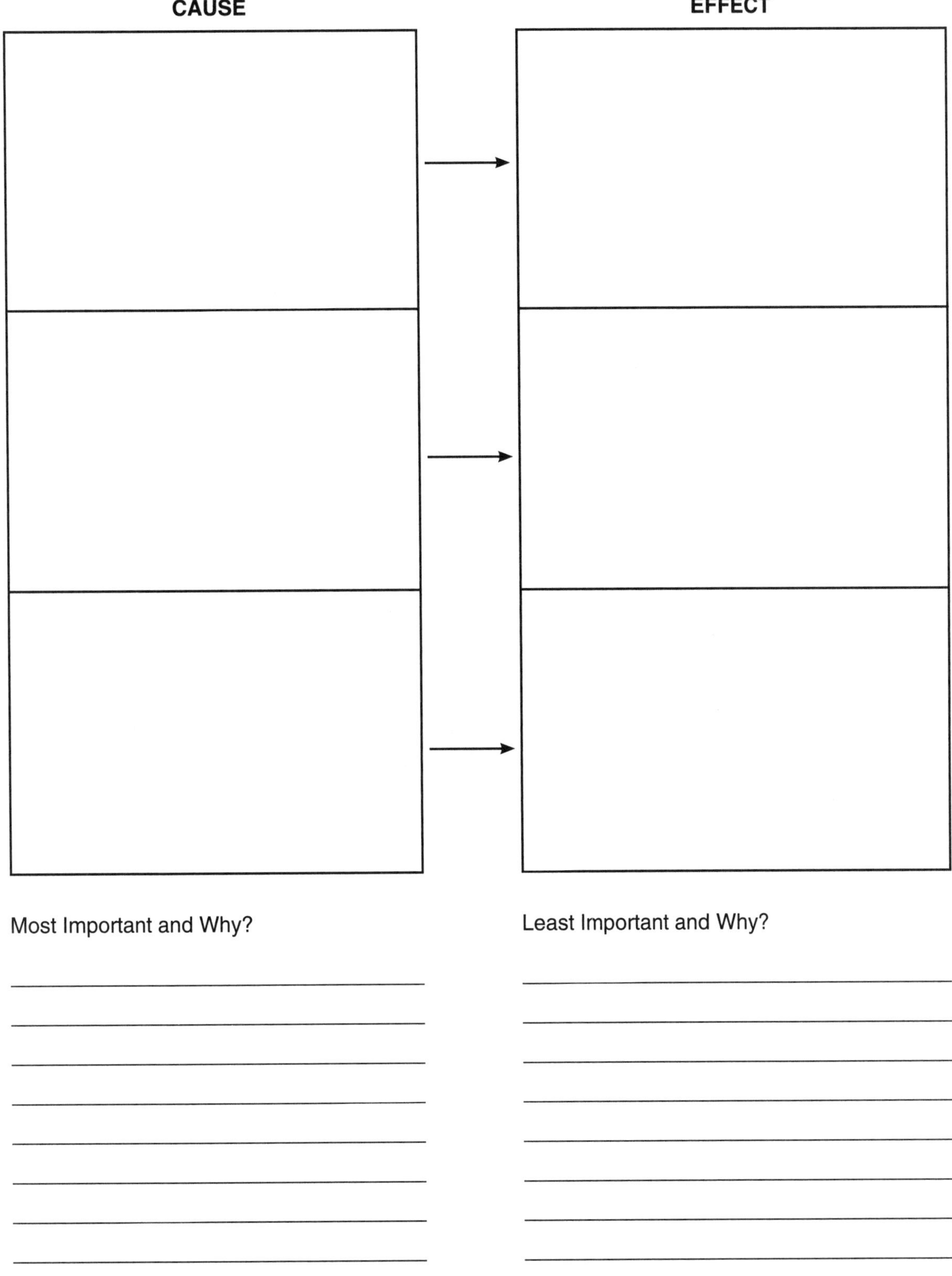

Most Important and Why?

____
____
____
____
____
____
____
____

Least Important and Why?

____
____
____
____
____
____
____
____

■ NAME: ______________________________ ■ Date: ______________

Causation: Bubonic Plague in 14th-Century Eurasia

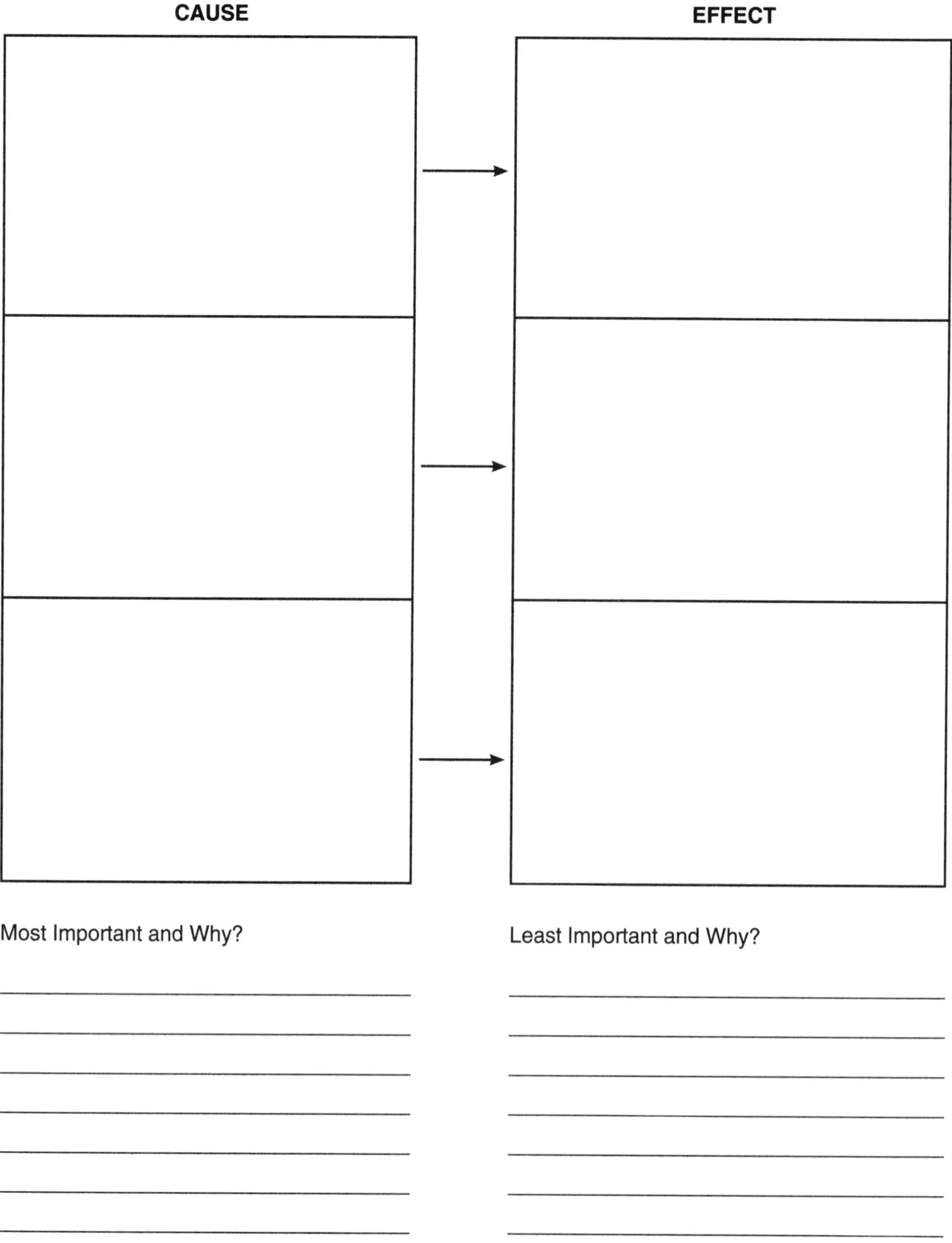

Most Important and Why?

____
____
____
____
____
____
____
____

Least Important and Why?

____
____
____
____
____
____
____
____

■ NAME: ____________________ ■ Date: __________

Causation: Interregional Conflict in the 12th Century

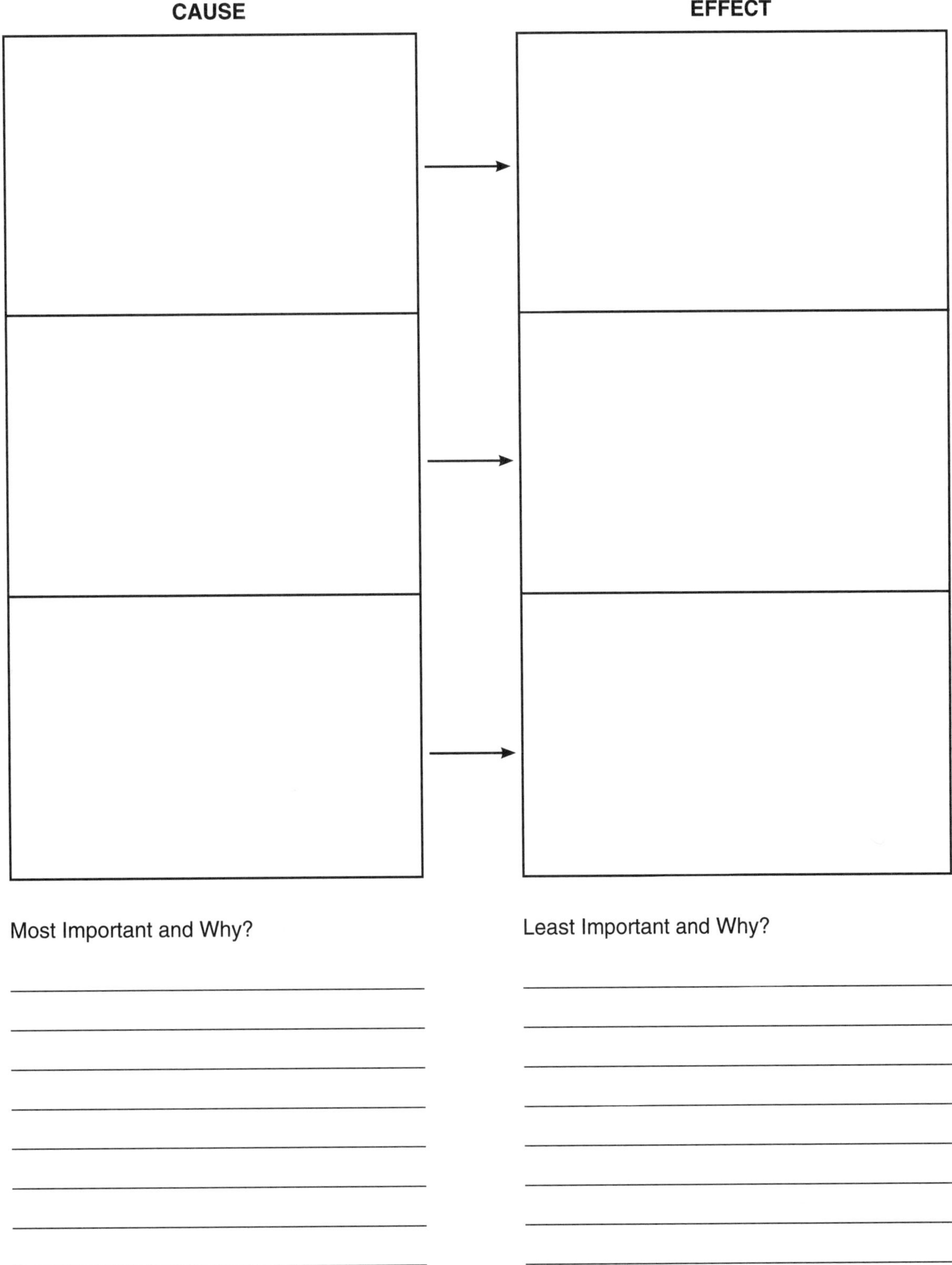

Most Important and Why?

Least Important and Why?

■ NAME: ______________________ ■ Date: __________

Causation: African Diaspora from 1500 to 1800

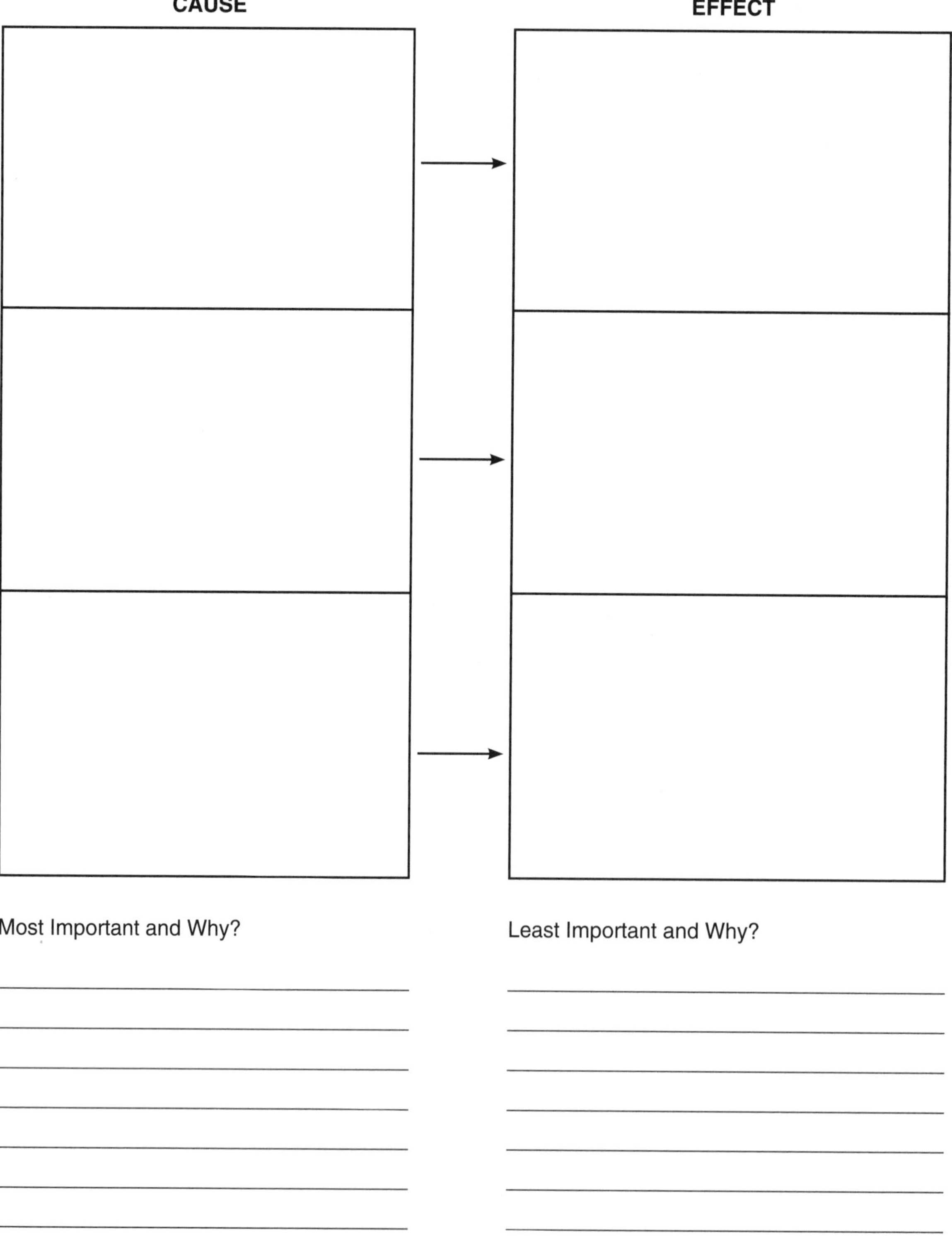

Most Important and Why?

____

____

____

____

____

____

____

____

Least Important and Why?

____

____

____

____

____

____

____

____

■ NAME: ______________________ ■ Date: ____________

Causation: Coerced Labor

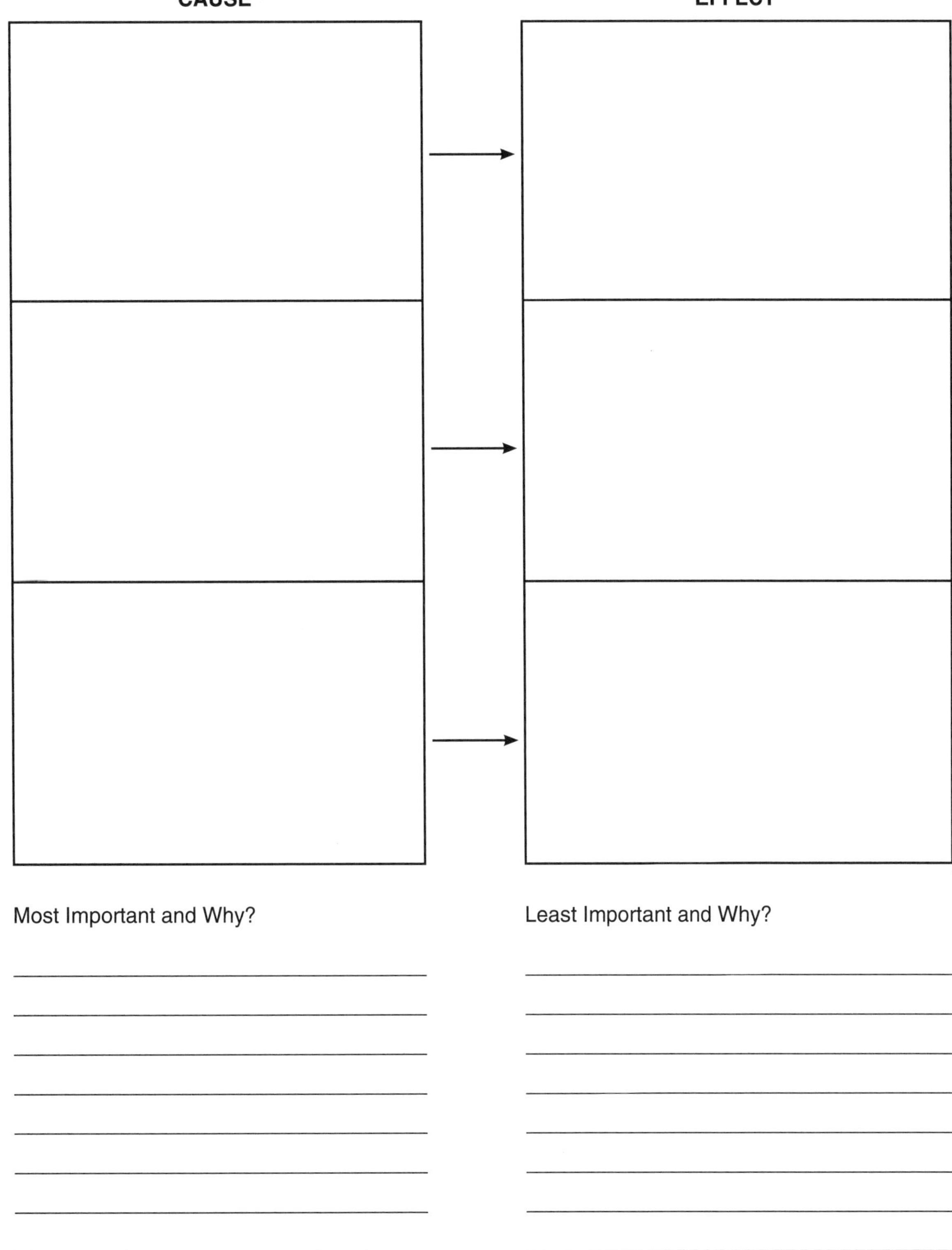

Most Important and Why?

Least Important and Why?

■ NAME: ______________________________ ■ Date: ____________

Causation: Extensive Plantation Agriculture

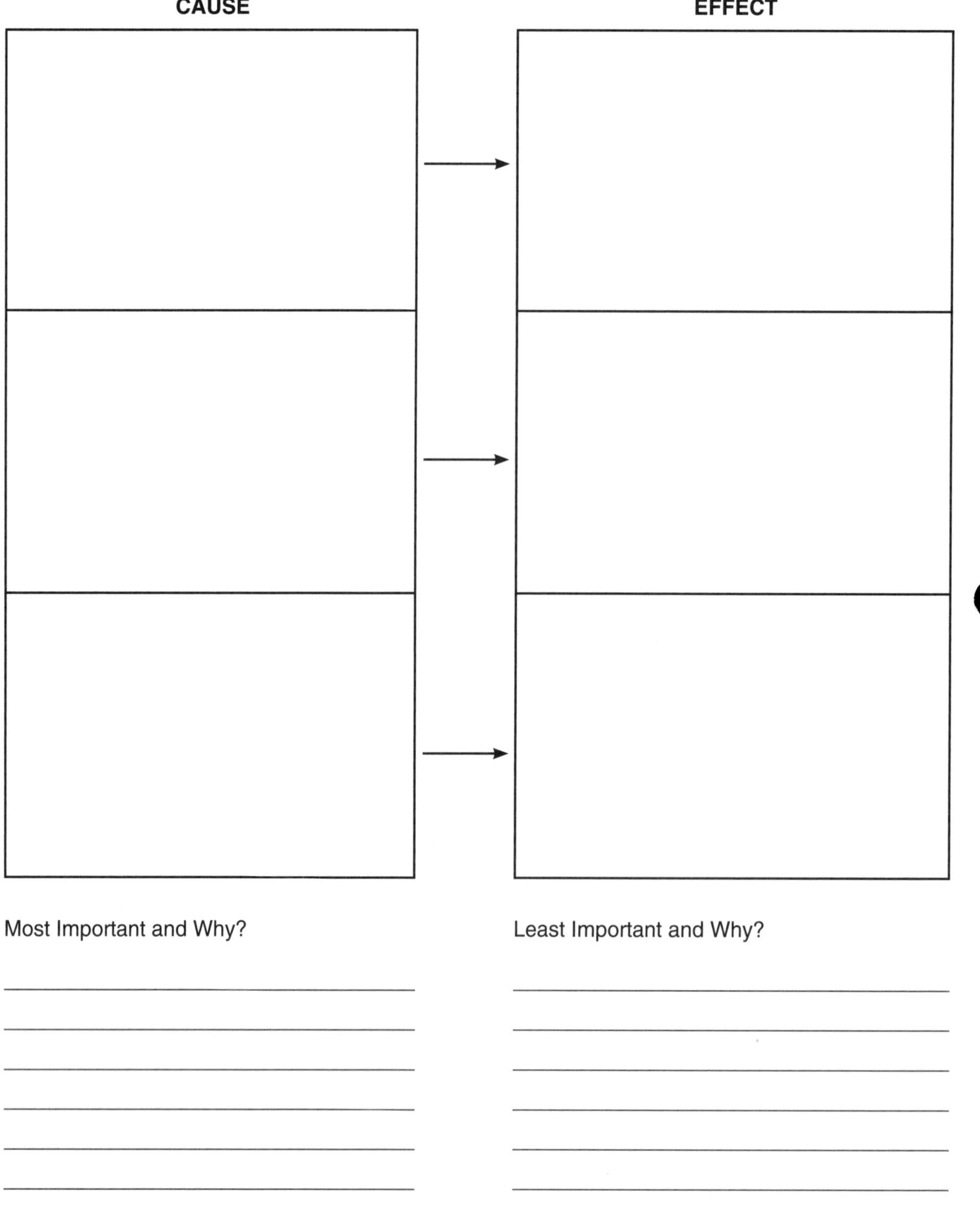

Most Important and Why?

Least Important and Why?

■ NAME: ____________________ ■ Date: __________

Causation: Marxism

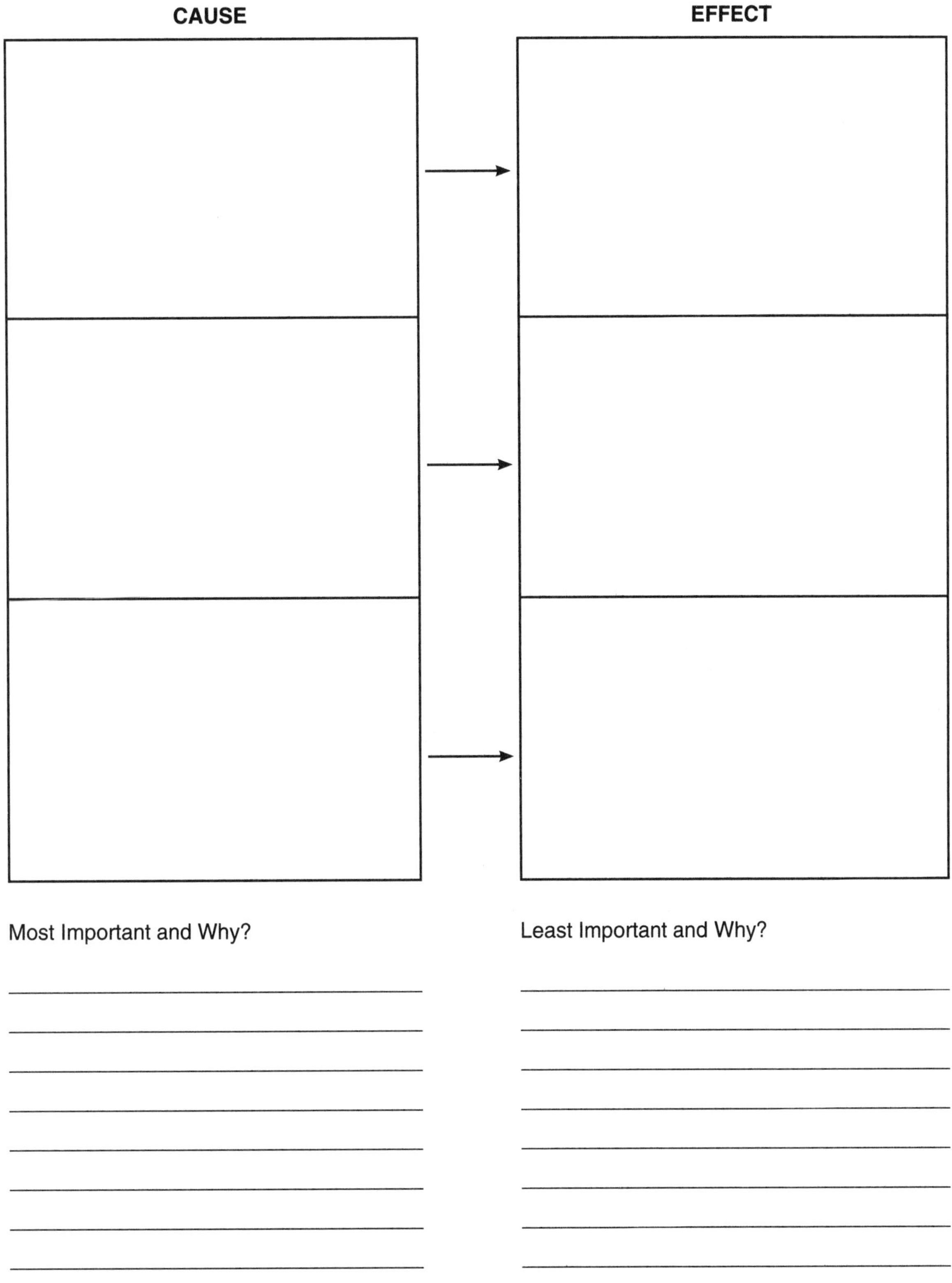

Most Important and Why?

Least Important and Why?

■ NAME: ________________________ ■ Date: ____________

Causation: Creation of the Middle Class

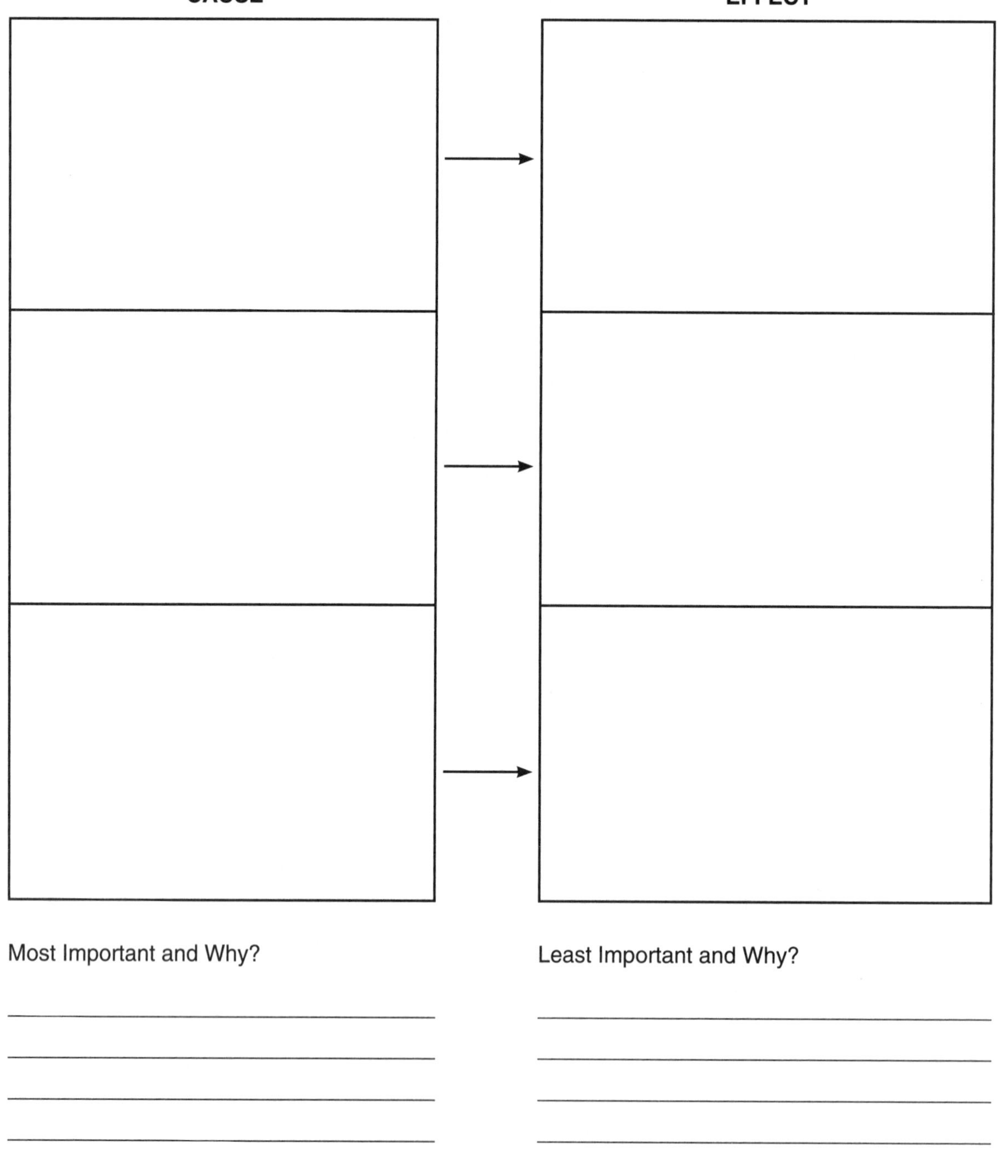

Most Important and Why?

____
____
____
____
____
____
____
____

Least Important and Why?

____
____
____
____
____
____
____
____

■ NAME: ______________________ ■ Date: __________

Causation: Capitalism

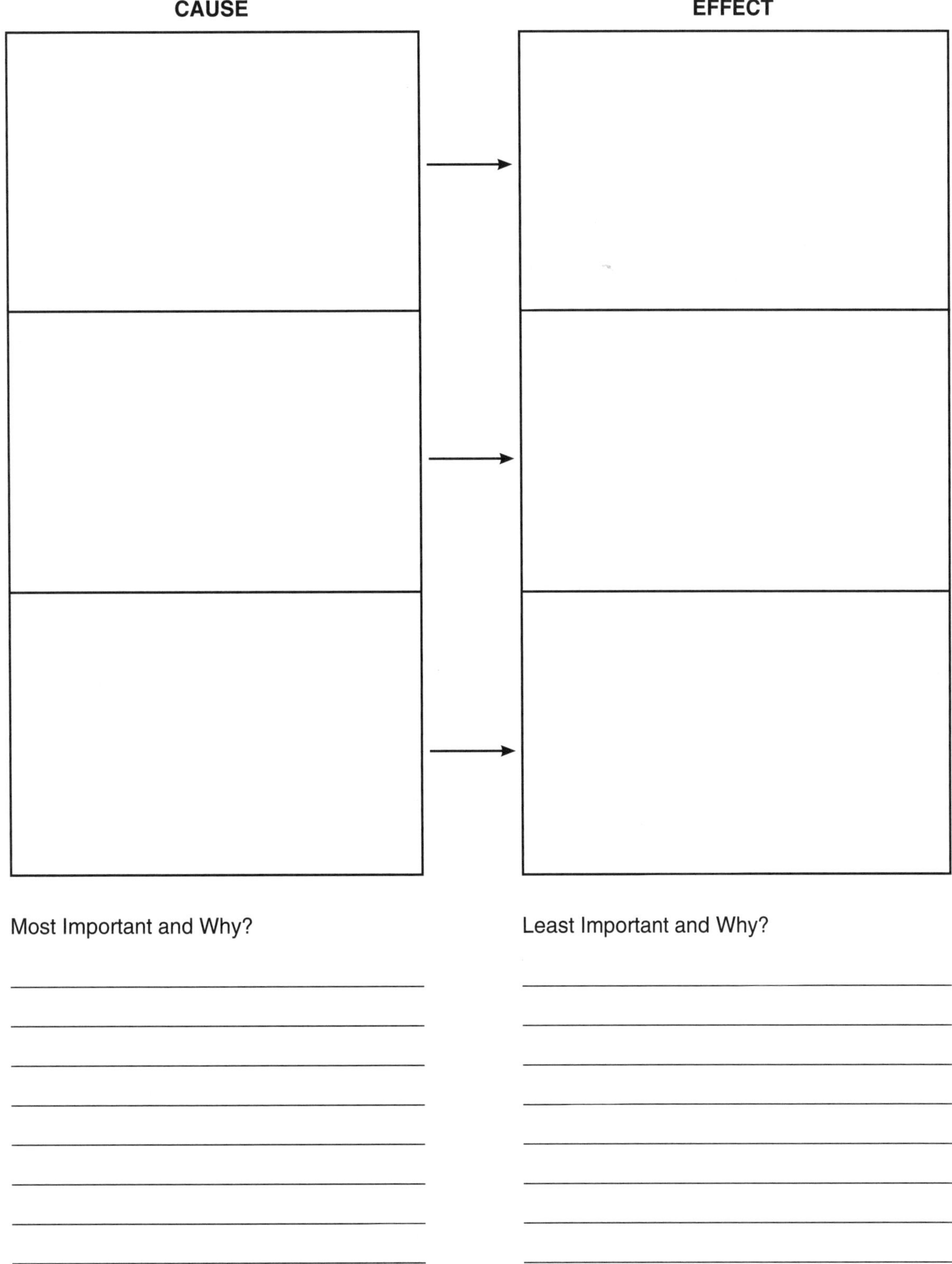

Most Important and Why?

Least Important and Why?

■ NAME: ______________________________ ■ Date: ______________

Causation: Rapid Urbanization

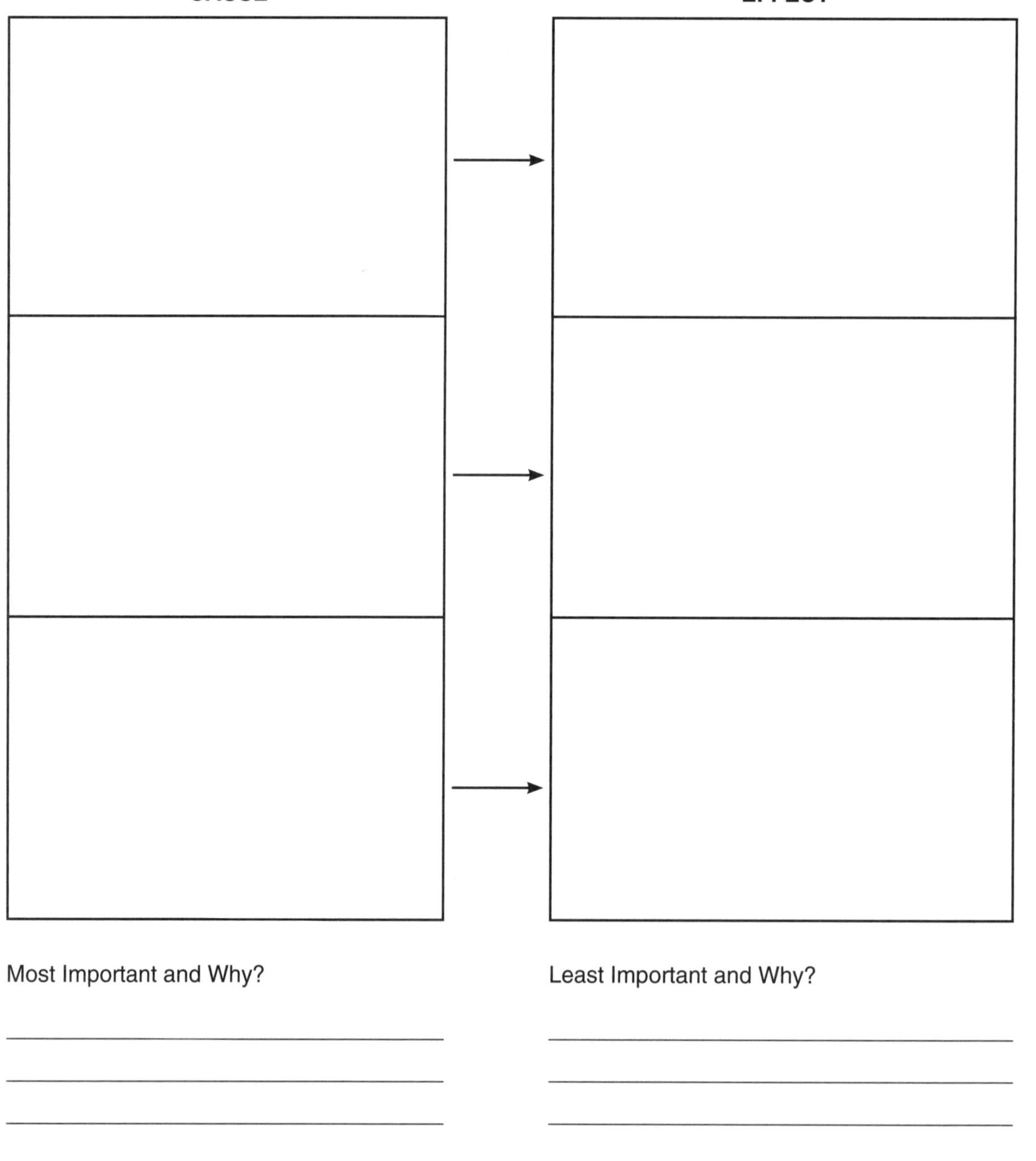

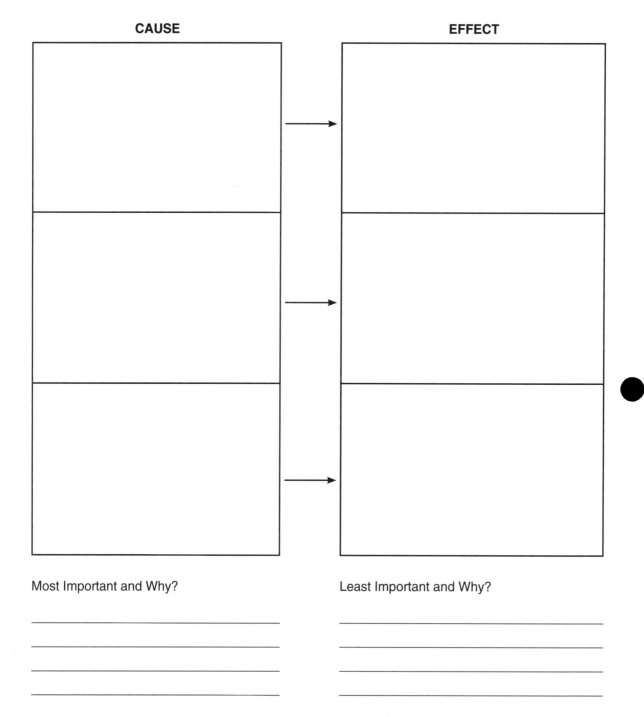

Most Important and Why?

____
____
____
____
____
____
____
____

Least Important and Why?

____
____
____
____
____
____
____
____

■ NAME: ______________________ ■ Date: __________

Causation: New Gender Roles

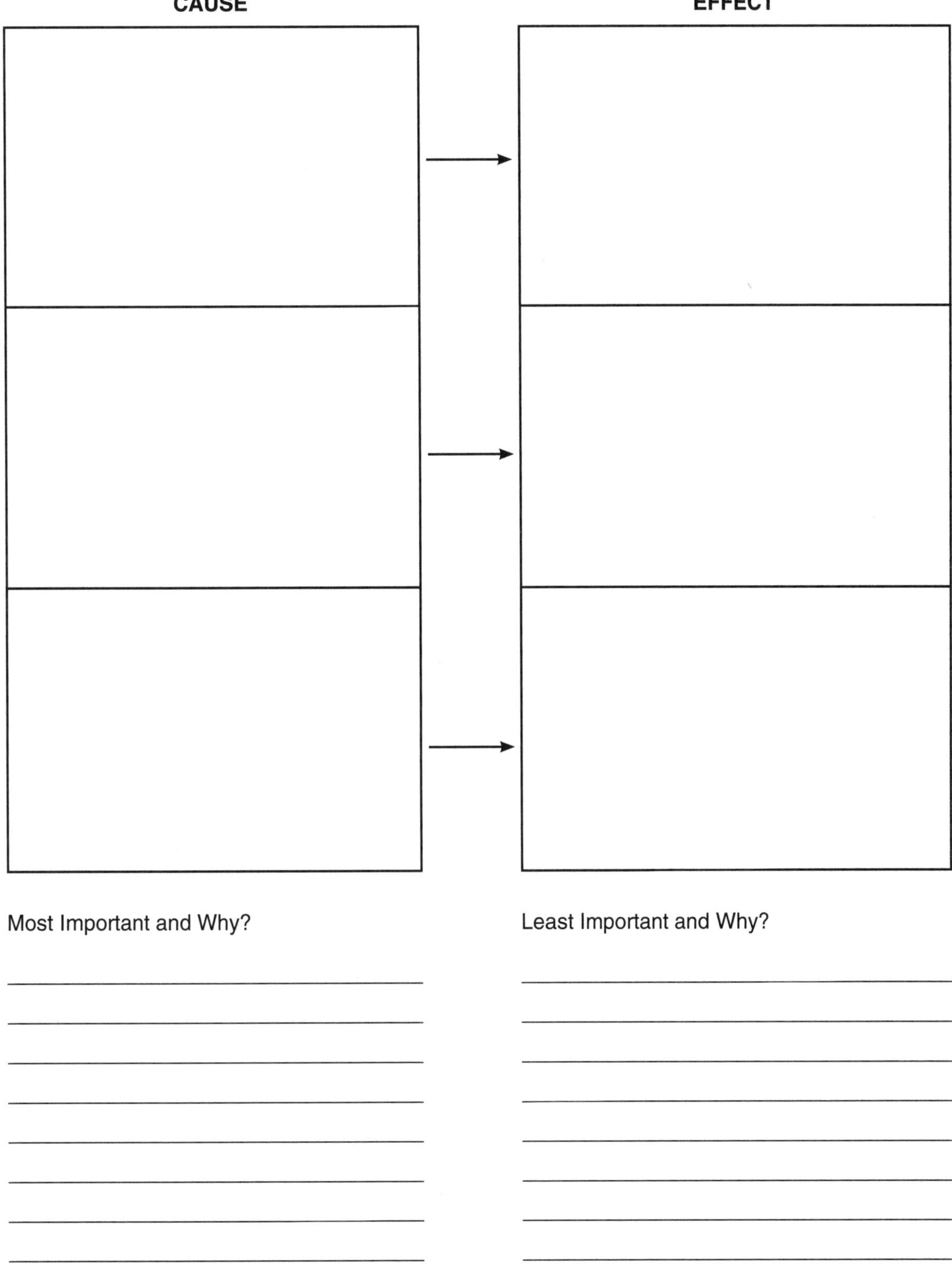

Most Important and Why?

Least Important and Why?

■ NAME: ______________________ ■ Date: ____________

Causation: Formation of the Nation-State

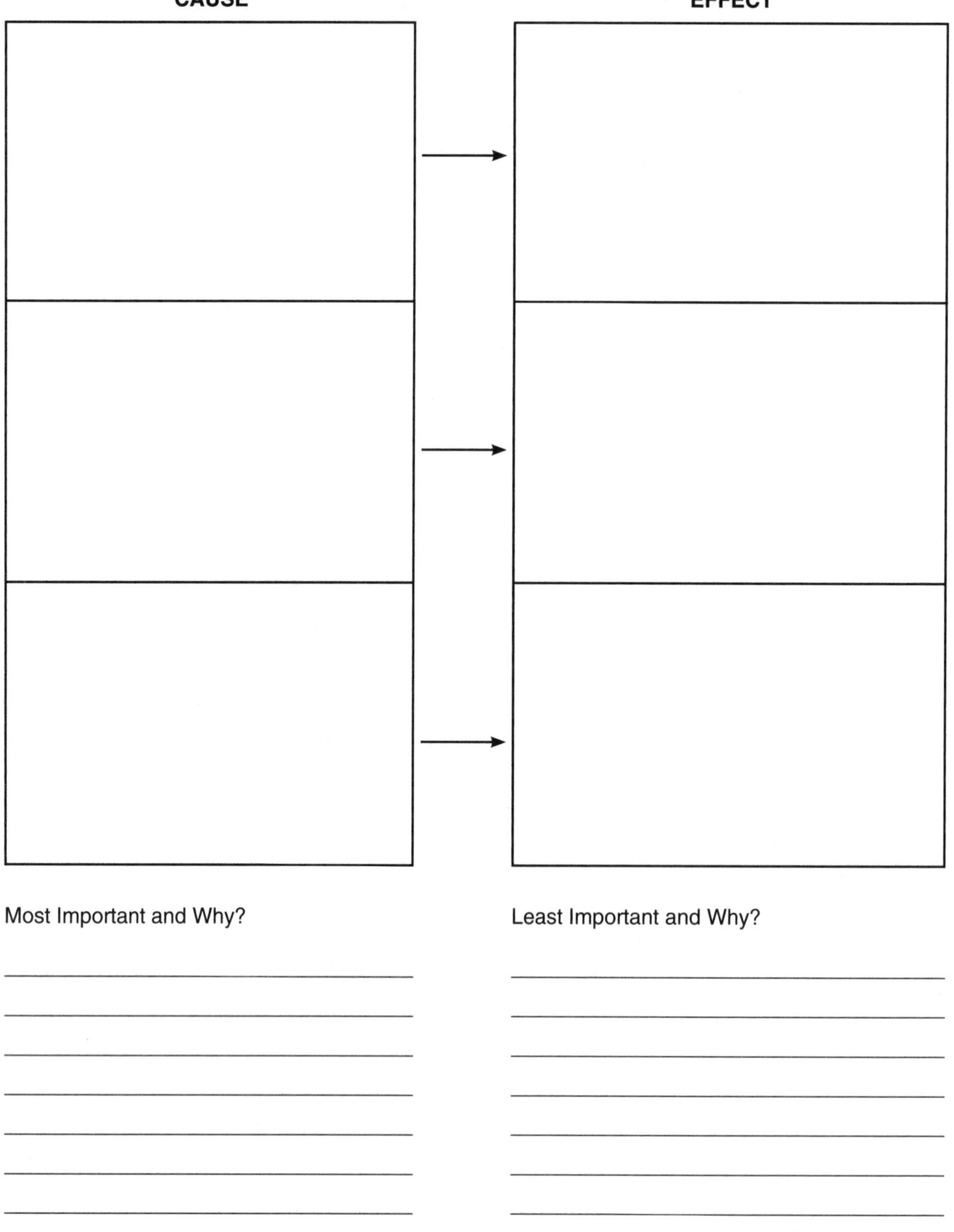

Most Important and Why?

Least Important and Why?

■ NAME: ______________________ ■ Date: __________

Causation: Social Darwinism

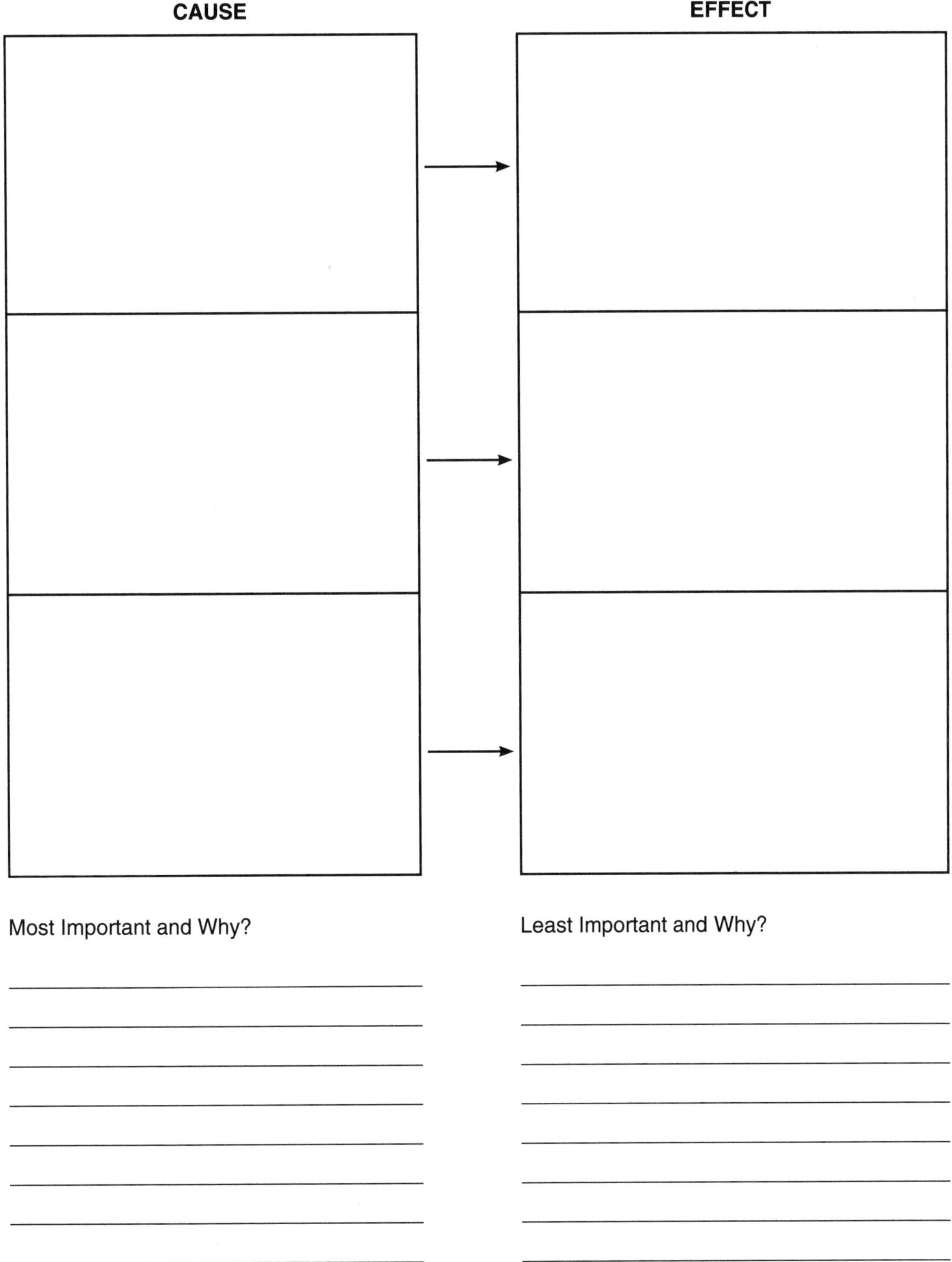

Most Important and Why?

____
____
____
____
____
____
____
____

Least Important and Why?

____
____
____
____
____
____
____
____

■ NAME: ______________________ ■ Date: __________

Causation: Green Revolution

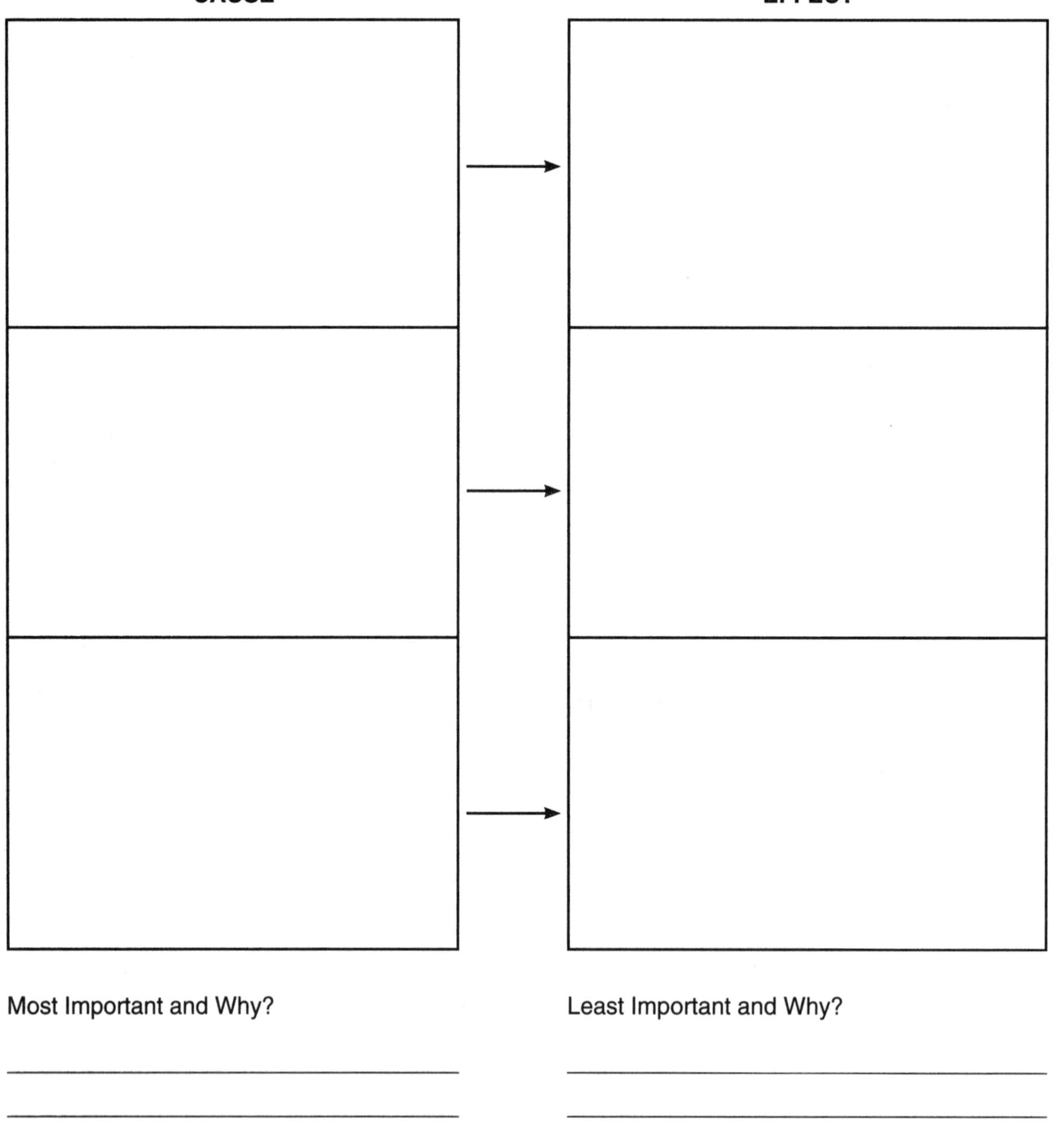

Most Important and Why?

Least Important and Why?

■ NAME: ______________________ ■ Date: __________

Causation: Medical Innovations

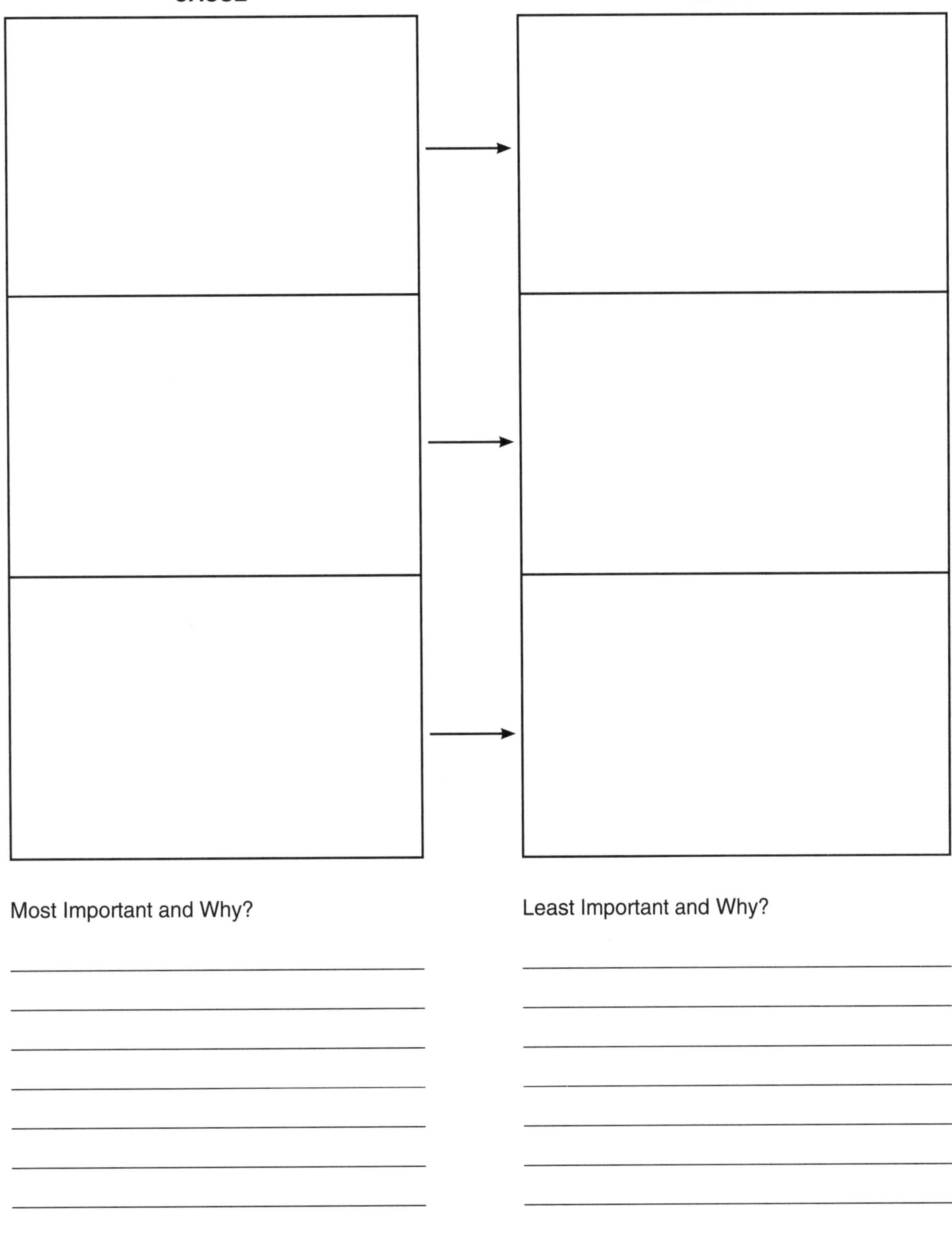

■ NAME: ______________________ ■ Date: __________

Causation: Pollution of Air and Water

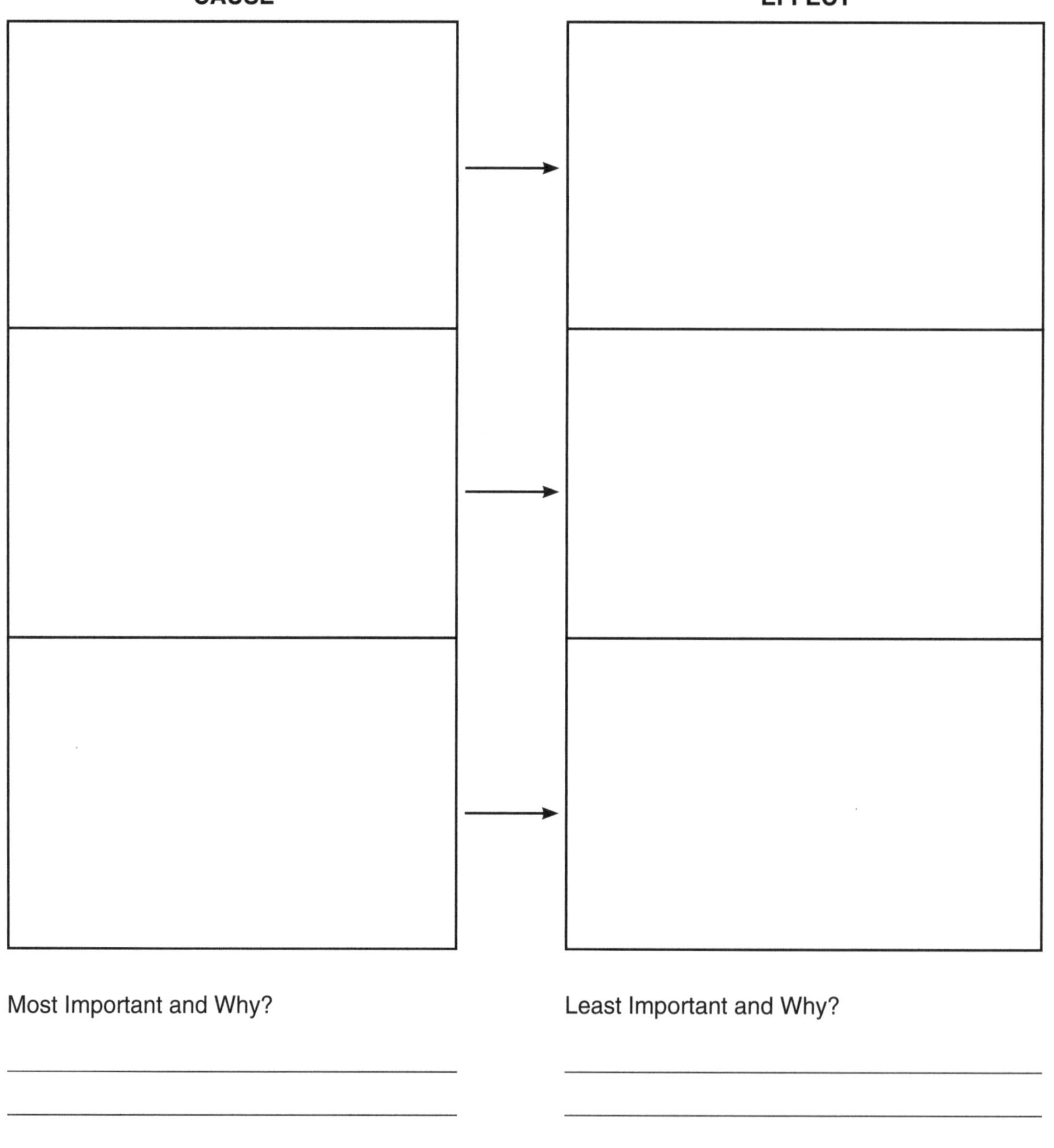

Most Important and Why?

____
____
____
____
____
____
____
____

Least Important and Why?

____
____
____
____
____
____
____
____

■ NAME: ______________________ ■ Date: __________

Causation: World War I

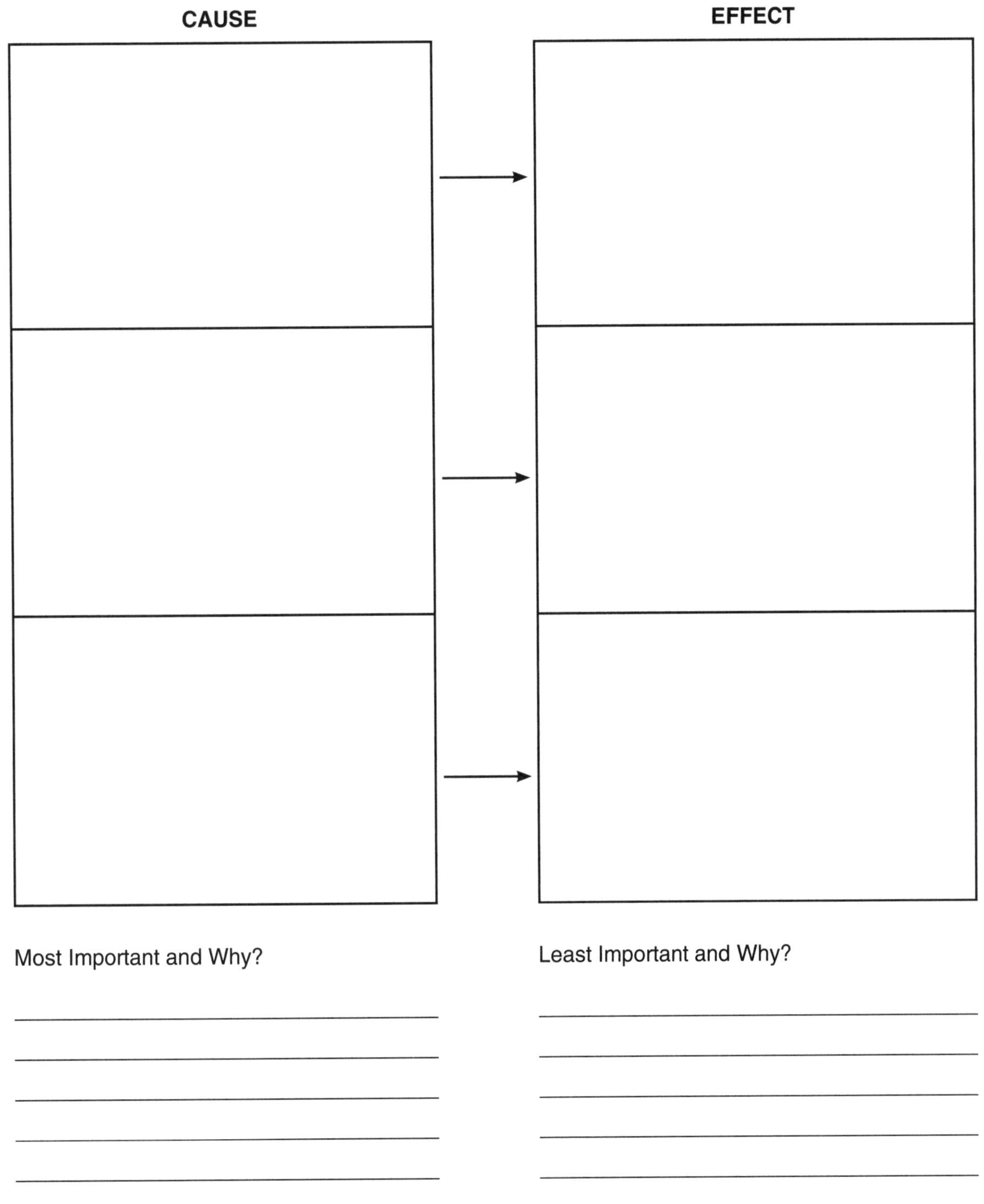

Most Important and Why?

____

____

____

____

____

____

____

____

Least Important and Why?

____

____

____

____

____

____

____

____

■ NAME: ____________________ ■ Date: __________

Causation: Great Depression

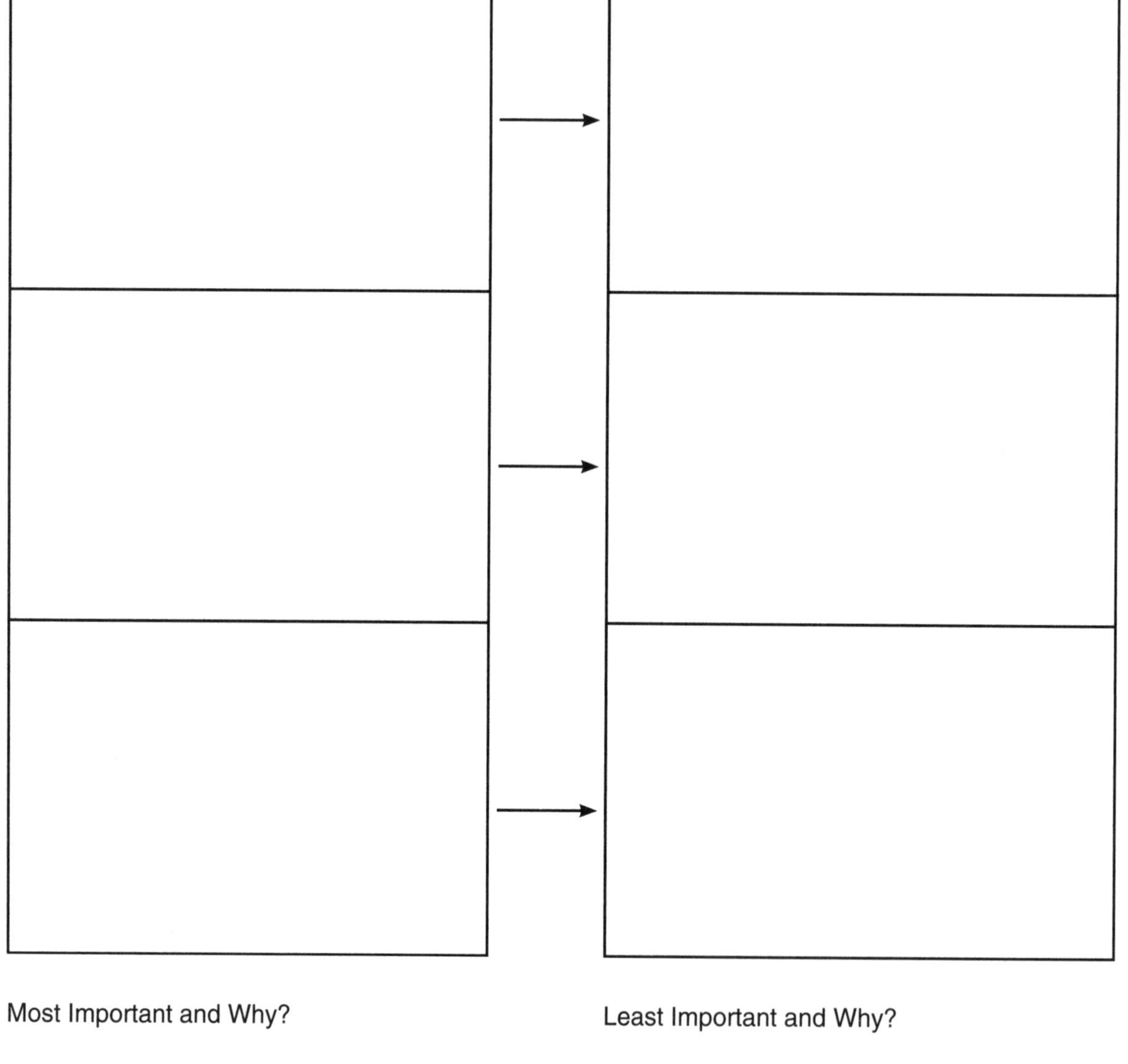

Most Important and Why?

Least Important and Why?

■ NAME: ______________________ ■ Date: ____________

Causation: Fascism

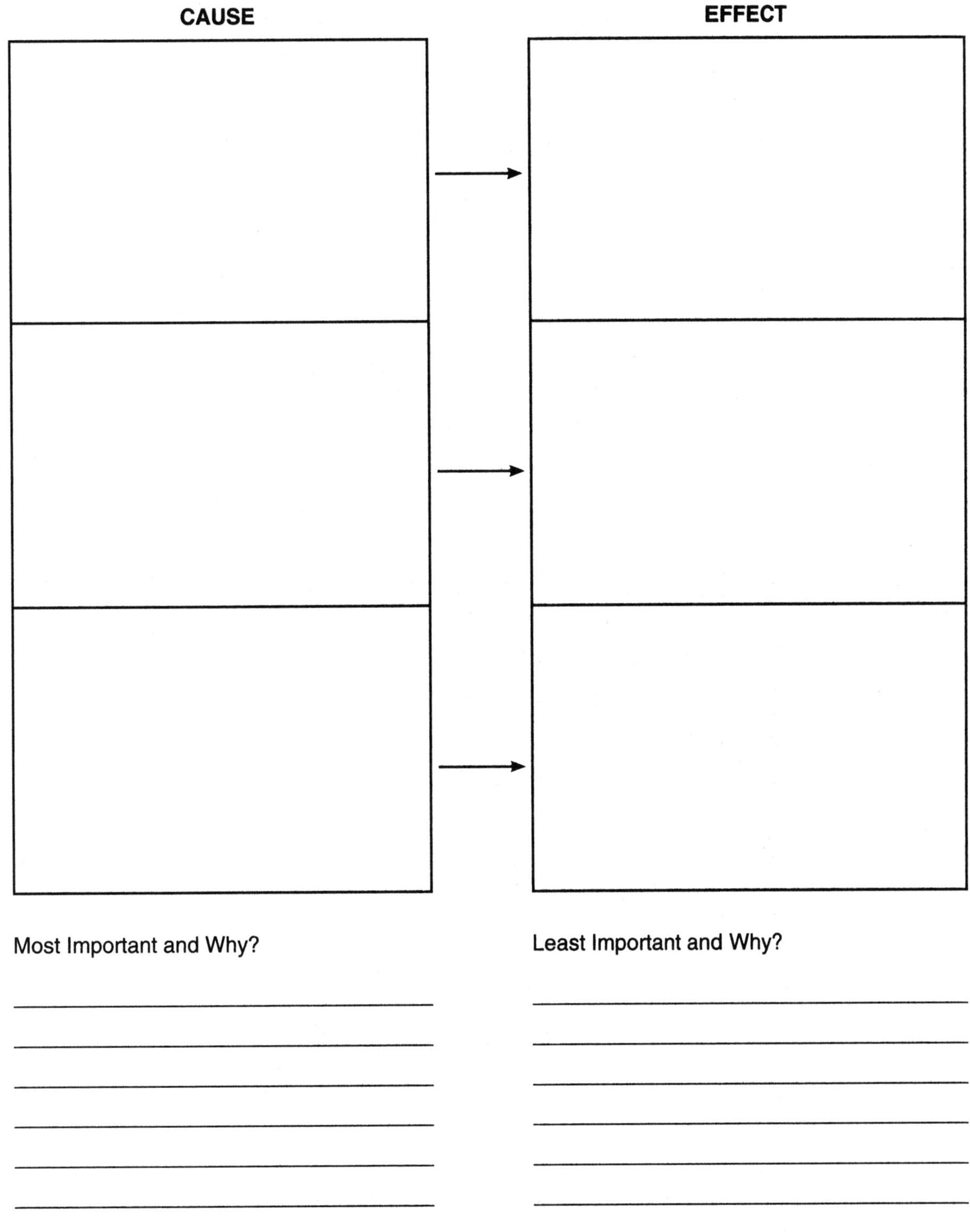

Most Important and Why?

____

____

____

____

____

____

____

____

Least Important and Why?

____

____

____

____

____

____

____

____

■ NAME: ______________________________ ■ Date: ____________

Causation: World War II

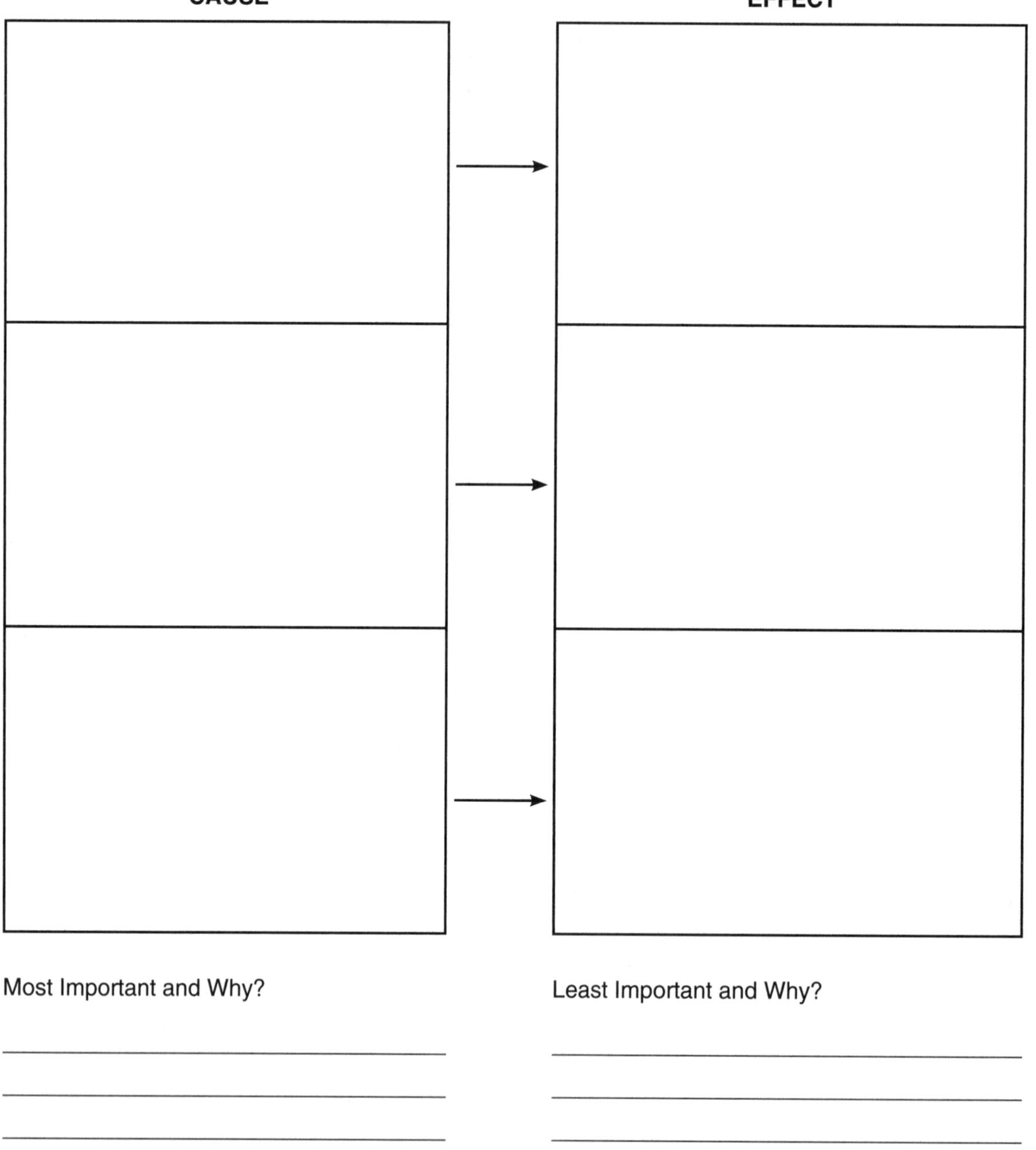

Most Important and Why?

____
____
____
____
____
____
____
____

Least Important and Why?

____
____
____
____
____
____
____
____

■ NAME: ____________________ ■ Date: __________

Causation: Space Race

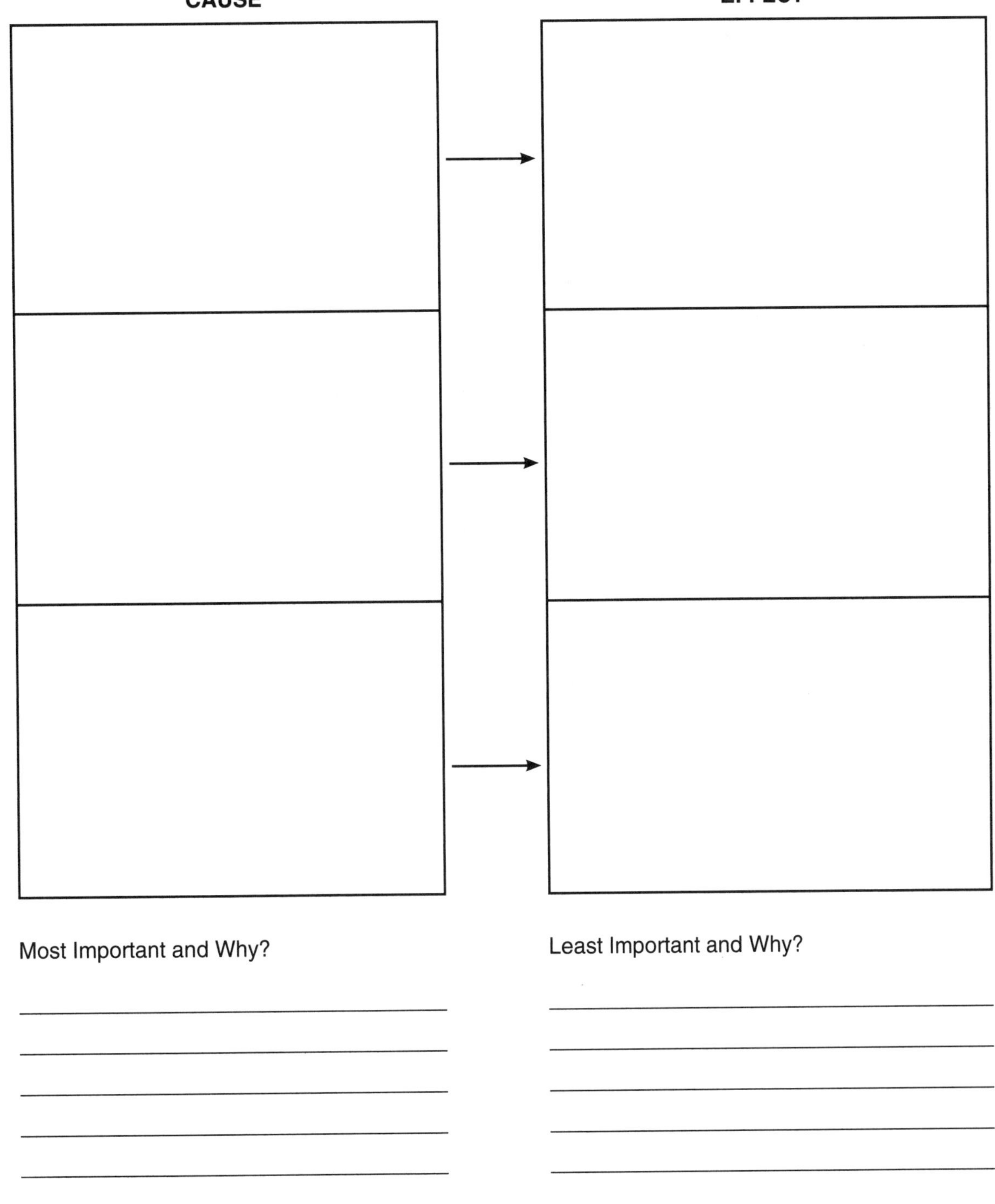

Most Important and Why?

____
____
____
____
____
____
____
____

Least Important and Why?

____
____
____
____
____
____
____
____

■ NAME: ______________________ ■ Date: __________

Causation: Terrorism

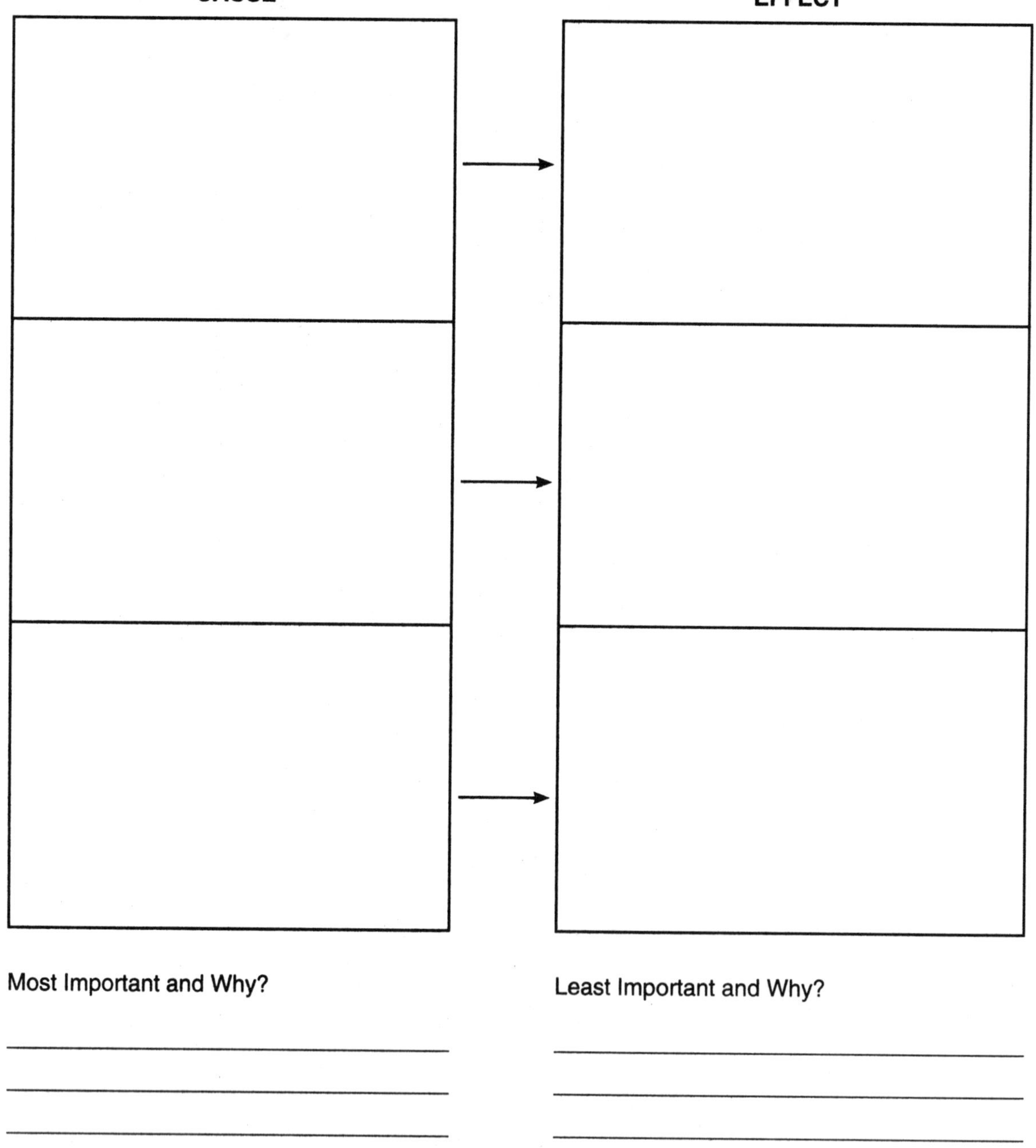

Most Important and Why?

Least Important and Why?

NAME: ______________________ Date: __________

Causation: United Nations

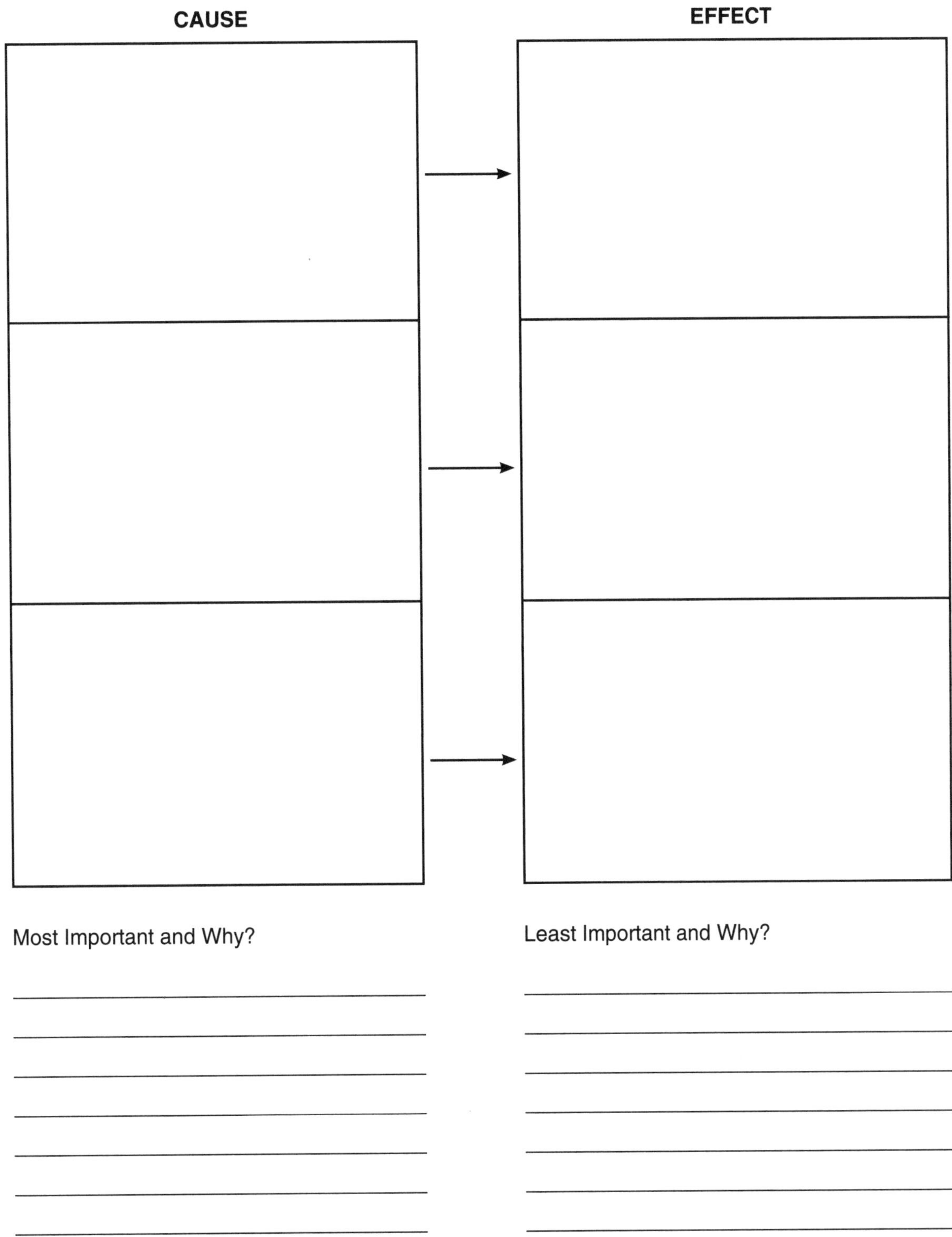

Most Important and Why?

____
____
____
____
____
____
____
____

Least Important and Why?

____
____
____
____
____
____
____
____

CA30

■ NAME: ____________________ ■ Date: __________

Causation: Modern International Sporting Events

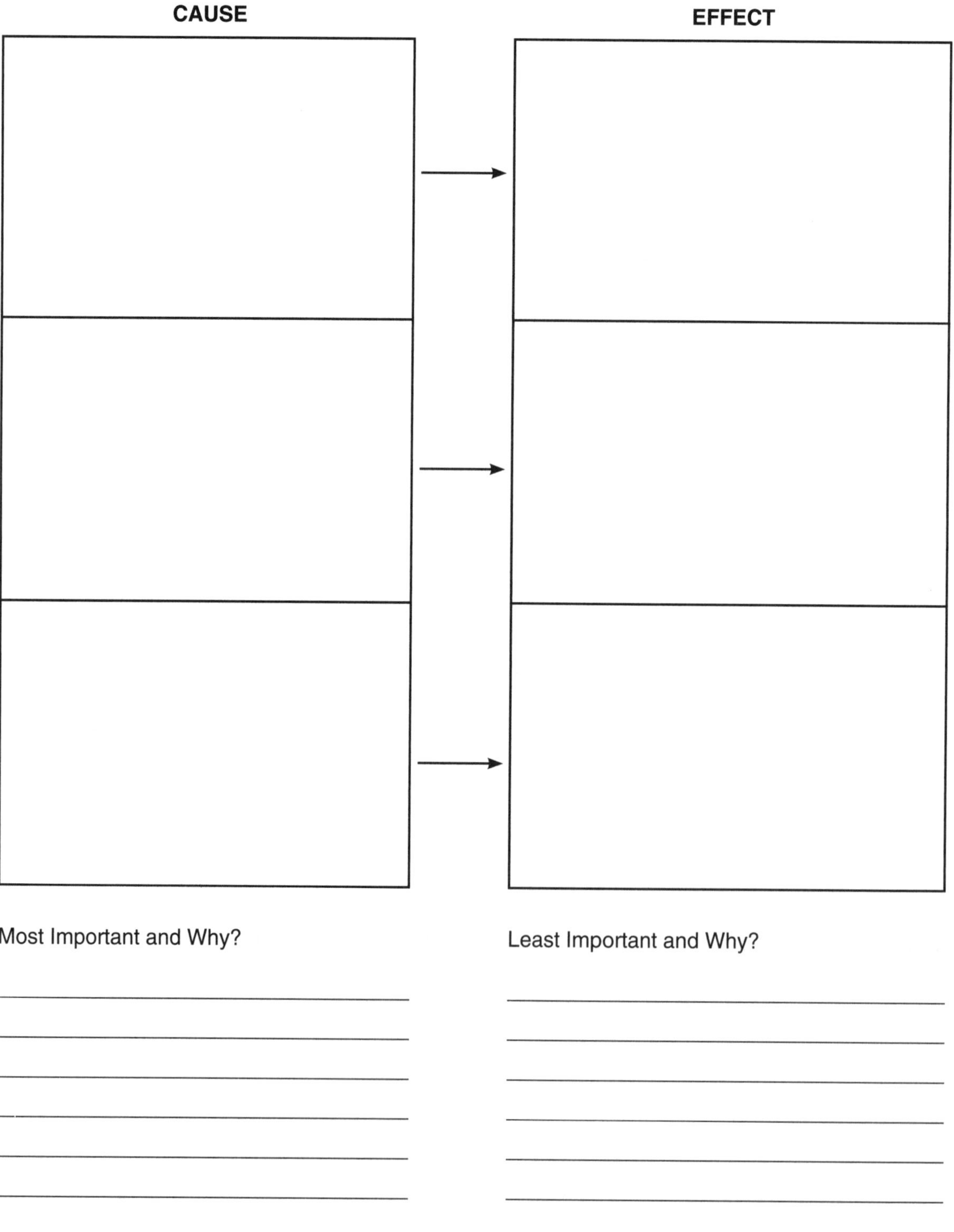

Most Important and Why?

Least Important and Why?

Student Instructions: Comparison

When we are asked to compare, we are asked to identify similarities and differences among the different entities under consideration. Similarities are the things that they have in common, that is, the things that are shared between the two entities. Differences are the things that are unique to that particular entity; in some cases, these can be things that are contradictory with other characteristics.

The purpose of these Comparison activities is to analyze how similar and different certain historical topics are within their historical contexts. On the surface, it may appear that different topics have no similarities or differences; but upon further inspection, we often see that, indeed, many historical topics are more complex than we realized. But recognizing the similarities and differences is only the beginning of these activities' purpose. They ask us to dig deeper into our observations and to move from observation to evaluation. We should evaluate *why* there are similarities and differences between the two historical topics.

■ NAME: ____________________ ■ Date: __________

Comparison: Chavin and Moche in the Americas (Example)

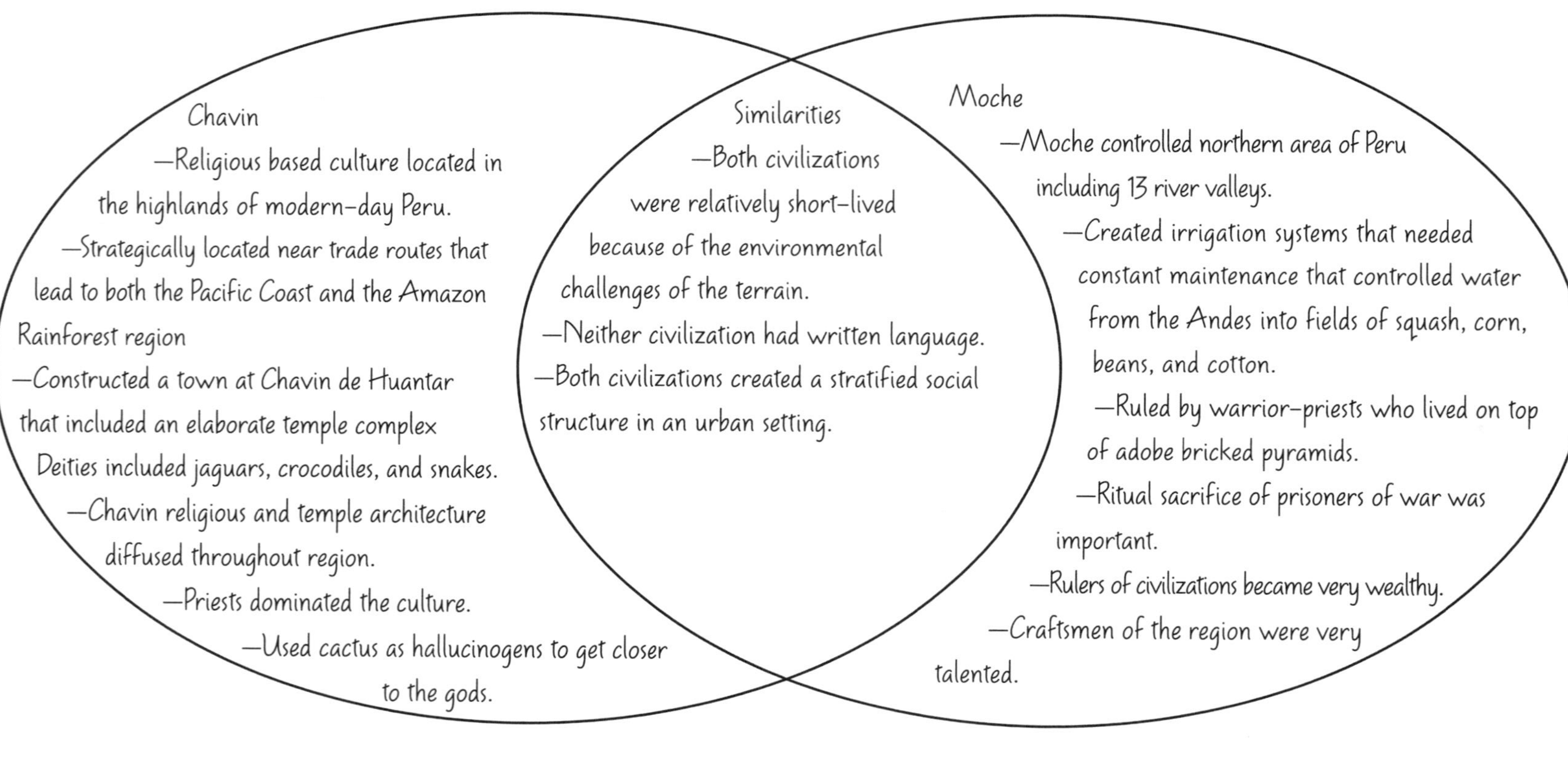

Chavin
—Religious based culture located in the highlands of modern-day Peru.
—Strategically located near trade routes that lead to both the Pacific Coast and the Amazon Rainforest region
—Constructed a town at Chavin de Huantar that included an elaborate temple complex
Deities included jaguars, crocodiles, and snakes.
—Chavin religious and temple architecture diffused throughout region.
—Priests dominated the culture.
—Used cactus as hallucinogens to get closer to the gods.
Similarities
—Both civilizations were relatively short-lived because of the environmental challenges of the terrain.
—Neither civilization had written language.
—Both civilizations created a stratified social structure in an urban setting.
Moche
—Moche controlled northern area of Peru including 13 river valleys.
—Created irrigation systems that needed constant maintenance that controlled water from the Andes into fields of squash, corn, beans, and cotton.
—Ruled by warrior-priests who lived on top of adobe bricked pyramids.
—Ritual sacrifice of prisoners of war was important.
—Rulers of civilizations became very wealthy.
—Craftsmen of the region were very talented.

Reasons for Similarities:

Both civilizations were located in essentially the same region: on the western slopes of the Andes. Earthquakes and droughts were frequent, as were torrential rains. Neither civilization had writing, although evidence indicates that they both made use of the quipu—a knot-based system of record keeping using different lengths and colors of string. This is probably the case because of the terrain and the difficulty of communicating over the mountains. It also could be that none of these civilizations was long-lived enough for the elite to create a system of writing.

Reasons for Differences:

The Moche were agricultural-based whereas the Chavin were trade-based. Moche culture was led by warrior elites whereas the Chavin culture centered on religion. Moche culture was located in the valley while Chavin culture was located in the Andean highlands.

■ NAME: ______________________ ■ Date: ________

Comparison: Chavin and Moche in the Americas

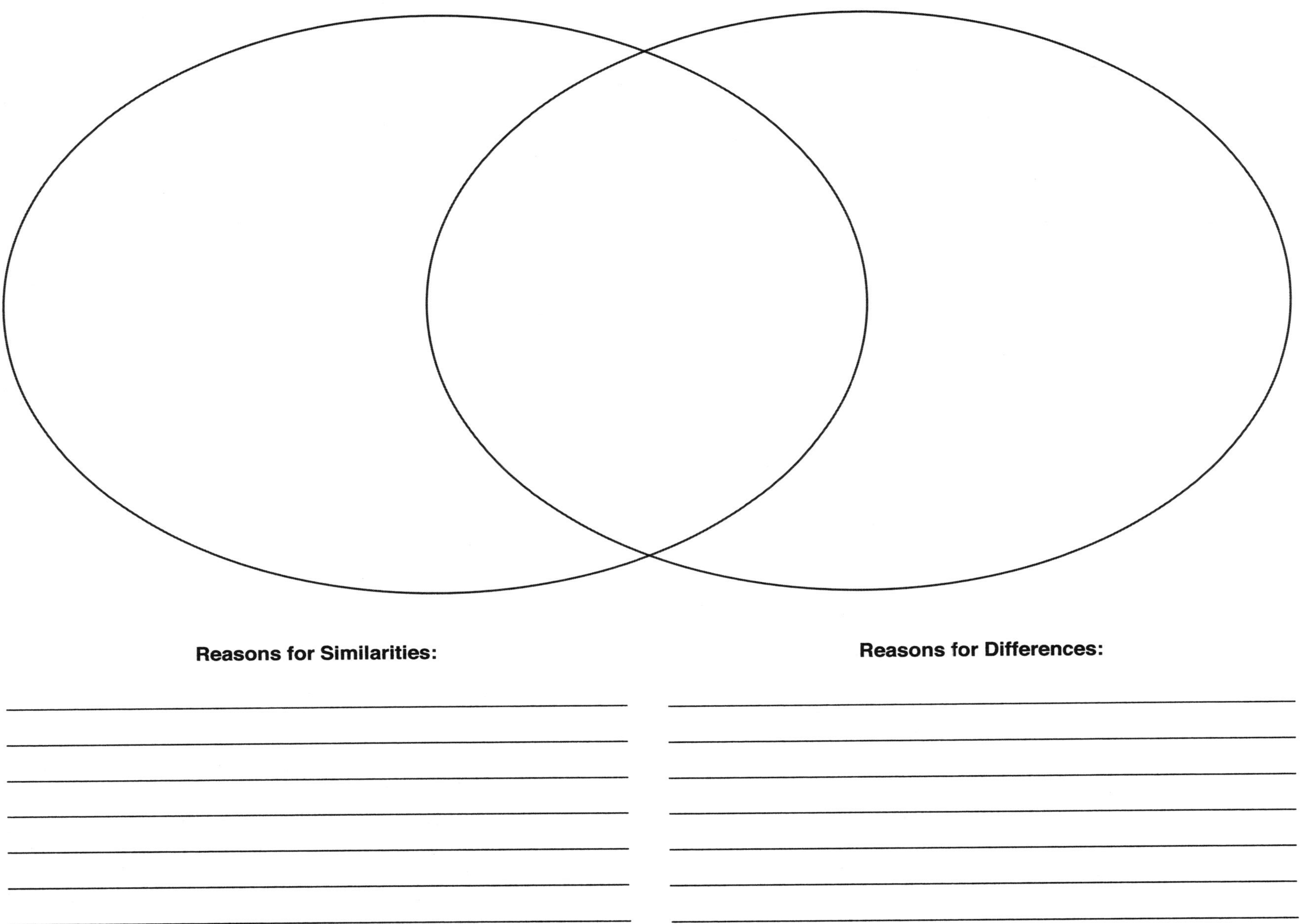

Reasons for Similarities:

Reasons for Differences:

■ NAME: ______________________ ■ Date: __________

Comparison: Agriculture and Pastoralism

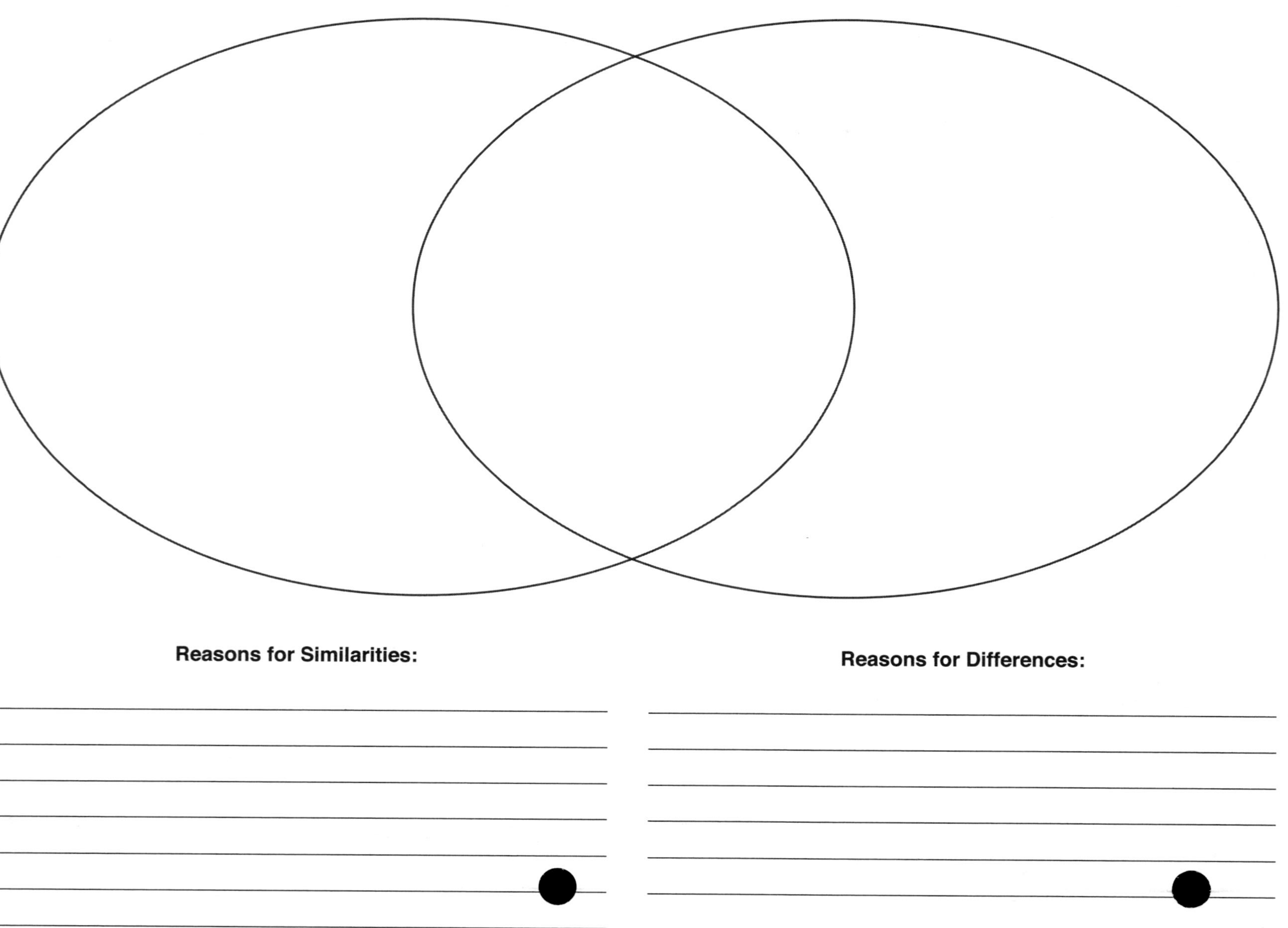

Reasons for Similarities:

Reasons for Differences:

■ NAME: ______________________ ■ Date: ________

Comparison: Confucianism and Daoism

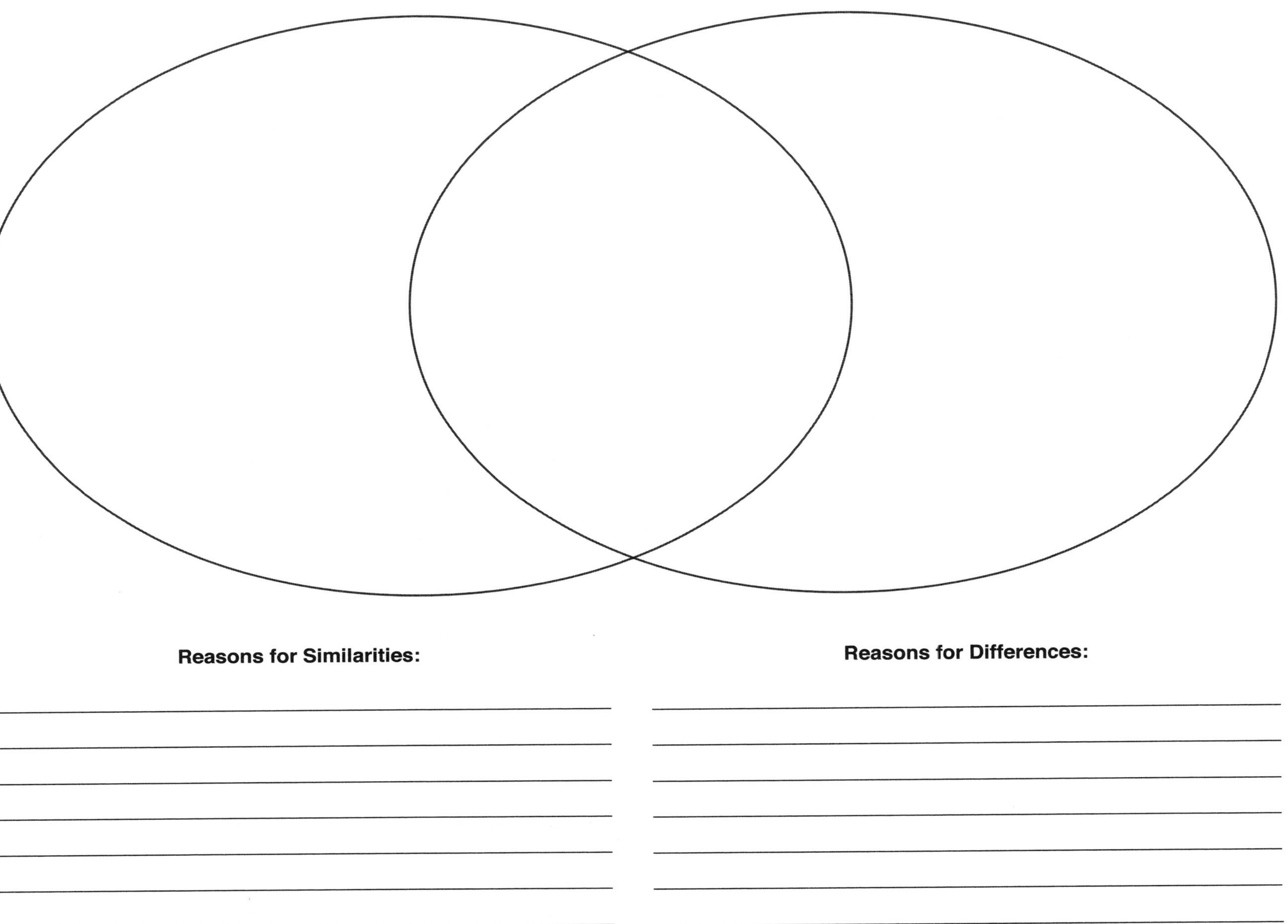

Reasons for Similarities:

Reasons for Differences:

■ NAME: ______________________ ■ Date: __________

Comparison: Buddhism and Christianity

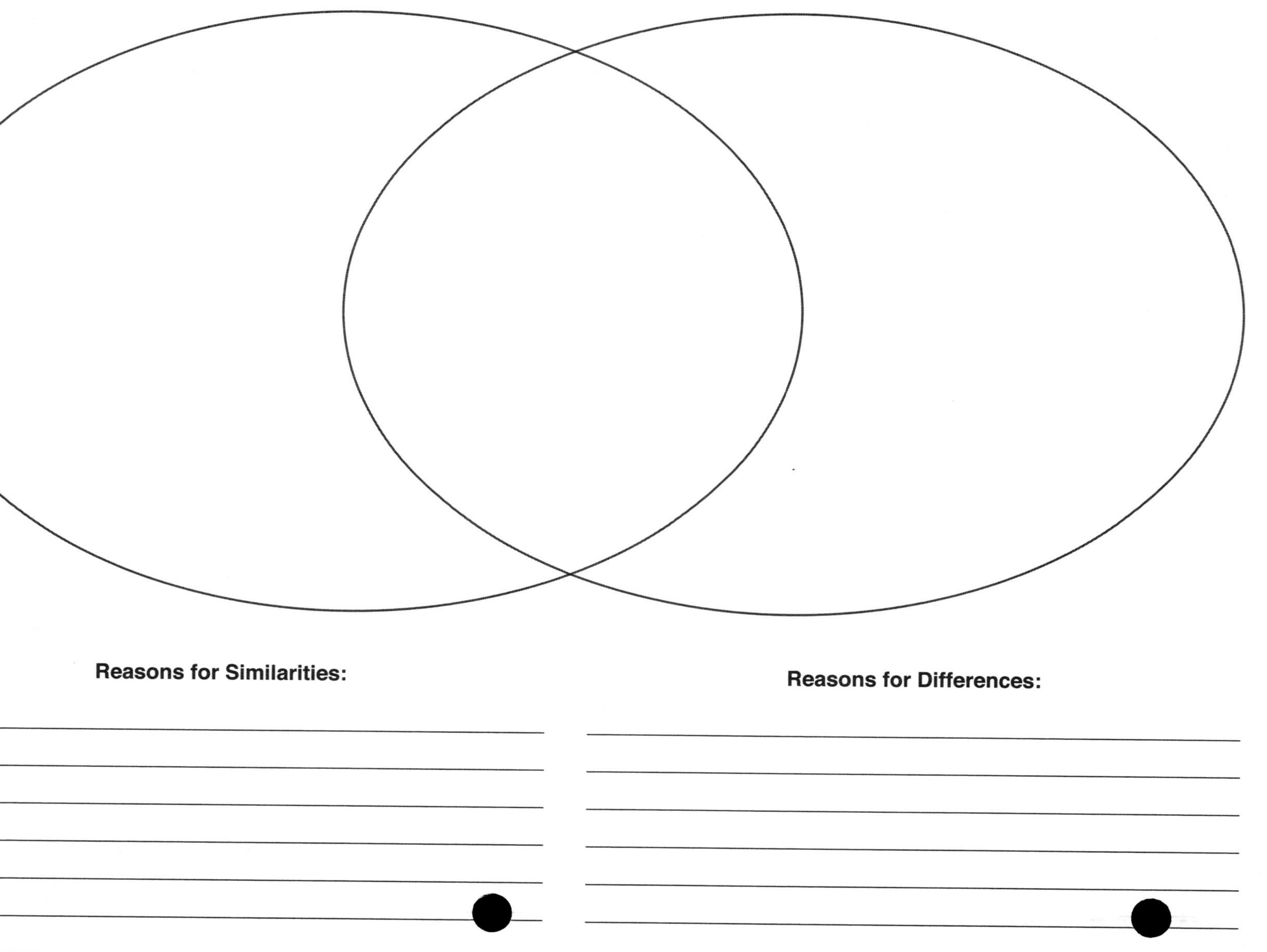

Reasons for Similarities:

Reasons for Differences:

■ NAME: ______________________________ ■ Date: ____________

Comparison: Slavery and Peasant Labor

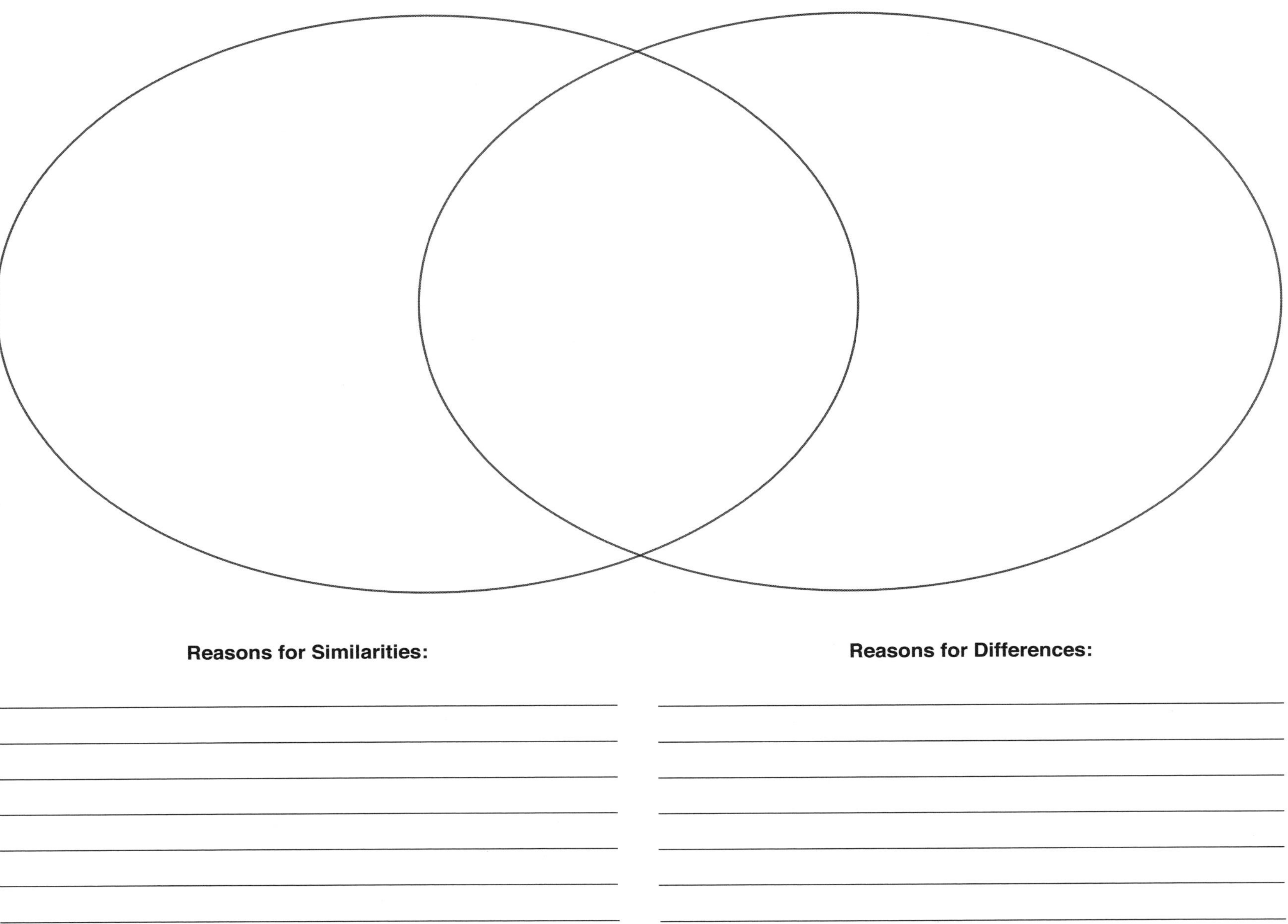

Reasons for Similarities:

Reasons for Differences:

■ NAME: ____________________ ■ Date: __________

Comparison: Trans-Saharan Trade and the Silk Roads

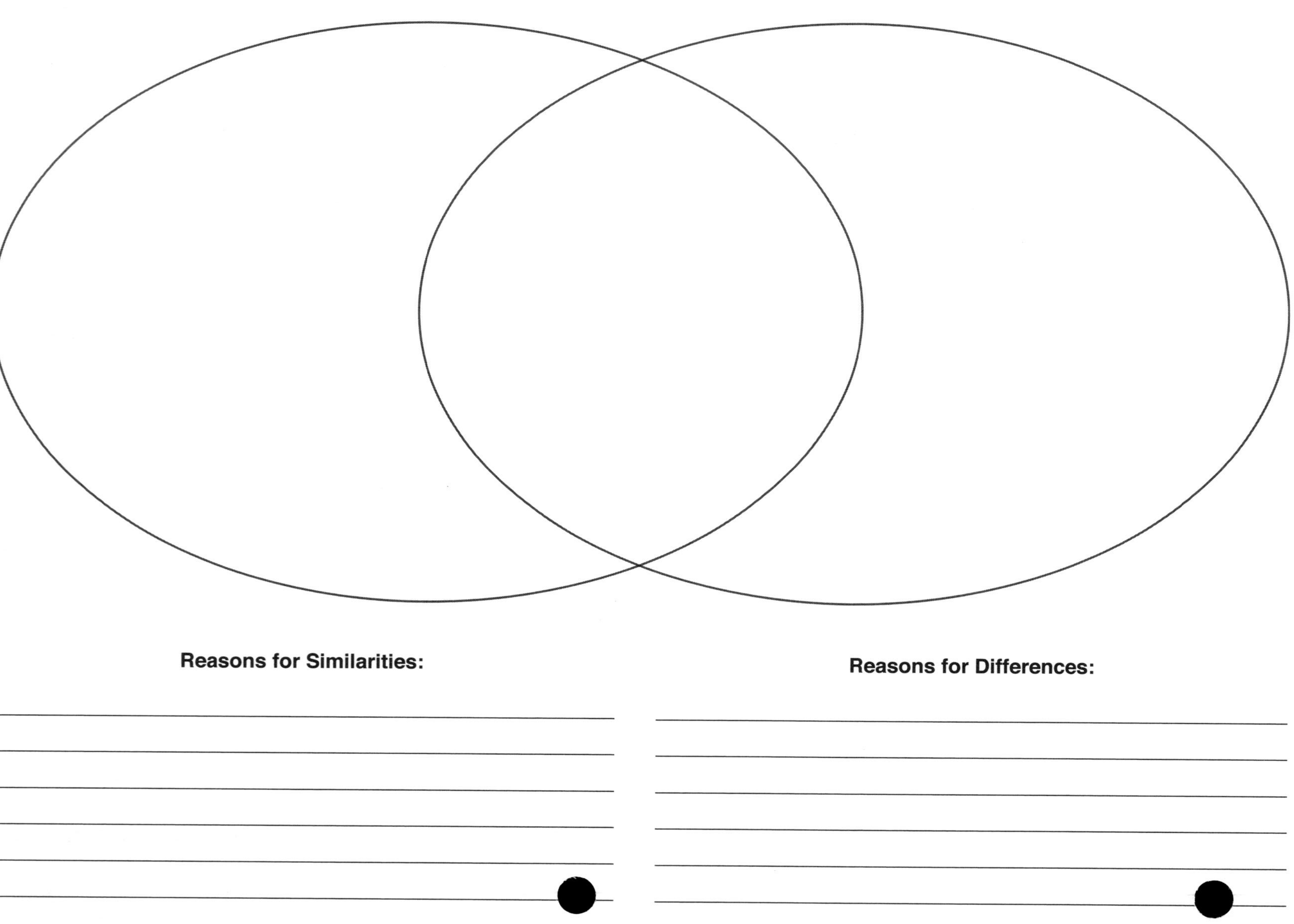

Reasons for Similarities:

Reasons for Differences:

■ NAME: ____________________ ■ Date: __________

Comparison: Effect of Disease on the Han and Roman Empires

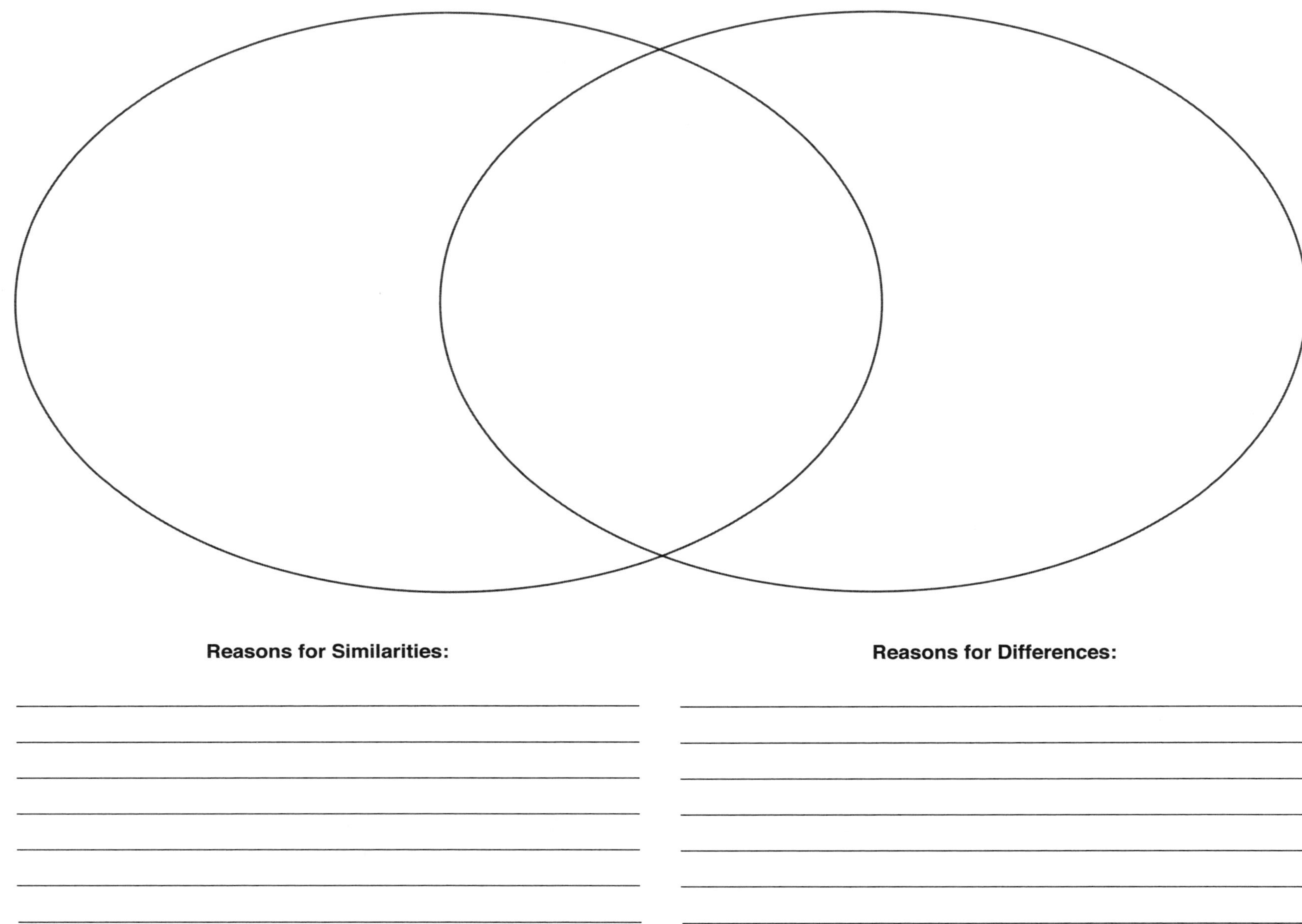

Reasons for Similarities:

Reasons for Differences:

■ NAME: ______________________ ■ Date: __________

Comparison: Mediterranean Sea and Indian Ocean Trades

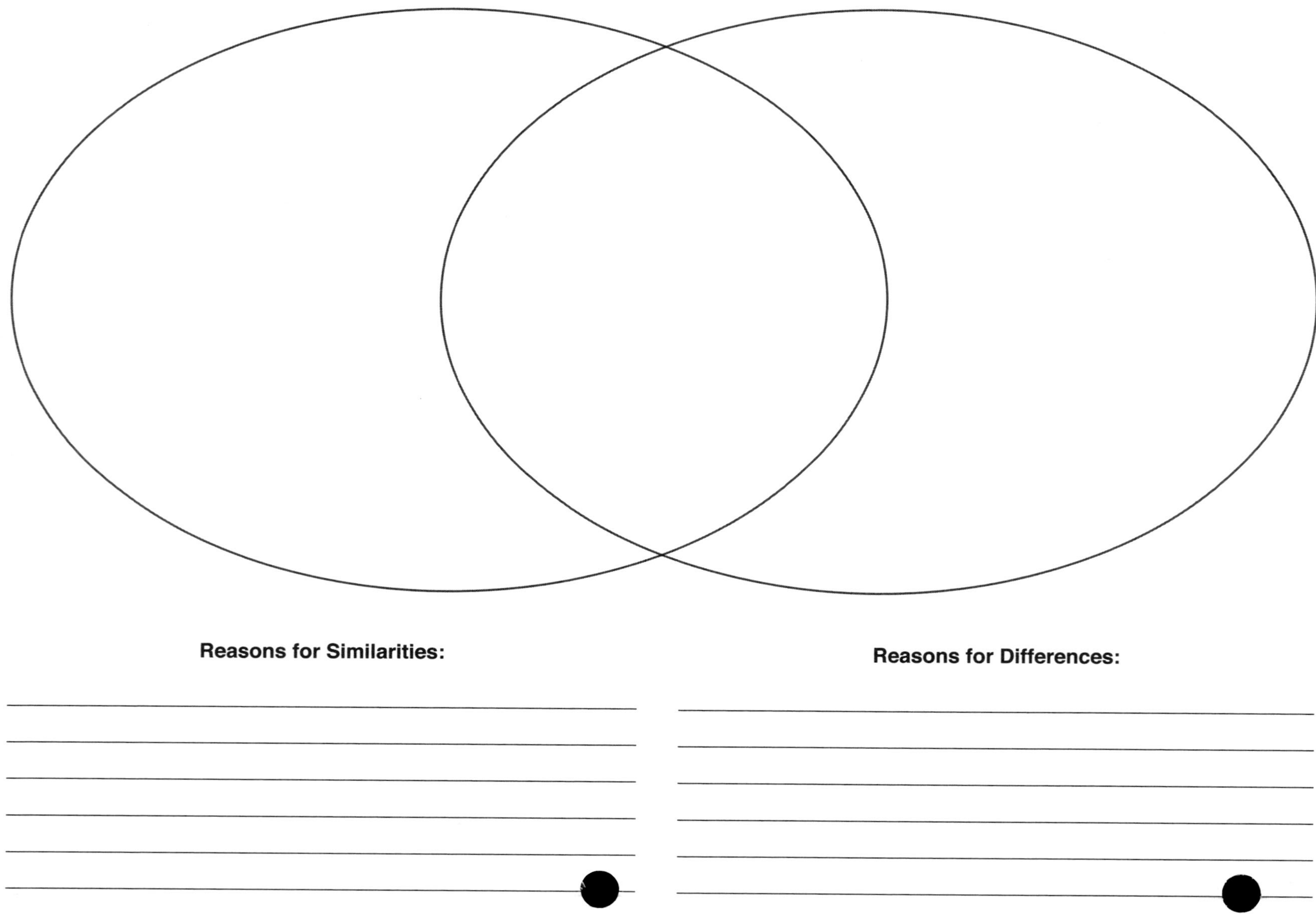

Reasons for Similarities:

Reasons for Differences:

■ NAME: ______________________________ ■ Date: __________

Comparison: Arabic and the Bantu

Reasons for Similarities:

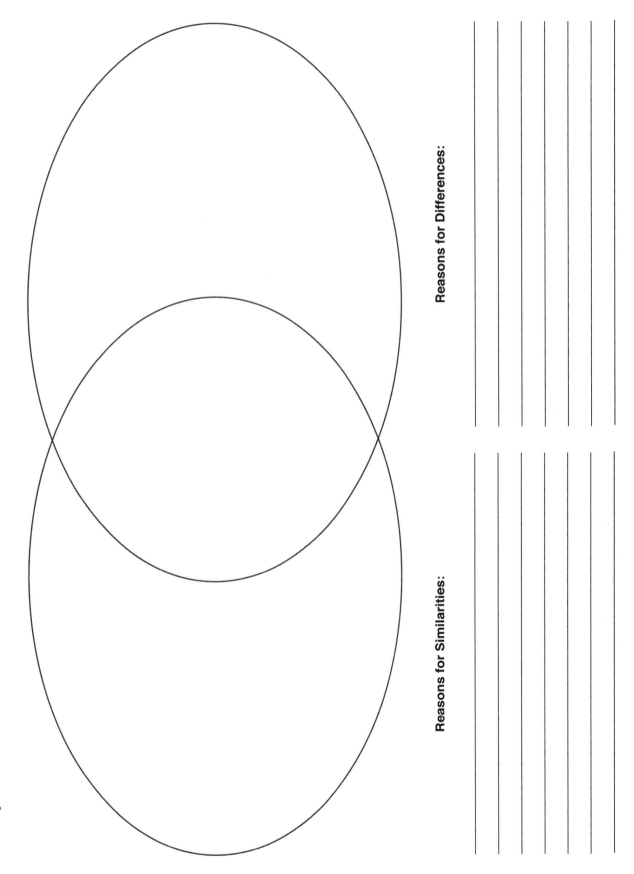

Reasons for Differences:

■ NAME: ______________________ ■ Date: __________

Comparison: Chinese Merchants in Southeast Asia and Jewish Communities in the Mediterranean

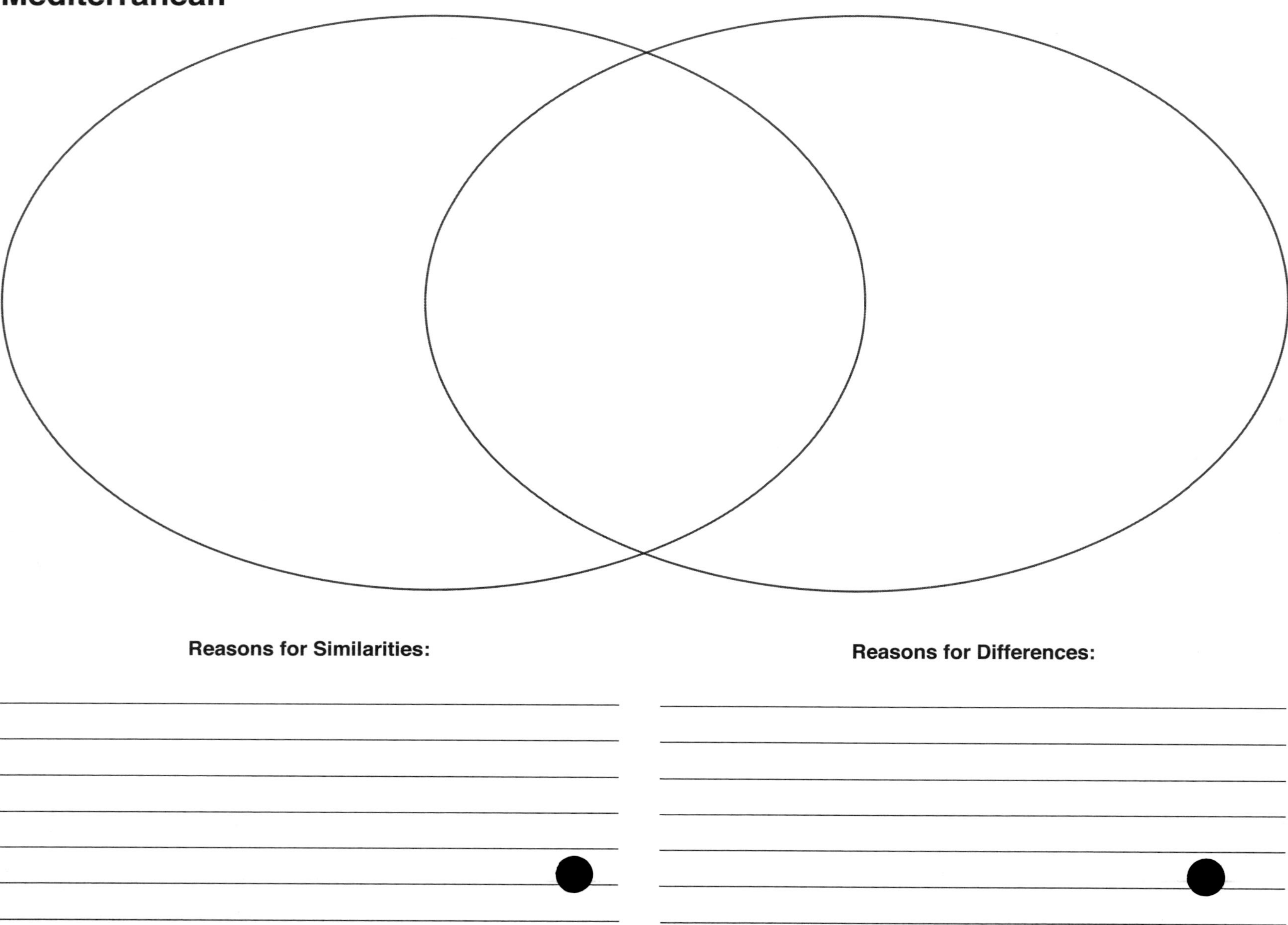

Reasons for Similarities:

Reasons for Differences:

■ NAME: ______________________________ ■ Date: ____________

Comparison: Persian Influences on Caliphates and Chinese Influences on Japan

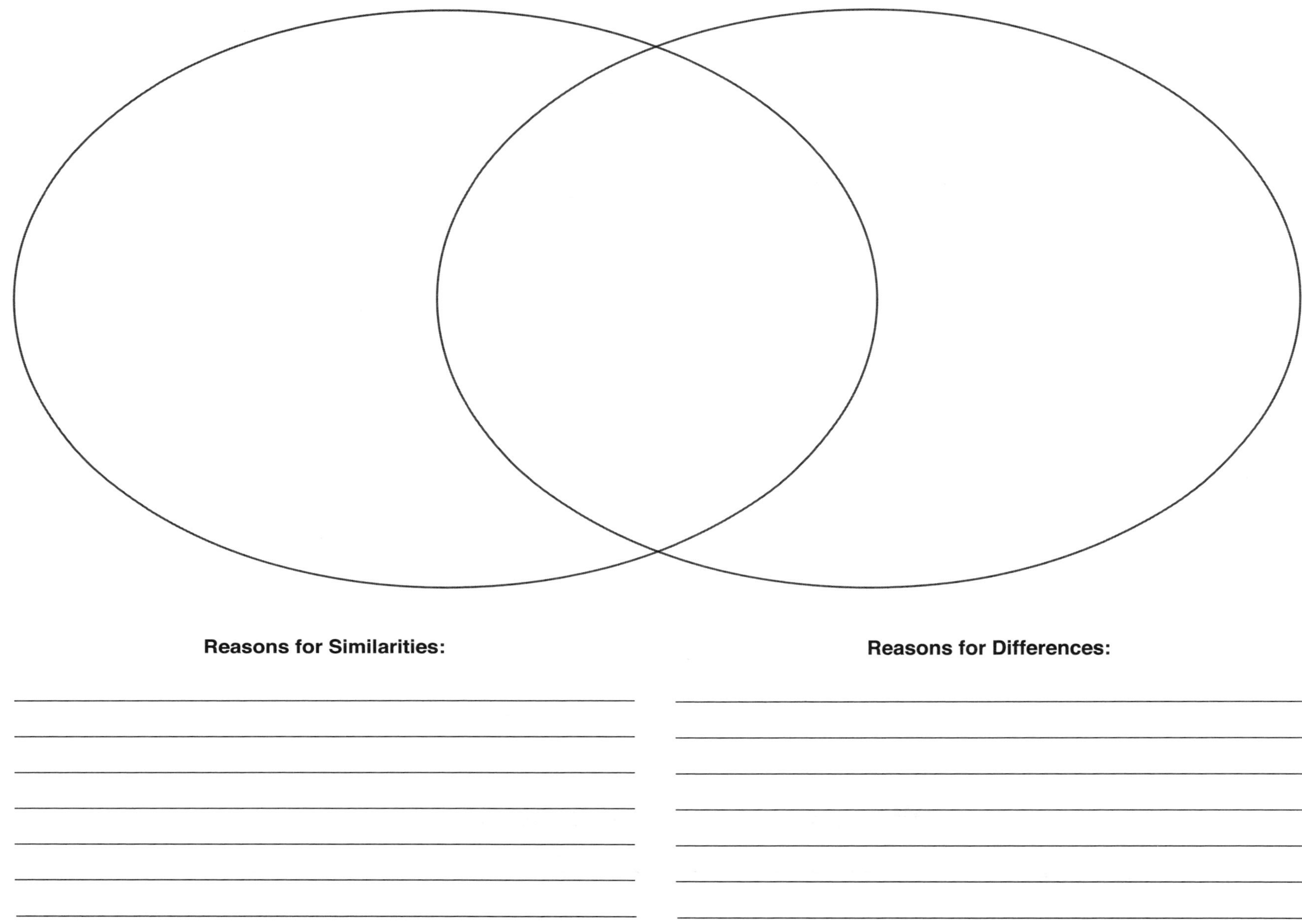

Reasons for Similarities:

____
____
____
____
____
____
____

Reasons for Differences:

____
____
____
____
____
____
____

■ NAME: ______________________ ■ Date: __________

Comparison: Mongol and Arab Muslim Conquest of Territory

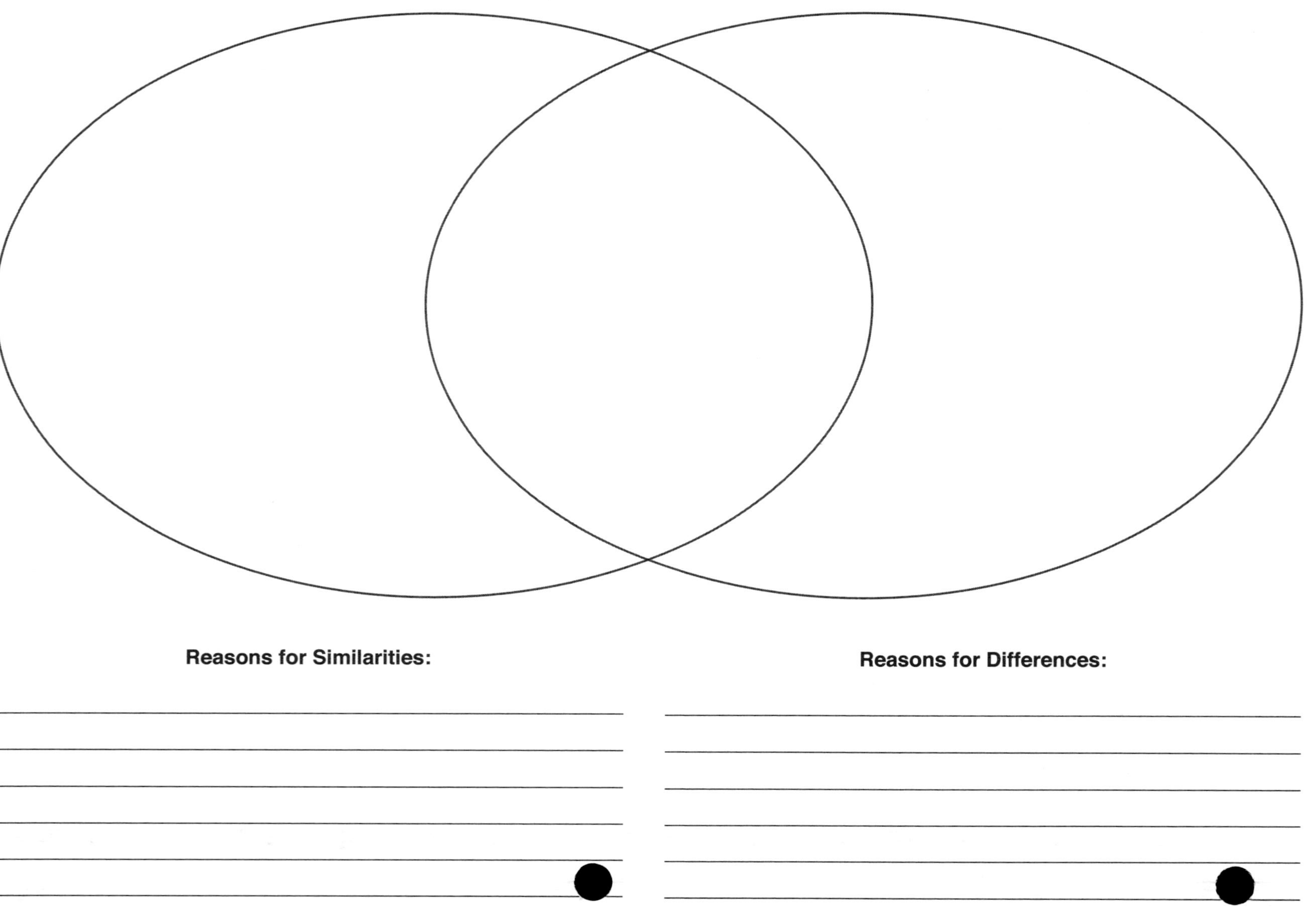

Reasons for Similarities:

Reasons for Differences:

■ NAME: ______________________________ ■ Date: __________

Comparison: Impact of the Columbian Exchange on Amerindians and on Chinese Peasants

Reasons for Similarities:

Reasons for Differences:

■ NAME: ______________________ ■ Date: __________

Comparison: European Roles in the Indian Ocean Trade and the Atlantic Trade

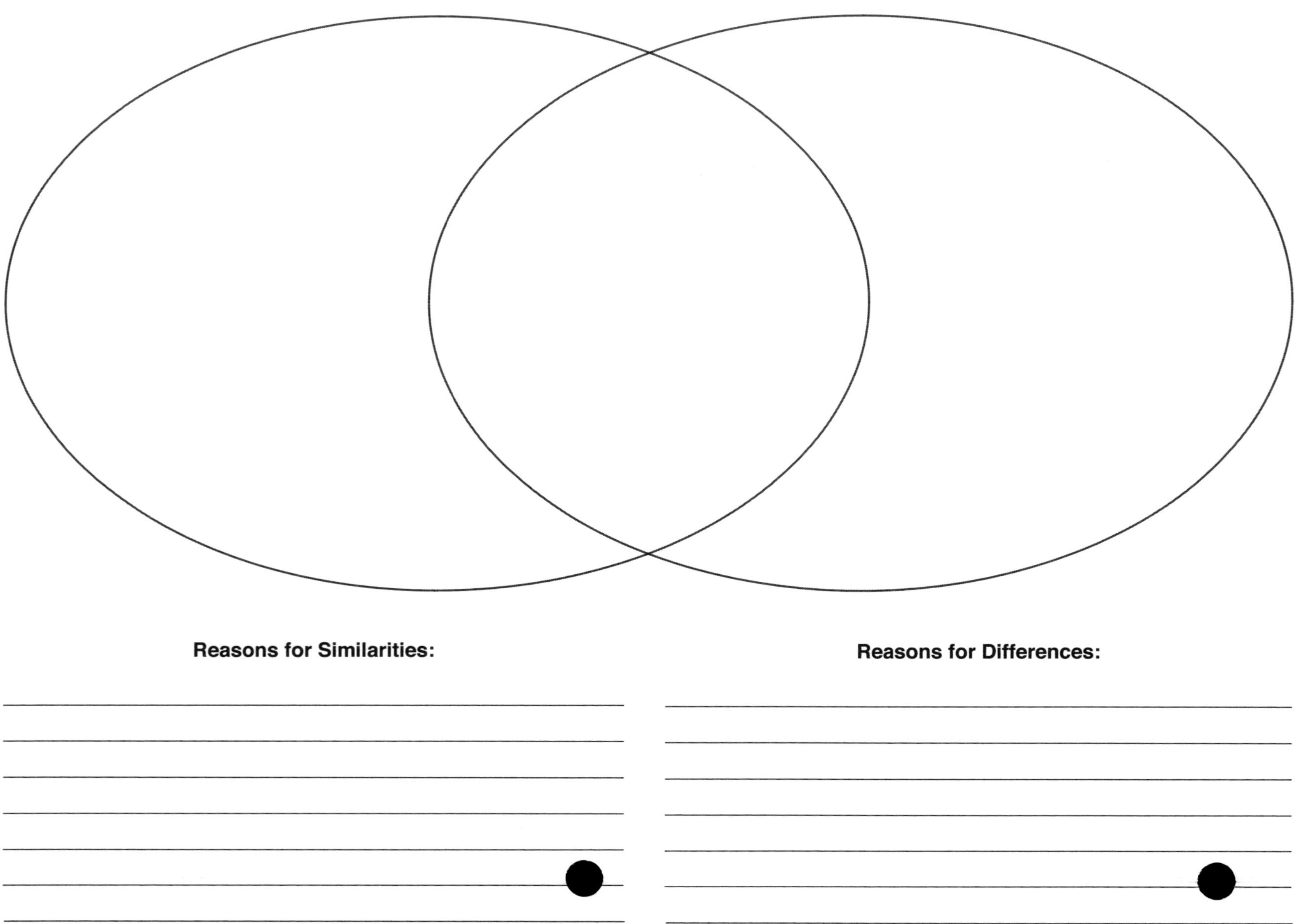

Reasons for Similarities:

Reasons for Differences:

■ NAME: ______________________ ■ Date: ________

Comparison: Vodun and Sikhism

Reasons for Similarities:

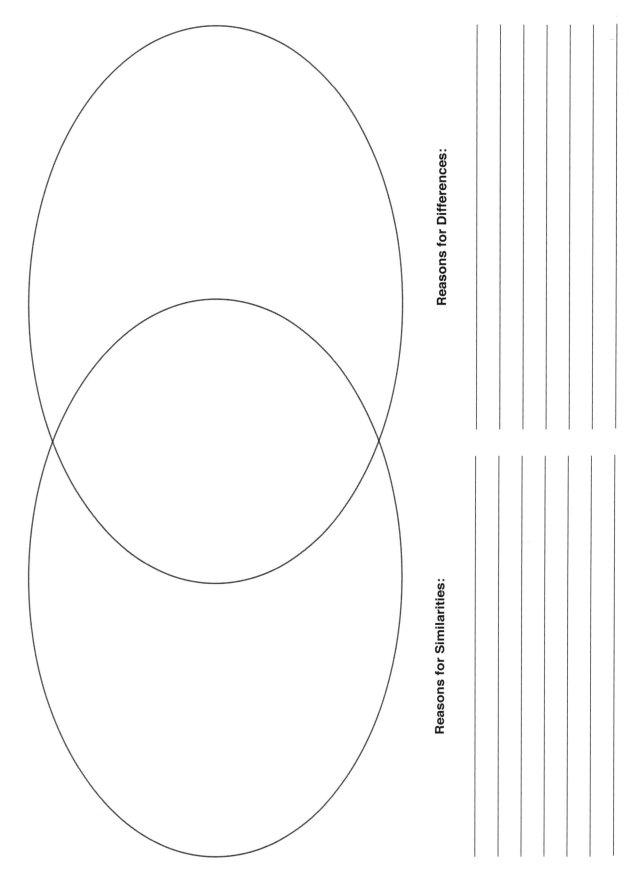

Reasons for Differences:

■ NAME: ______________________________ ■ Date: __________

Comparison: Indian Caste System and the Castas System of New Spain

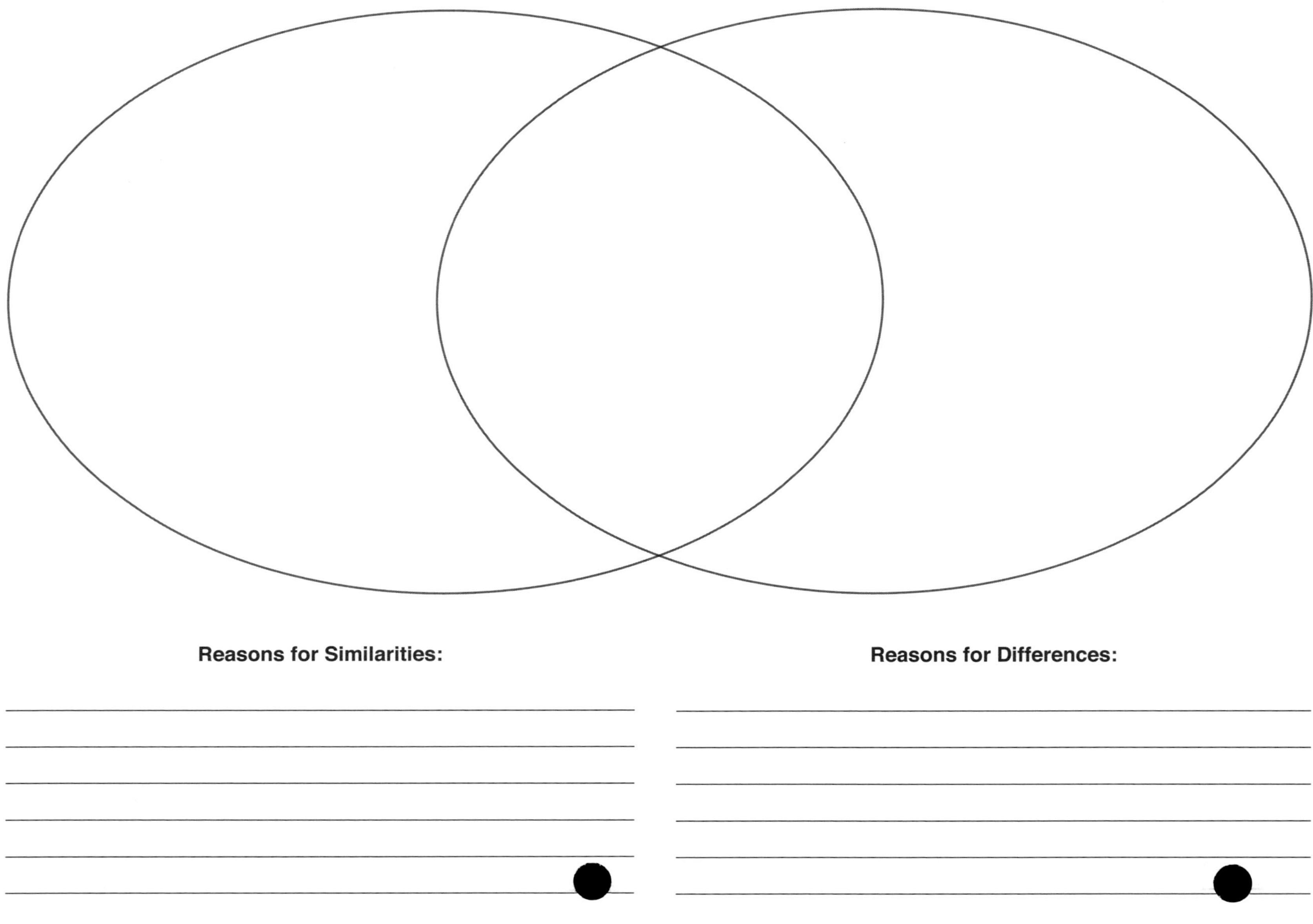

Reasons for Similarities:

Reasons for Differences:

■ NAME: ______________________ ■ Date: __________

Comparison: Chinese Silk Production under the Song and English Cotton Cloth Production at the Beginning of Industrialization

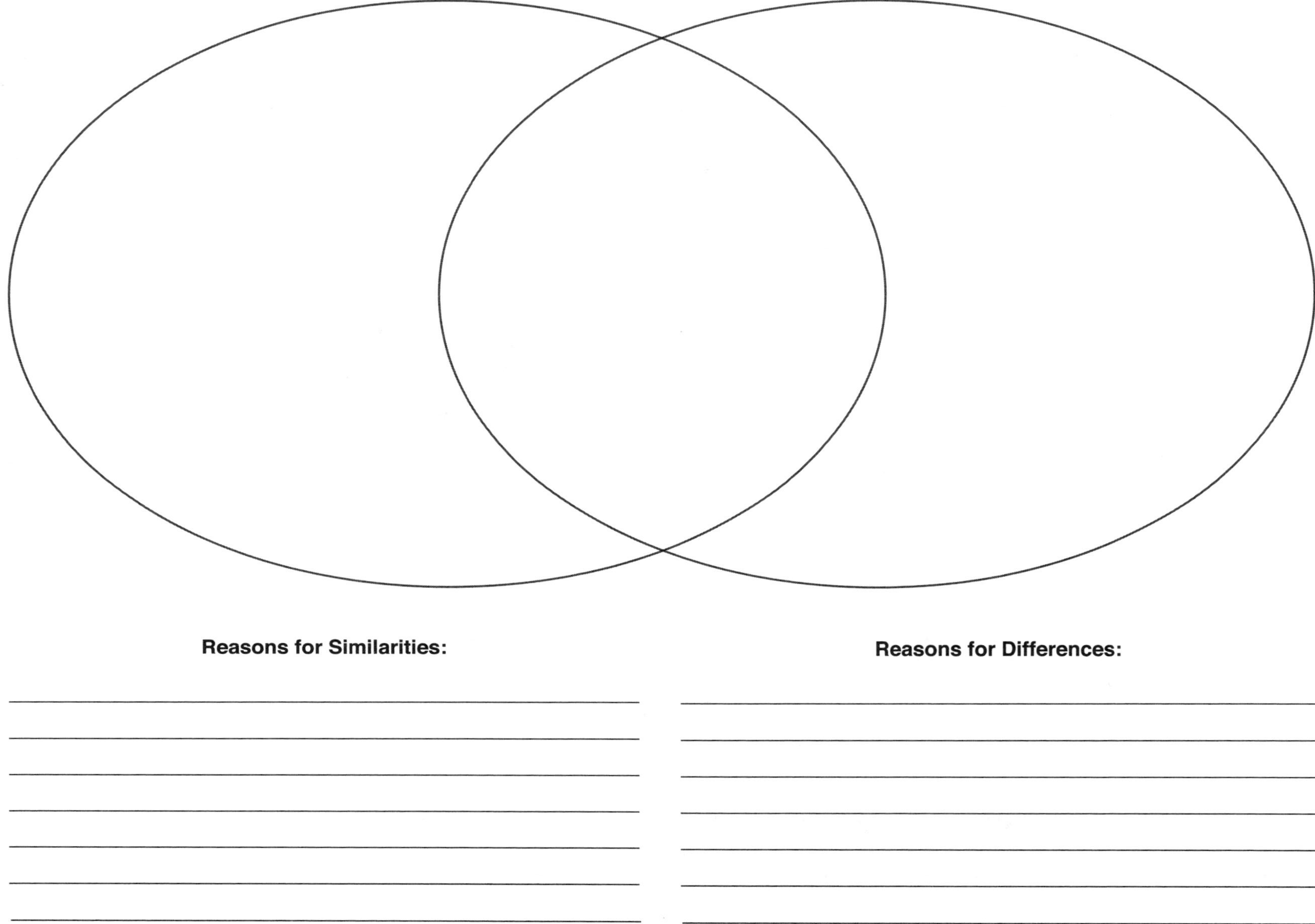

Reasons for Similarities:

Reasons for Differences:

■ NAME: ______________________ ■ Date: __________

Comparison: Industrialization under Meiji Japan and Tsarist Russia

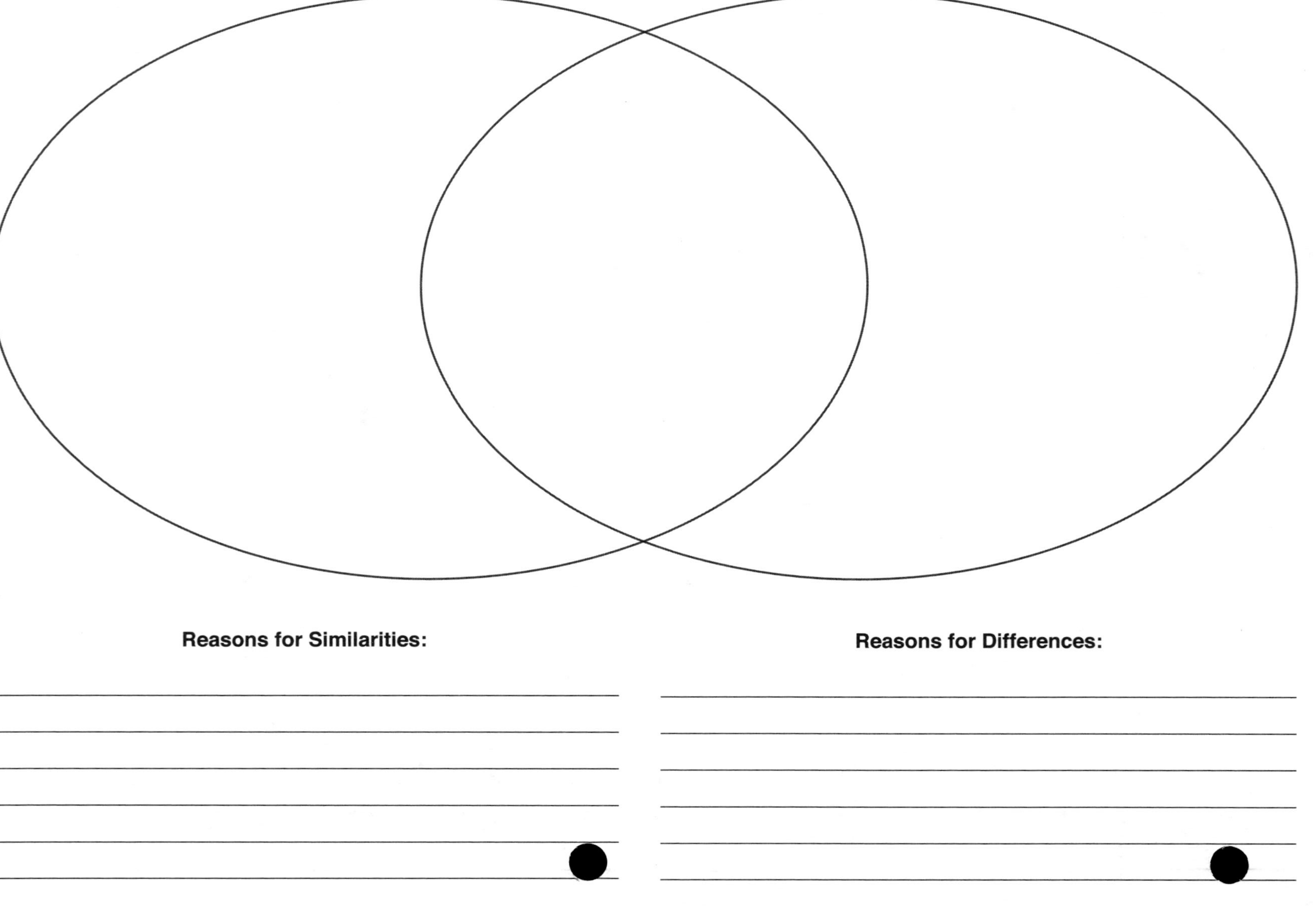

Reasons for Similarities:

Reasons for Differences:

■ NAME: ______________________ ■ Date: __________

Comparison: Resistance to Industrialization in the Ottoman Empire and in Qing China

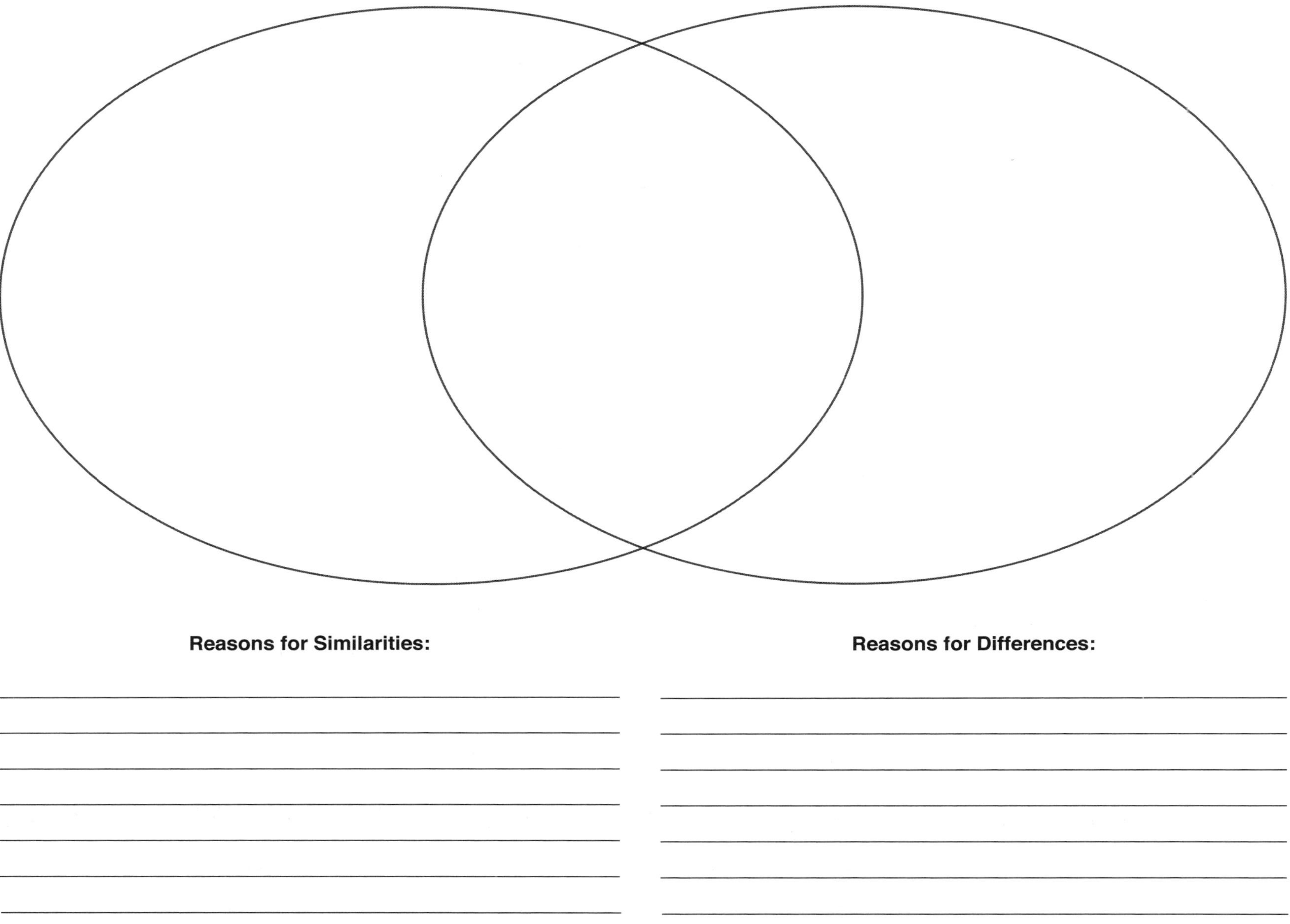

Reasons for Similarities:

Reasons for Differences:

■ NAME: ______________________ ■ Date: __________

Comparison: British Empire in West Africa and the Belgian Empire in the Congo

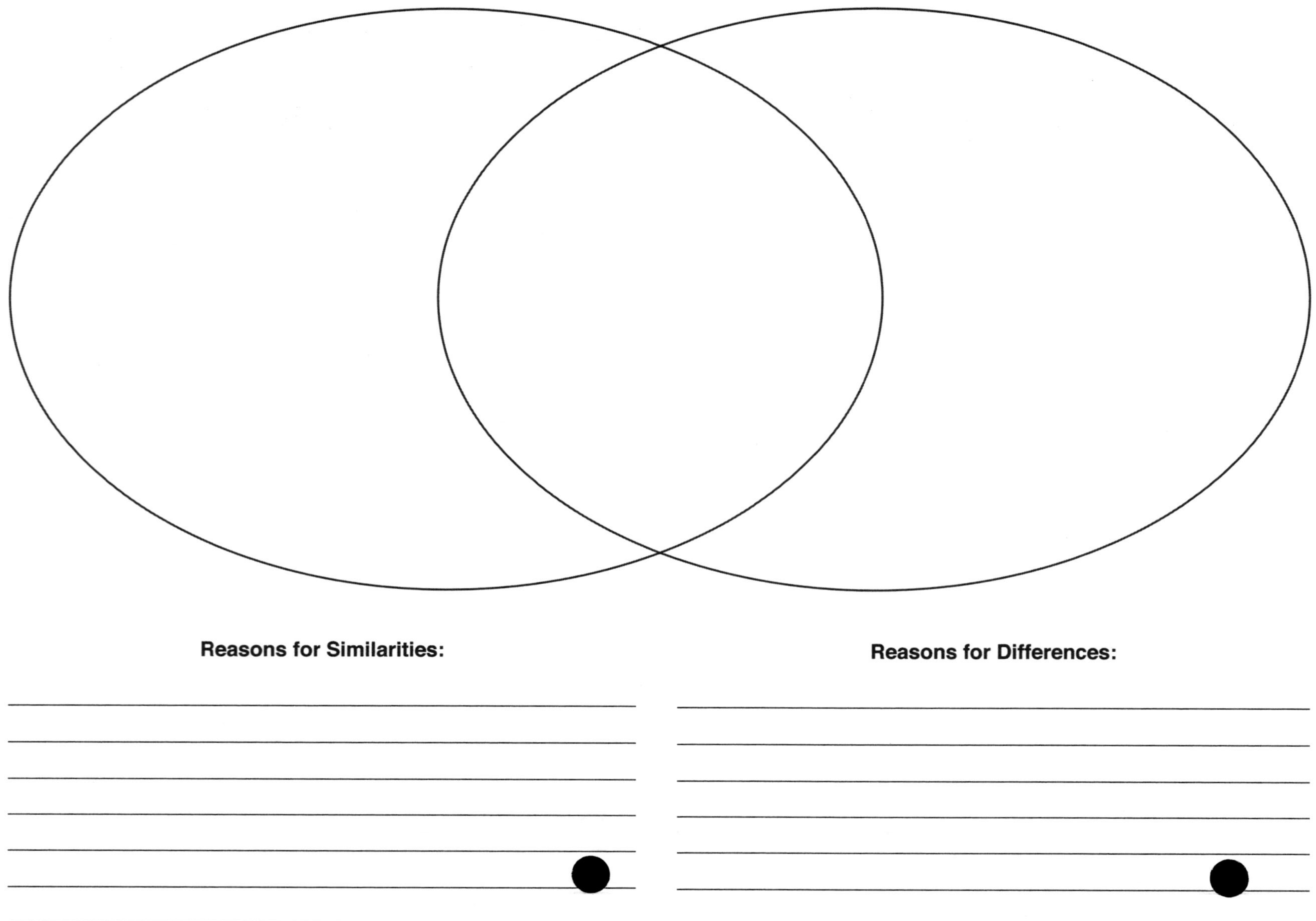

Reasons for Similarities:

Reasons for Differences:

■ NAME: ______________________ ■ Date: __________

Comparison: Haitian Revolution and French Revolution

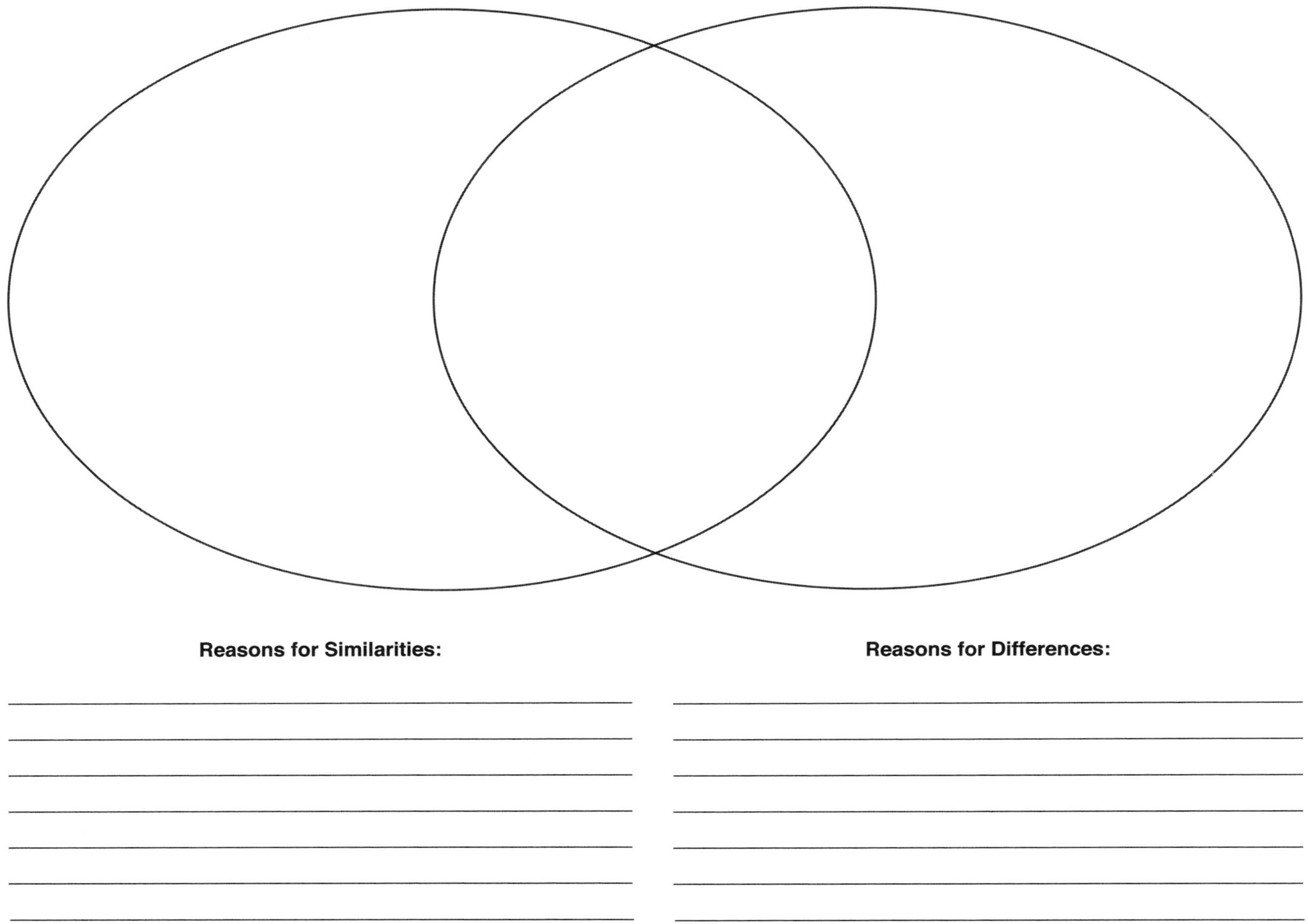

Reasons for Similarities:

Reasons for Differences:

■ NAME: ______________________ ■ Date: __________

Comparison: Indian Revolt of 1857 and the Boxer Rebellion

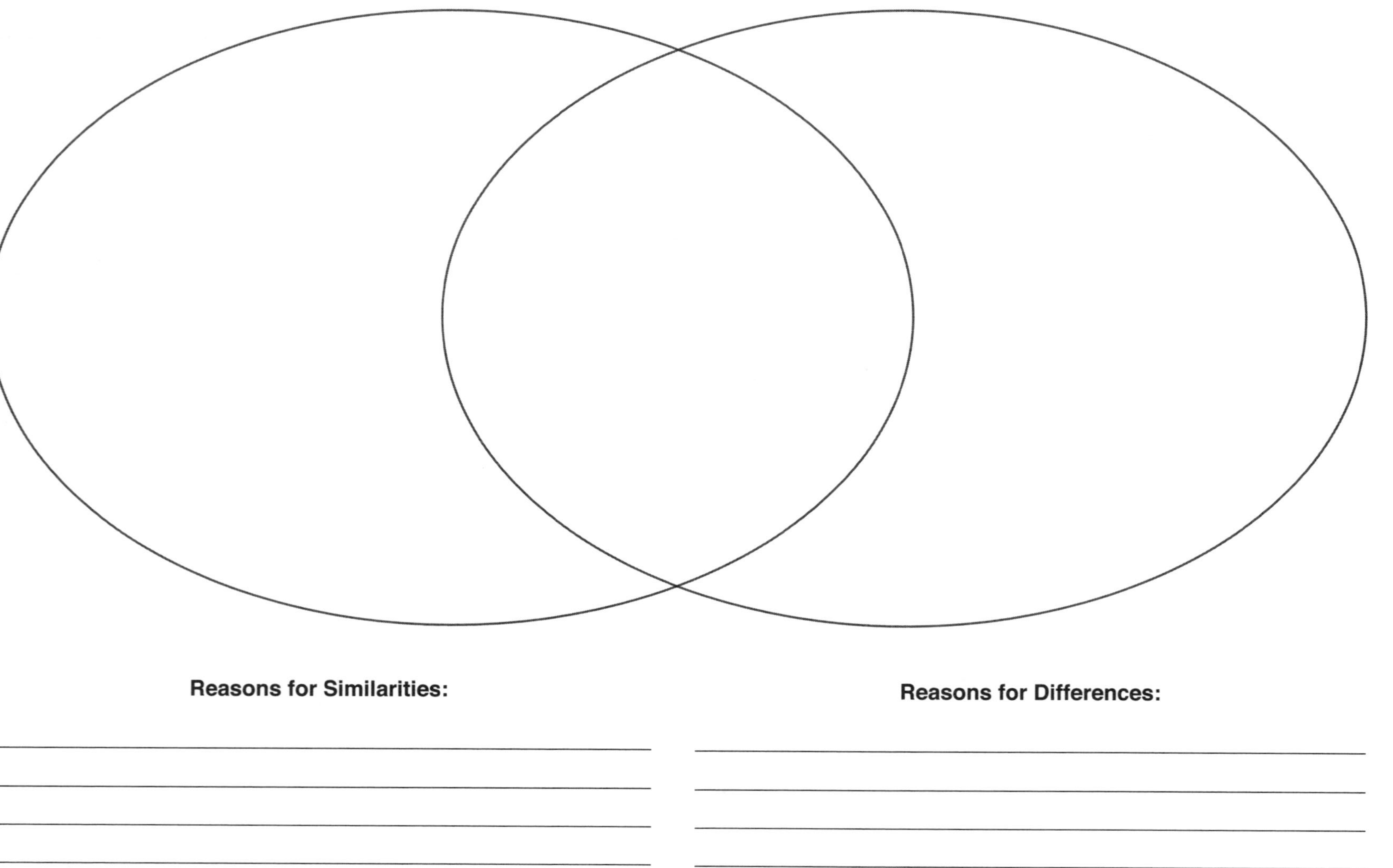

Reasons for Similarities:

Reasons for Differences:

■ NAME: ______________________ ■ Date: __________

Comparison: Chinese Exclusion Acts and White Australia Policy

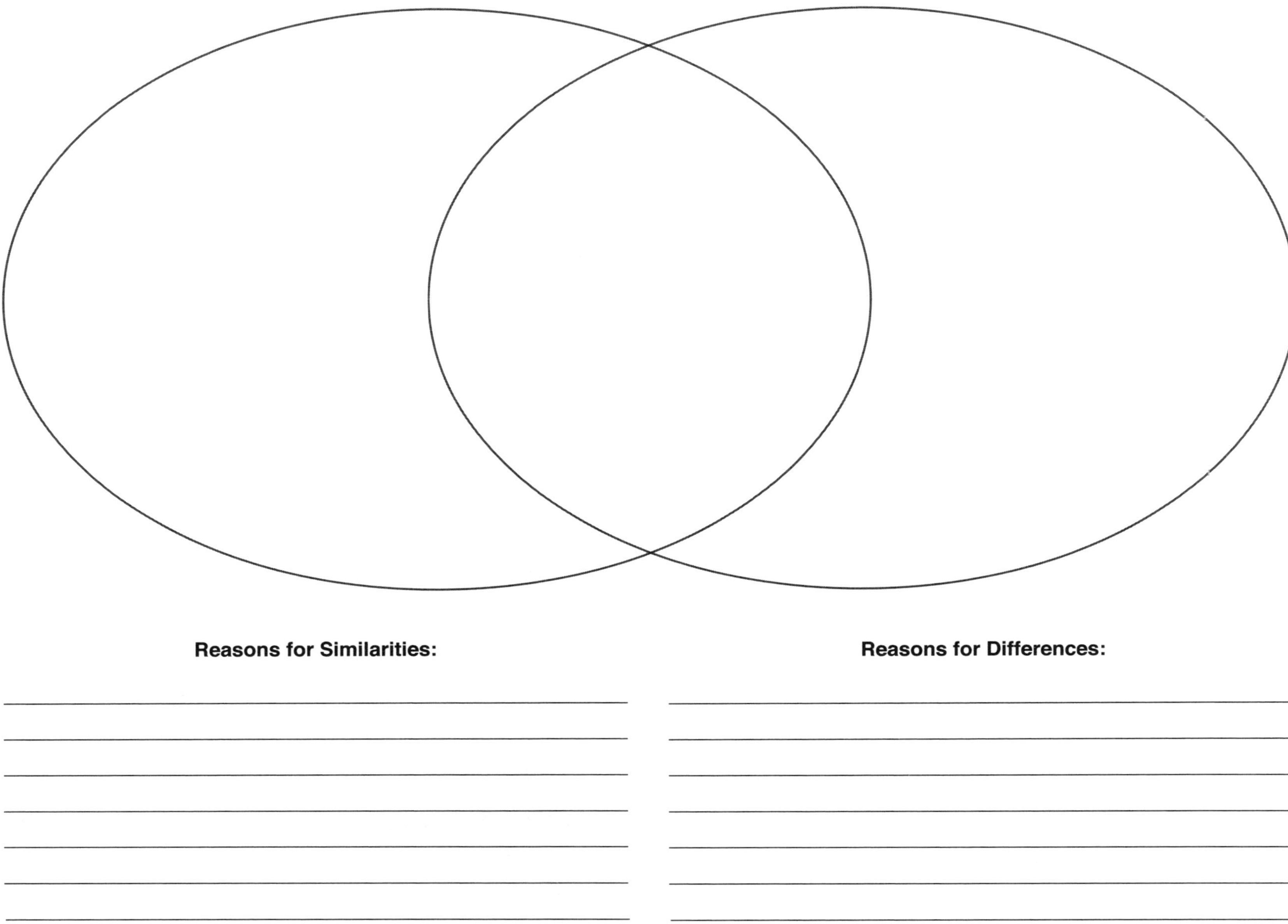

Reasons for Similarities:

____

Reasons for Differences:

____

■ NAME: ______________________ ■ Date: __________

Comparison: Independence Movements in Vietnam and India

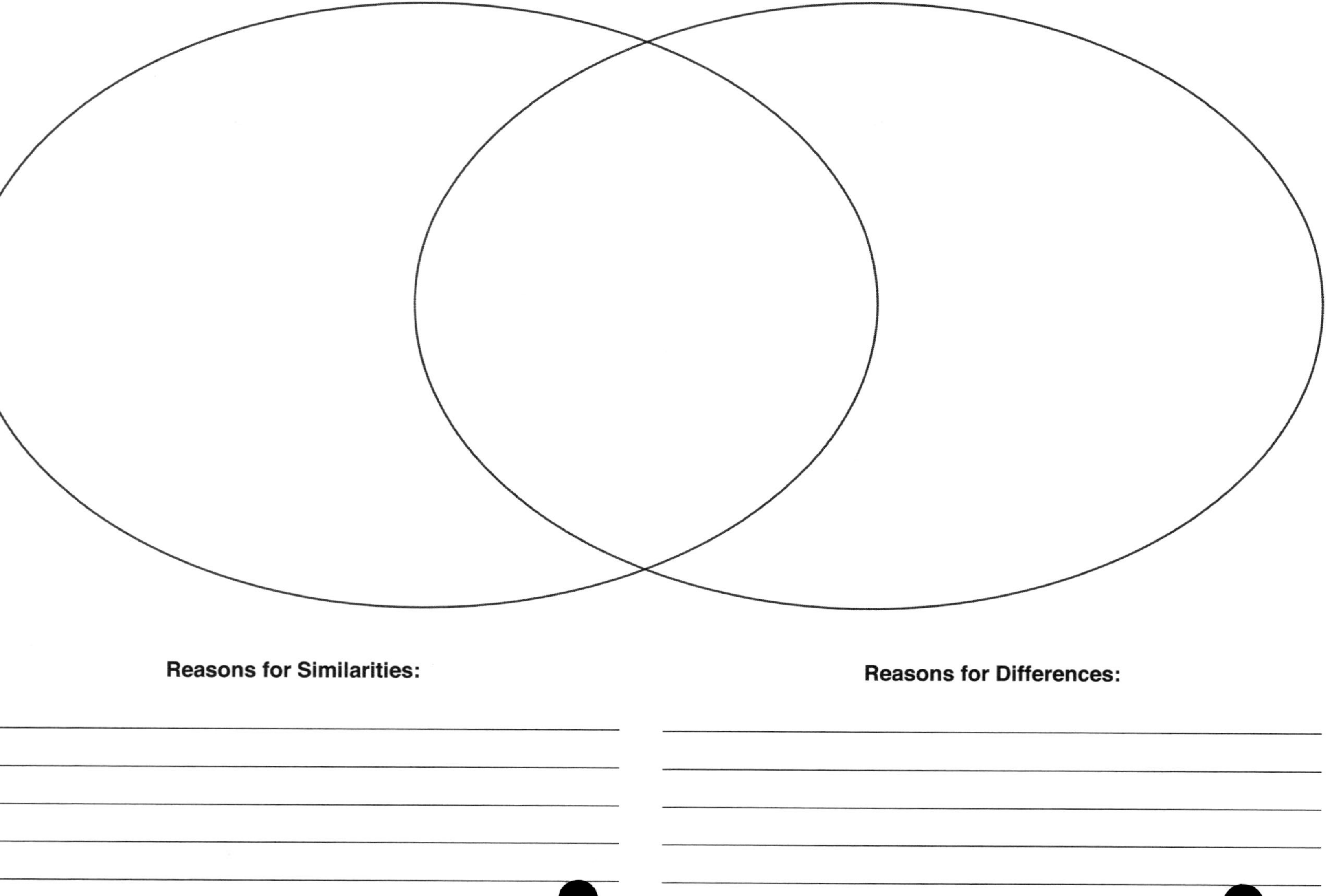

Reasons for Similarities:

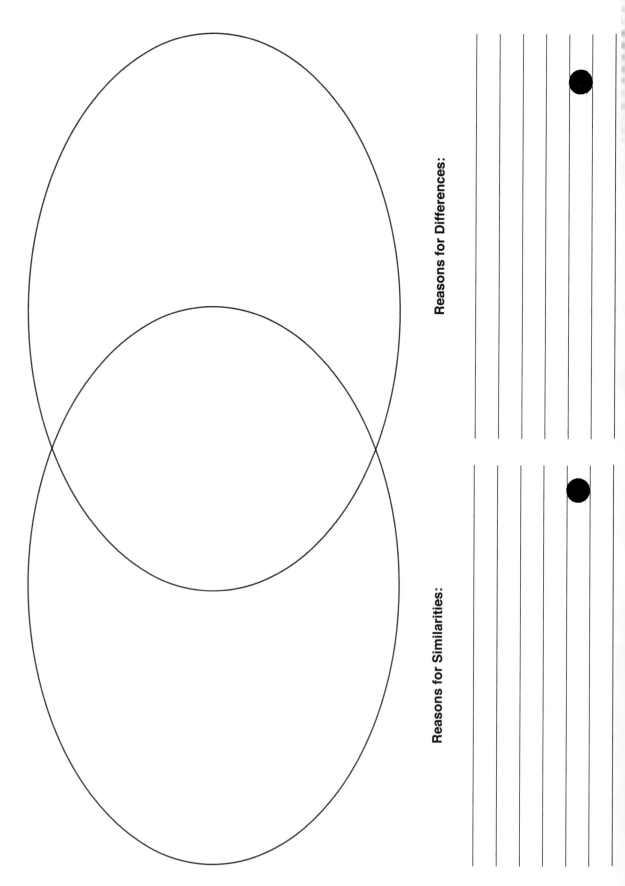

Reasons for Differences:

■ NAME: ______________________ ■ Date: __________

Comparison: Pan-Arabism and Pan-Africanism

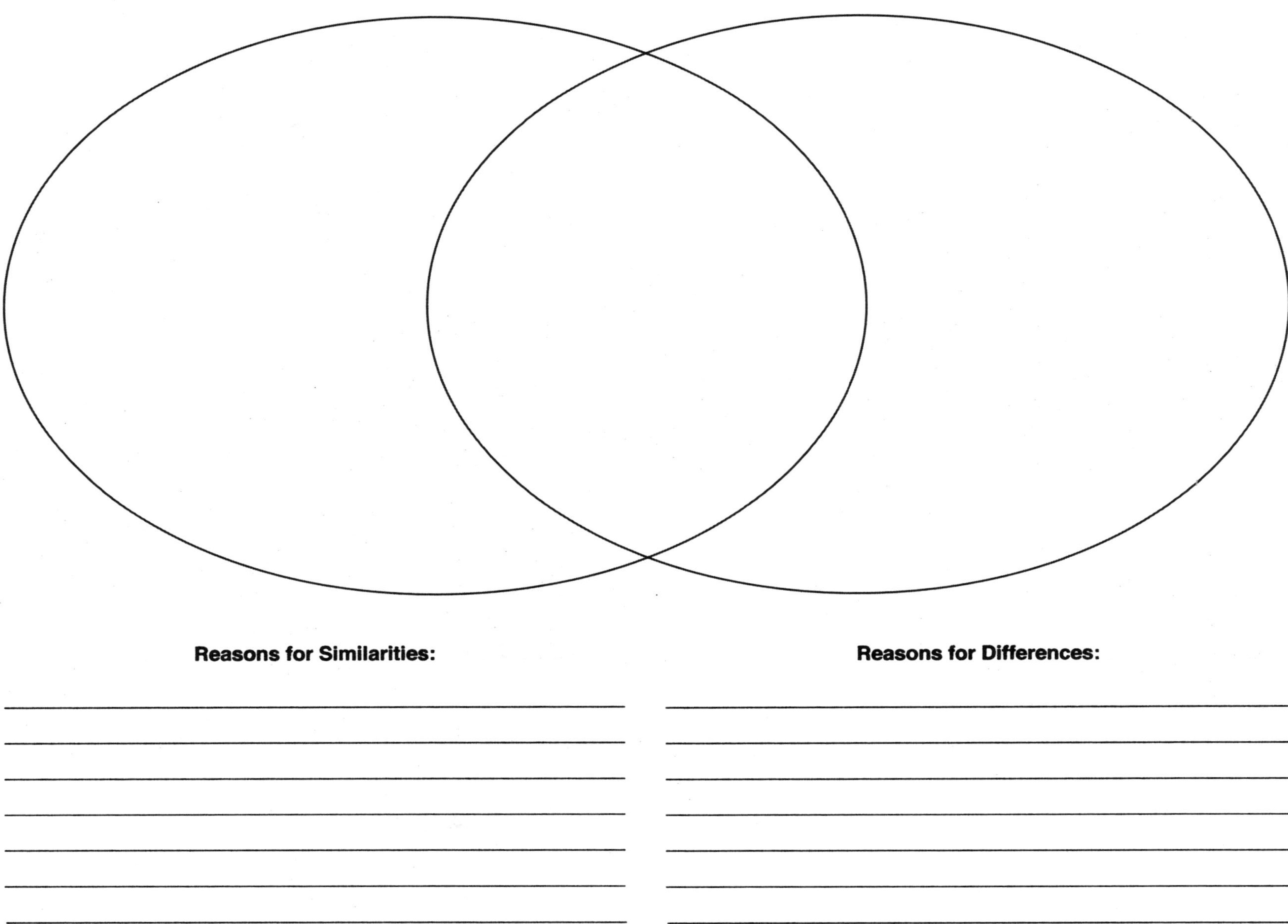

Reasons for Similarities:

Reasons for Differences:

■ NAME: ______________________ ■ Date: __________

Comparison: Nationalism in France and Pakistan

Reasons for Similarities:

Reasons for Differences:

■ NAME: ______________________ ■ Date: __________

Comparison: Ethnic Violence in Rwanda and Armenia

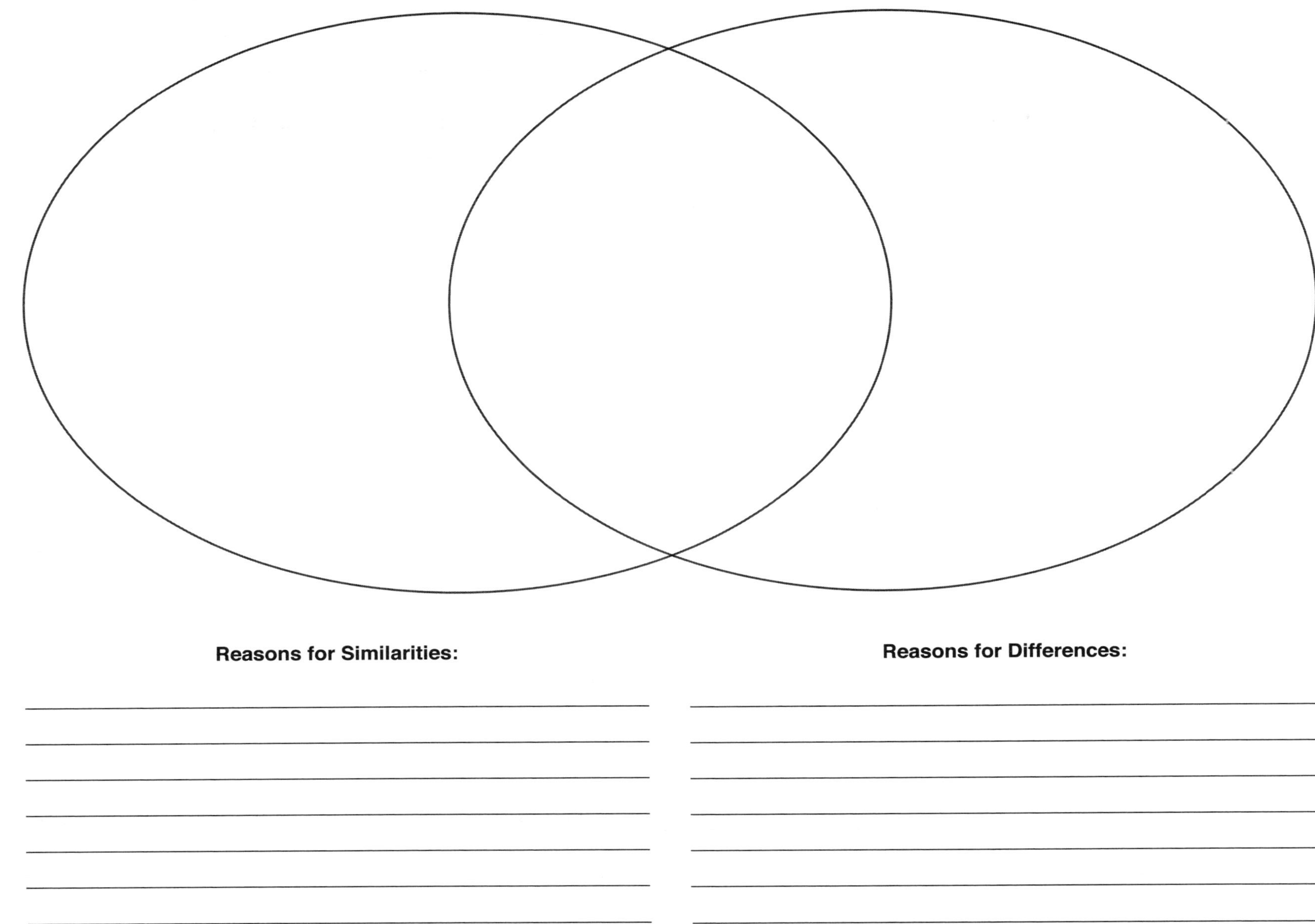

Reasons for Similarities:

Reasons for Differences:

■ NAME: ______________________________ ■ Date: __________

Comparison: Liberation Leaders Mao Zedong and Fidel Castro

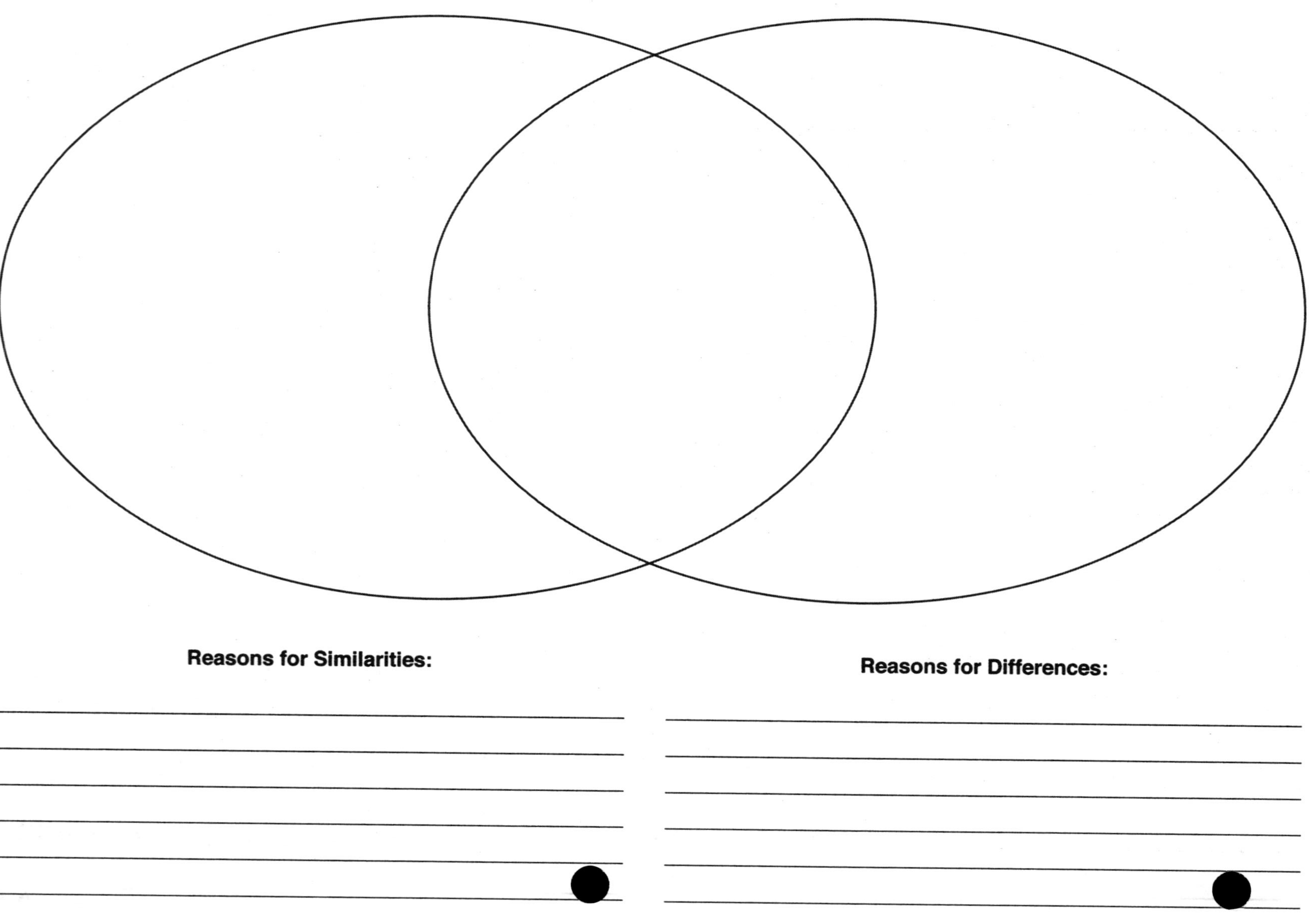

Reasons for Similarities:

Reasons for Differences:

■ NAME: ____________________ ■ Date: __________

Comparison: ETA and al-Qaeda

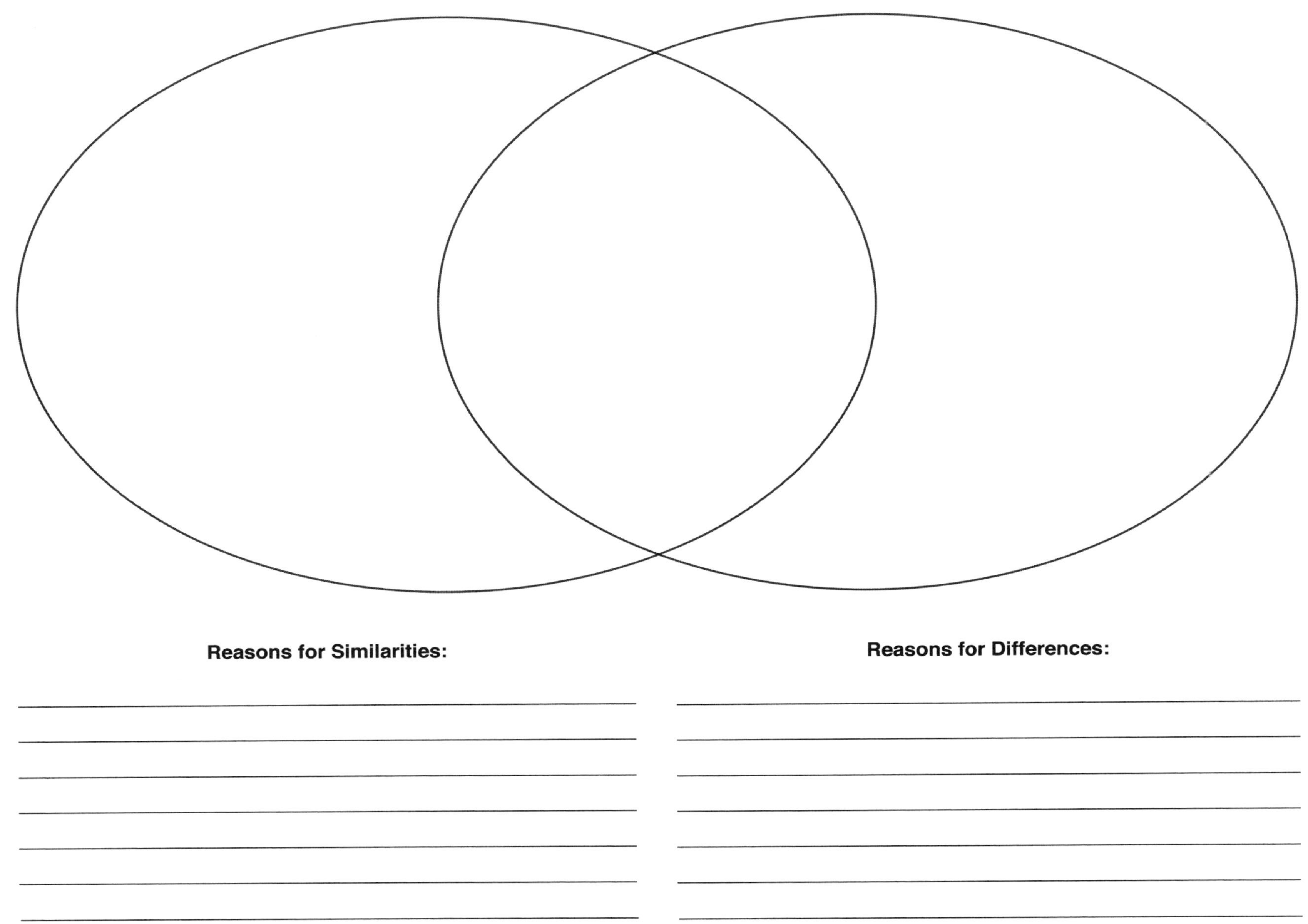

Reasons for Similarities:

Reasons for Differences:

■ NAME: ______________________ ■ Date: __________

Comparison: Hollywood and Bollywood

Reasons for Similarities:

Reasons for Differences:

■ NAME: ______________________ ■ Date: __________

Comparison: Spanish Civil War and World War II

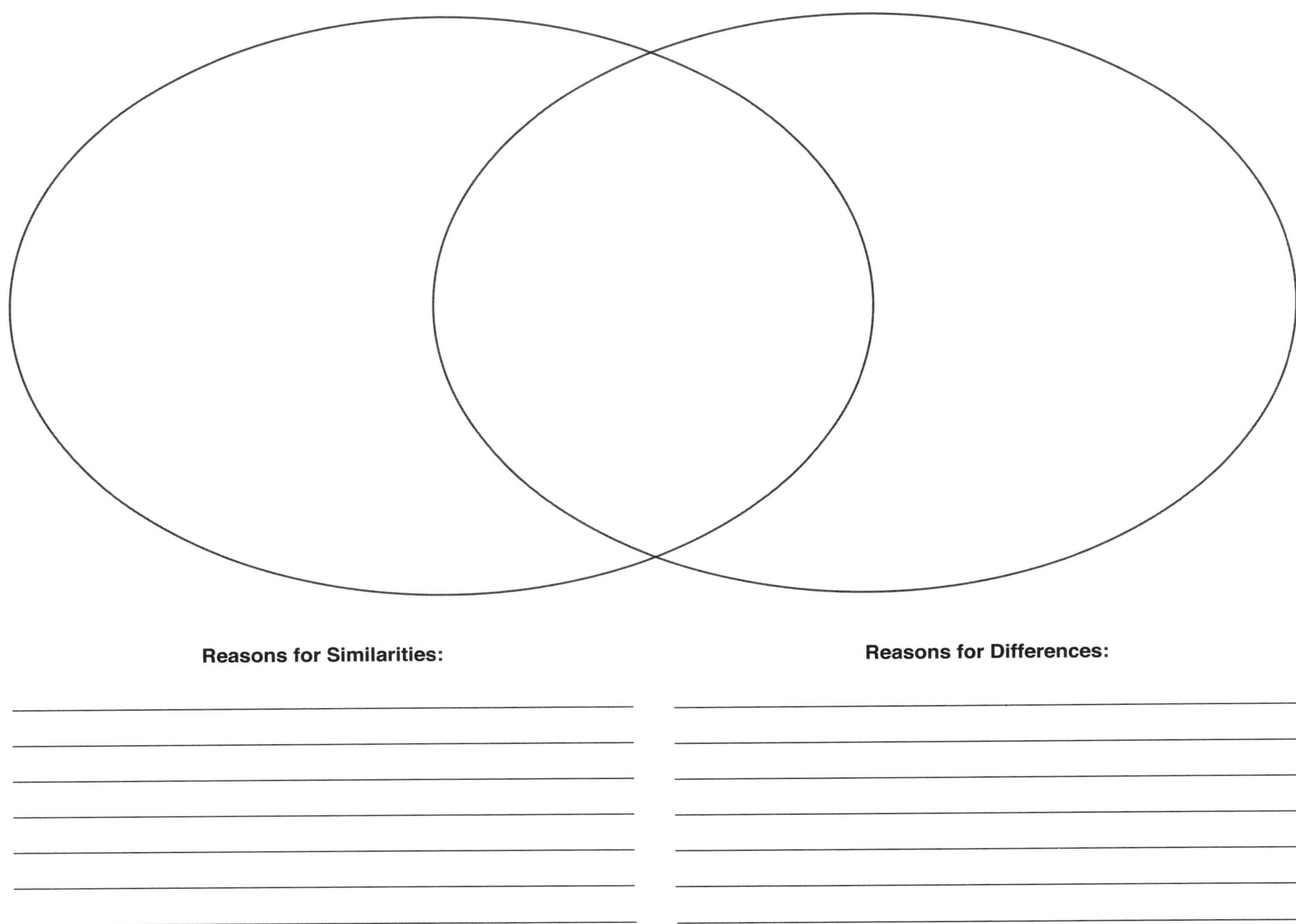

Reasons for Similarities:

Reasons for Differences:

Student Instructions: Defining the Period

When we are asked to define a historical period, we are asked to determine specific start and stop dates of events for the period under investigation. Many historical periods do not have clearly defined beginnings and endings; therefore, the task of defining the period is an important one and leads to much debate within historical scholarship.

The purpose of these Defining the Period activities is to investigate when important periods in history begin and end. Each worksheet has a broad historical period about which you are asked to determine when that period begins and ends. In other words, is there some specific historical event or date that you believe defines the beginning and ending of the period under investigation? In addition to determining the beginning and end dates, you will also be asked to provide specific details that help define and contradict the historical period.

■ NAME: ______________________ ■ Date: __________

Defining the Period: Bantu Migrations (Example)

Start Date / Event: 1000 BCE

Why?

Bantu-speaking agricultural peoples, who had learned the art of ironworking and who had largely occupied the forest regions of west Africa, began moving out of their region and moved throughout eastern and southern Africa.

End Date / Event: 500 CE

Why?

By this time, pioneering groups of Bantu had made it through the rainforests of central Africa and into the savannahs south of the forest region. In eastern Africa, Bantu-speaking farmers followed the rivers where agriculture was possible.

DEFINING CHARACTERISTICS	CONTRADICTORY CHARACTERISTICS
• Gradual movement of people • No conflict or warfare, but a gradual diffusion of patterns of living involving language, root crops, grains, sheep, cattle, ironworking technology, and even pottery. • Existing villages could "become Bantu." • Hunting and gathering people were displaced by Bantu agriculturalists.	• Although Bantu migrations were peaceful, new research suggests that only descendants of the Bantu survive in present-day western Africa, suggesting a complete population replacement. • Immunity to diseases gave Bantu advantages over the hunting and gathering peoples they encountered. • Bantus changed as they moved southward and eastward. Some farmers who moved eastward from the original Bantu homeland grew coconuts, sugarcane, and bananas, while those who moved southward but stayed in the western regions of Africa grew more grains and raised more animals.

■ NAME: ______________________ ■ Date: __________

Defining the Period: Bantu Migrations

Start Date / Event:

Why?

___

___

___

End Date / Event:

Why?

___

___

___

DEFINING CHARACTERISTICS	CONTRADICTORY CHARACTERISTICS

■ NAME: ____________________ ■ Date: __________

Defining the Period: Development of Chinese Imperial Structure

Start Date / Event:

Why?

____

____

____

End Date / Event:

Why?

____

____

____

DEFINING CHARACTERISTICS	CONTRADICTORY CHARACTERISTICS

■ NAME: ______________________ ■ Date: __________

Defining the Period: Pax Romana

Start Date / Event:

Why?

____

____

____

End Date / Event:

Why?

____

____

____

DEFINING CHARACTERISTICS	CONTRADICTORY CHARACTERISTICS

DP4

■ NAME: ______________________ ■ Date: __________

Defining the Period: Caliphates

Start Date / Event:

Why?

____

____

____

End Date / Event:

Why?

____

____

____

DEFINING CHARACTERISTICS	CONTRADICTORY CHARACTERISTICS

■ NAME: ______________________________ ■ Date: ____________

Defining the Period: Byzantine Empire

Start Date / Event:

Why?

____

____

____

End Date / Event:

Why?

____

____

____

DEFINING CHARACTERISTICS	CONTRADICTORY CHARACTERISTICS

DP6

■ **NAME:** ______________________ ■ **Date:** __________

Defining the Period: Influence of Buddhism in China, Korea, Japan, and Vietnam

Start Date / Event:

Why?

____

____

____

End Date / Event:

Why?

____

____

____

DEFINING CHARACTERISTICS	**CONTRADICTORY CHARACTERISTICS**

■ NAME: ______________________ ■ Date: __________

Defining the Period: Polynesian Migrations

Start Date / Event:

Why?

____

____

____

End Date / Event:

Why?

____

____

____

DEFINING CHARACTERISTICS	CONTRADICTORY CHARACTERISTICS

■ NAME: ______________________________ ■ Date: ____________

Defining the Period: Pax Mongolica

Start Date / Event:
Why?

____

____

____

End Date / Event:
Why?

____

____

____

DEFINING CHARACTERISTICS	CONTRADICTORY CHARACTERISTICS

■ NAME: ____________________ ■ Date: __________

Defining the Period: Japanese Shogunates

Start Date / Event:

Why?

____

____

____

End Date / Event:

Why?

____

____

____

DEFINING CHARACTERISTICS	CONTRADICTORY CHARACTERISTICS

■ NAME: ________________________ ■ Date: ____________

Defining the Period: Gunpowder Empires

Start Date / Event:
Why?

____

____

____

End Date / Event:
Why?

____

____

____

DEFINING CHARACTERISTICS	CONTRADICTORY CHARACTERISTICS

■ NAME: ______________________ ■ Date: __________

Defining the Period: Rise of Russia

Start Date / Event:

Why?

____

____

____

End Date / Event:

Why?

____

____

____

DEFINING CHARACTERISTICS	CONTRADICTORY CHARACTERISTICS

■ NAME: ______________________ ■ Date: __________

Defining the Period: Columbian Exchange

Start Date / Event:
Why?

____

____

____

End Date / Event:
Why?

____

____

____

DEFINING CHARACTERISTICS	CONTRADICTORY CHARACTERISTICS

■ NAME: ______________________ ■ Date: __________

Defining the Period: Transatlantic Slave Trade

Start Date / Event:

Why?

End Date / Event:

Why?

DEFINING CHARACTERISTICS	CONTRADICTORY CHARACTERISTICS

■ NAME: ______________________________ ■ Date: ____________

Defining the Period: Industrialization

Start Date / Event:

Why?

____

____

____

End Date / Event:

Why?

____

____

____

DEFINING CHARACTERISTICS	CONTRADICTORY CHARACTERISTICS

■ NAME: ______________________ ■ Date: ____________

Defining the Period: Imperialism

Start Date / Event:

Why?

____

____

____

End Date / Event:

Why?

____

____

____

DEFINING CHARACTERISTICS	CONTRADICTORY CHARACTERISTICS

■ NAME: ______________________ ■ Date: __________

Defining the Period: Global Migration

Start Date / Event:

Why?

____

____

____

End Date / Event:

Why?

____

____

____

DEFINING CHARACTERISTICS	CONTRADICTORY CHARACTERISTICS

■ NAME: ____________________ ■ Date: __________

Defining the Period: Scientific Revolution and Age of Enlightenment

Start Date / Event:

Why?

End Date / Event:

Why?

DEFINING CHARACTERISTICS	CONTRADICTORY CHARACTERISTICS

■ NAME: ____________________ ■ Date: __________

Defining the Period: Internationalization

Start Date / Event:

Why?

End Date / Event:

Why?

DEFINING CHARACTERISTICS	CONTRADICTORY CHARACTERISTICS

■ NAME: ______________________ ■ Date: __________

Defining the Period: Cold War

Start Date / Event:

Why?

End Date / Event:

Why?

DEFINING CHARACTERISTICS	CONTRADICTORY CHARACTERISTICS

■ NAME: ______________________ ■ Date: __________

Defining the Period: Total War

Start Date / Event:

Why?

____

____

____

End Date / Event:

Why?

____

____

____

DEFINING CHARACTERISTICS	CONTRADICTORY CHARACTERISTICS

Student Instructions: Contextualization and Synthesis

When we are asked to consider contextualization and synthesis, we are asked to first consider the historical setting of a particular event (i.e., the who, what, when, where, and why) and then to connect that event to another event in history.

The purpose of the Contextualization and Synthesis activities is to explore the different ways in which historians work with context. The first is what we call broad context: the big picture. The second is what we call other context: the connection of the topic under investigation to another period by looking either backward or forward —"similar in kind, but at a different time."

■ NAME: ________________ ■ Date: ________

Contextualization and Synthesis: Harappa (Example)

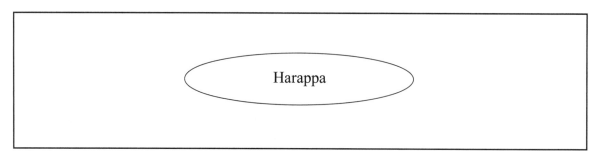

Contextualization

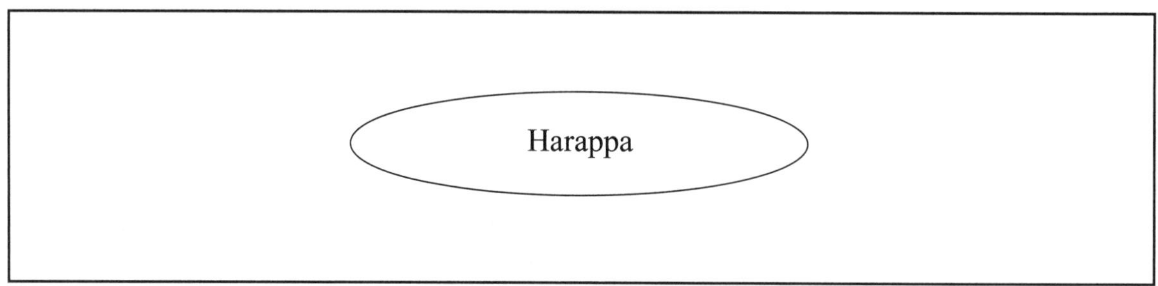

Synthesis

Harappa is similar to . . .

Backward Looking

Humans discover fire

One Similarity

Harappa, in the massive change that it represented, is similar to humans discovering fire because the discovery of fire allowed humans control over their environment that they had not had previously. Similarly, urban living changed the way humans interacted with the environment around them.

Second Similarity

Once humans discovered fire, just like once they discovered urban living, the new discovery spread quickly and was also discovered independently in various areas.

Forward Looking

Industrialization

One Similarity

With the Industrial Revolution, cities grew even larger.

Second Similarity

Larger cities, created by the Industrial Revolution, required more laws, more organization, and bigger government.

Harappa was one of the world's first cities. As agriculture became more productive, a few agricultural villages became cities with streets, organized stone houses, and up to 40,000 inhabitants. Cities arose only in areas that could sustain very intensive agriculture, so they were rare initially.

■ NAME: ______________________ ■ Date: __________

Contextualization and Synthesis: Harappa

Contextualization

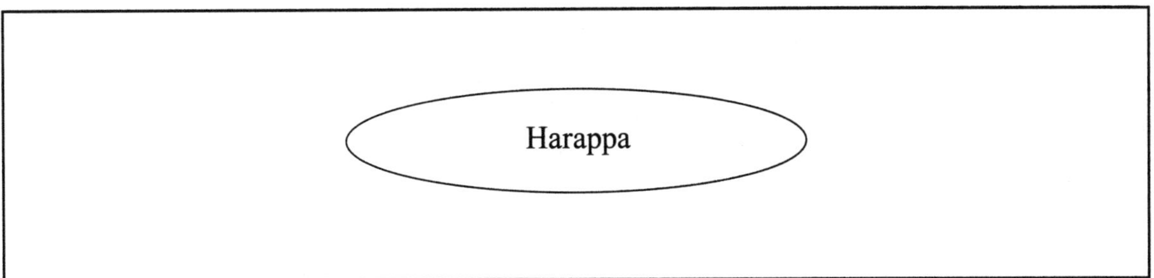

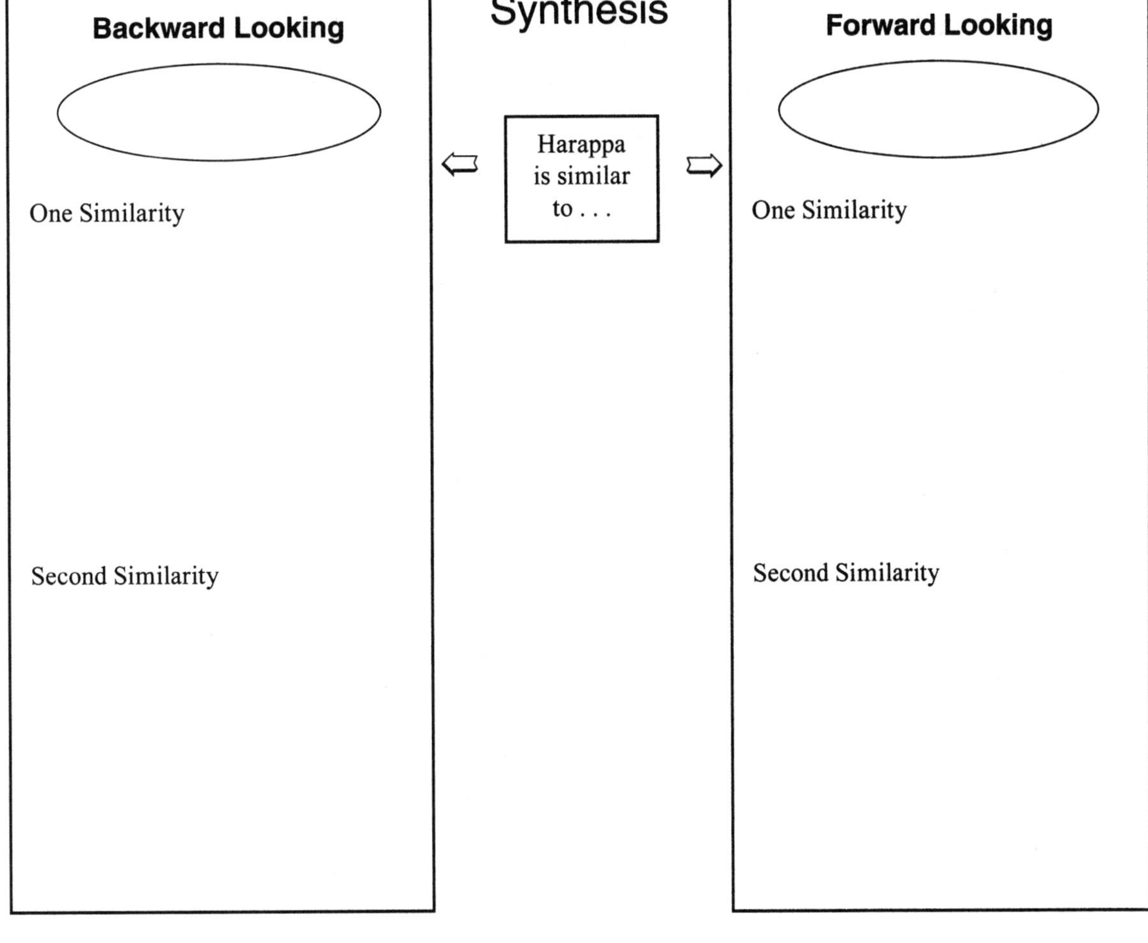

____

____

____

____

■ NAME: ______________________ ■ Date: __________

Contextualization and Synthesis: Mandate of Heaven

Contextualization

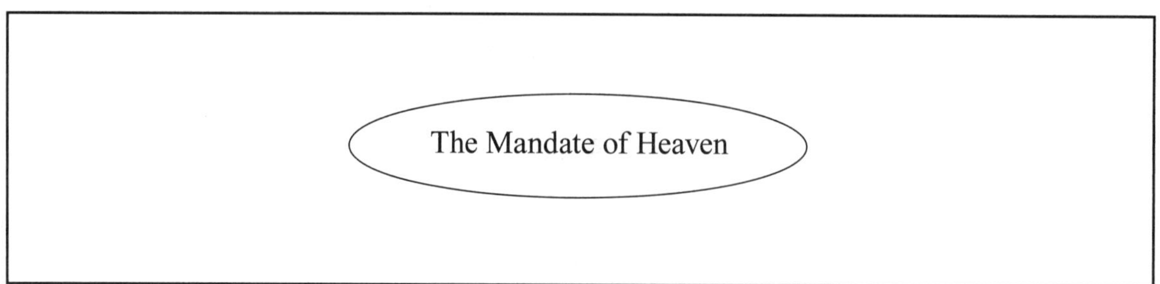

Synthesis

Backward Looking

One Similarity

Second Similarity

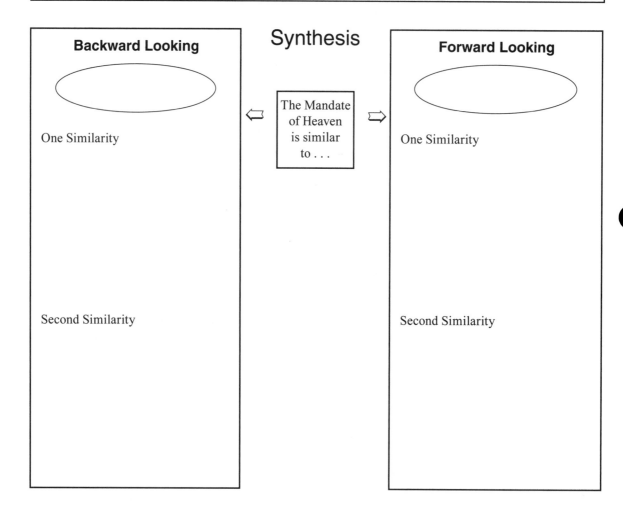

The Mandate of Heaven is similar to . . .

Forward Looking

One Similarity

Second Similarity

■ NAME: ____________________ ■ Date: __________

Contextualization and Synthesis: Mahayana Buddhism

Contextualization

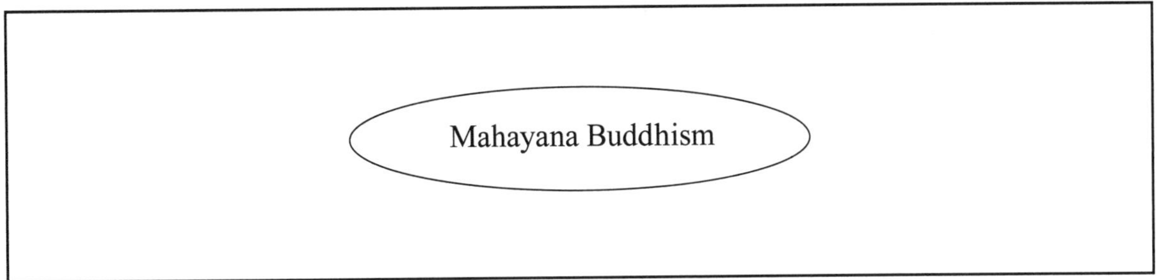

Synthesis

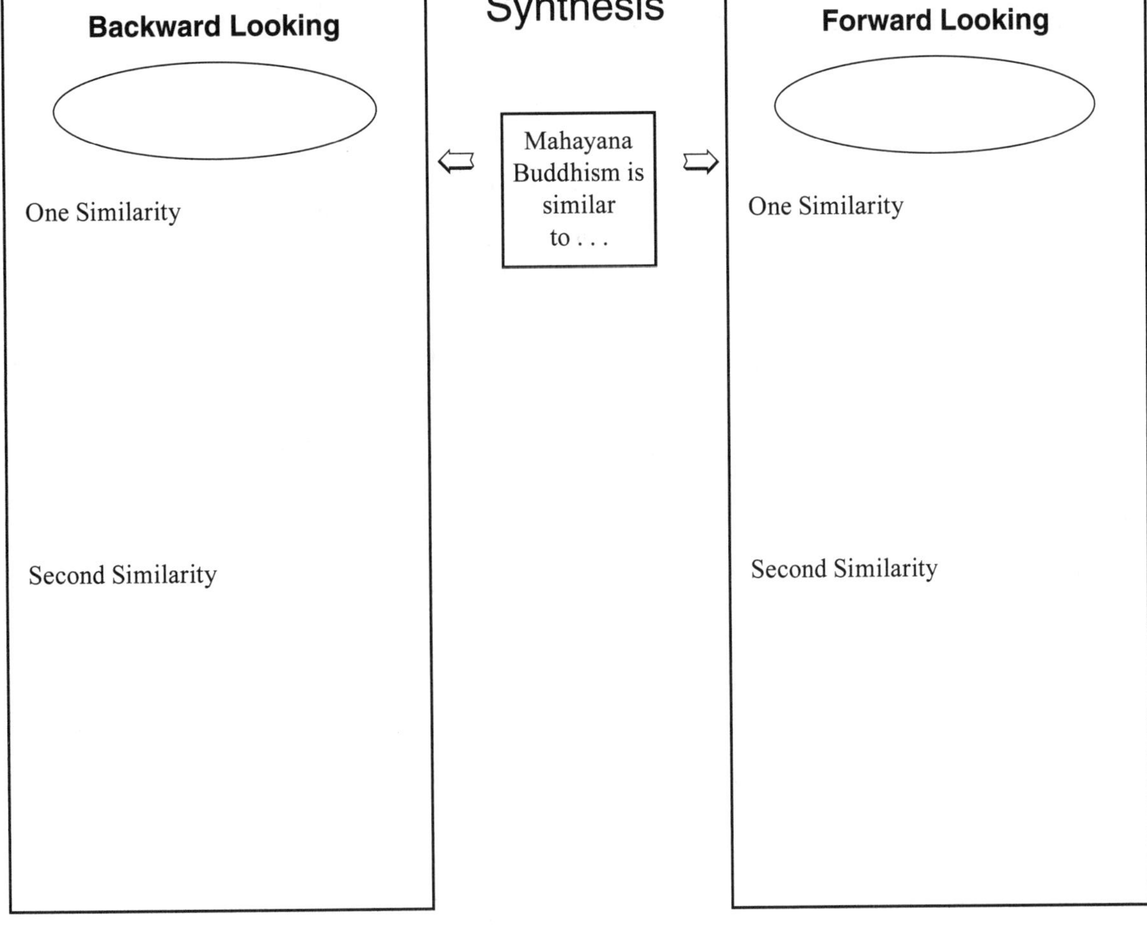

____

____

____

____

■ NAME: ______________________ ■ Date: __________

Contextualization and Synthesis: Conversion of Constantine

Contextualization

Conversion of Constantine

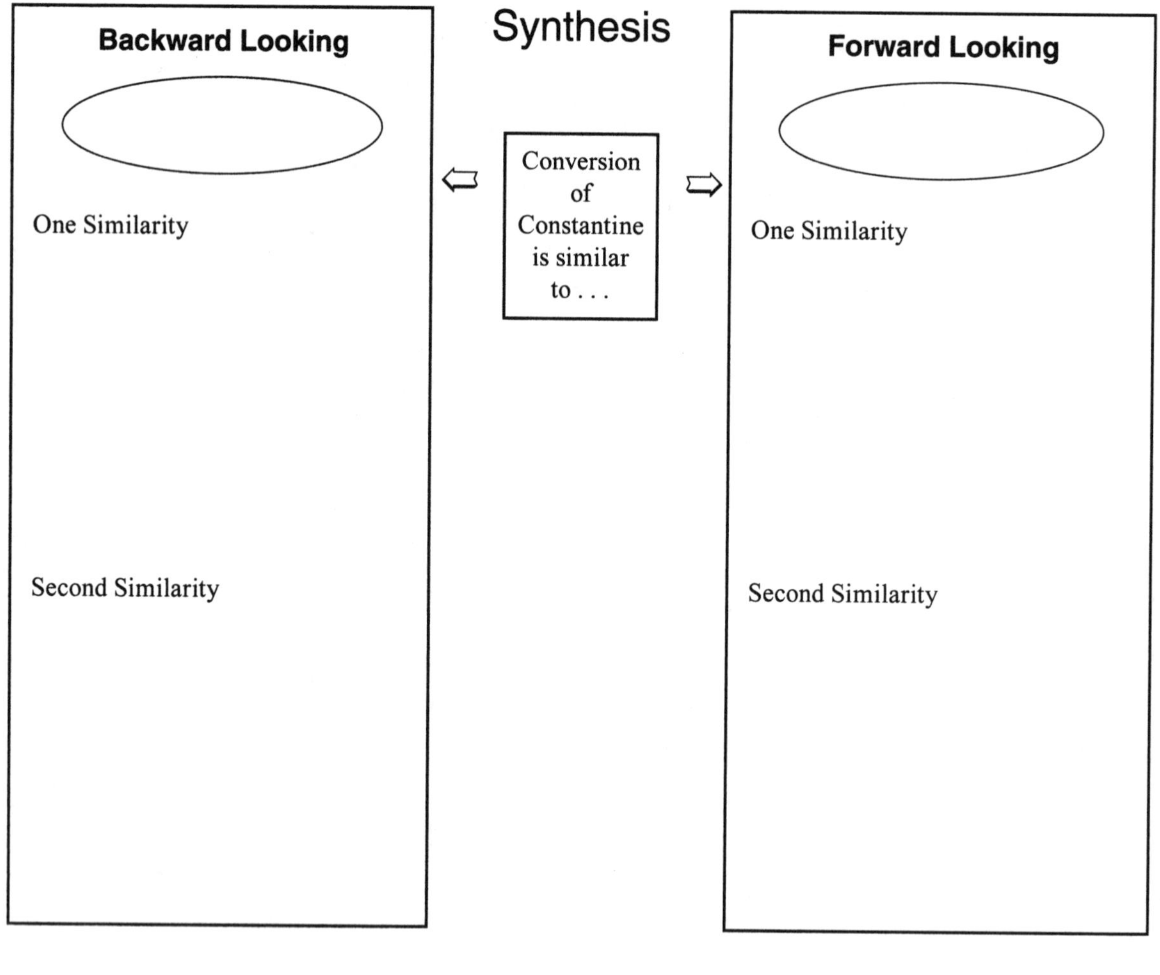

____

____

____

____

■ NAME: ______________________ ■ Date: __________

Contextualization and Synthesis: Justinian's Code

Contextualization

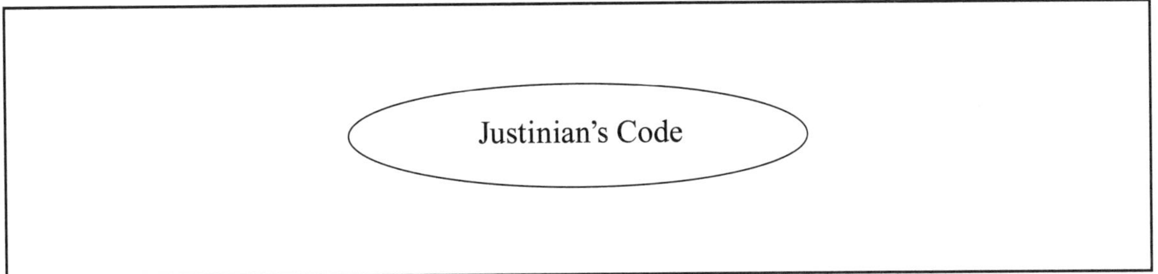

Synthesis

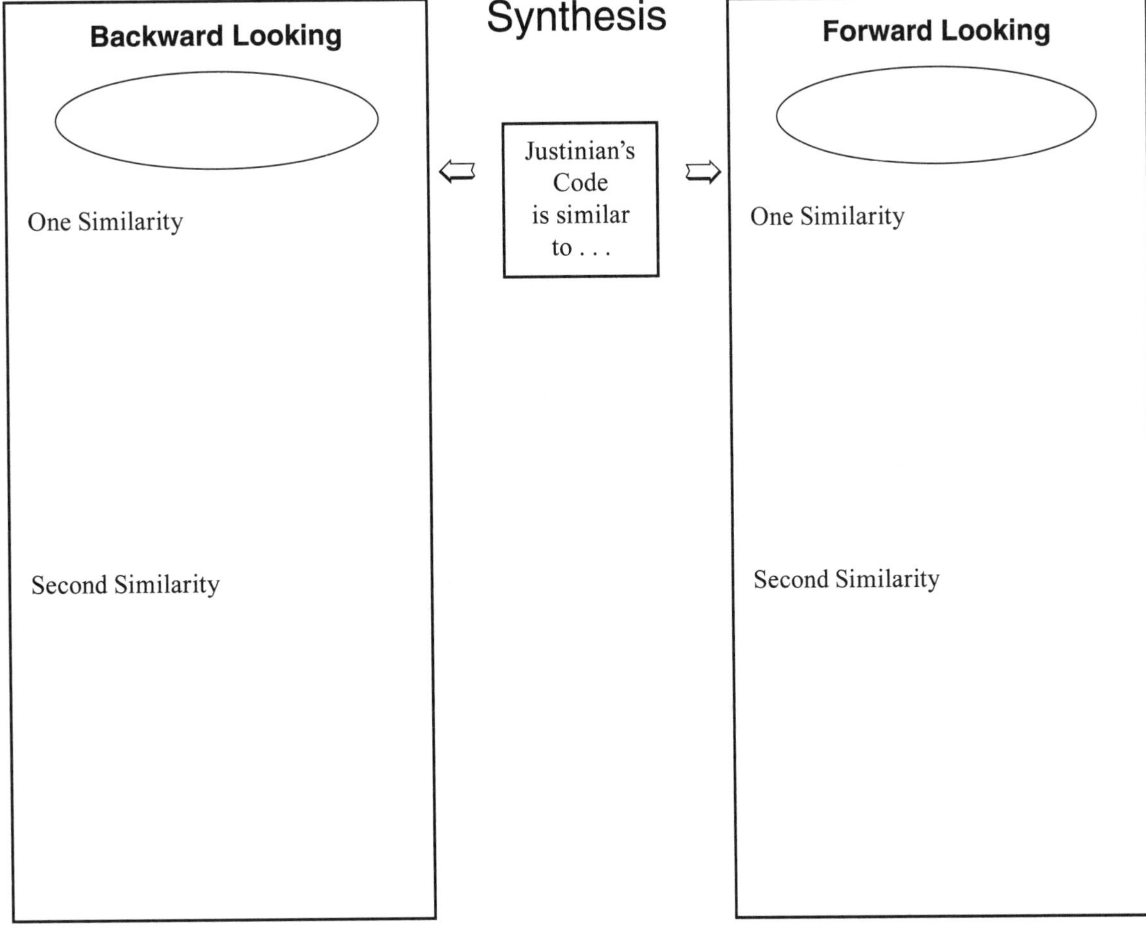

____

____

____

____

■ NAME: ______________________ ■ Date: __________

Contextualization and Synthesis: Laws of Manu

Contextualization

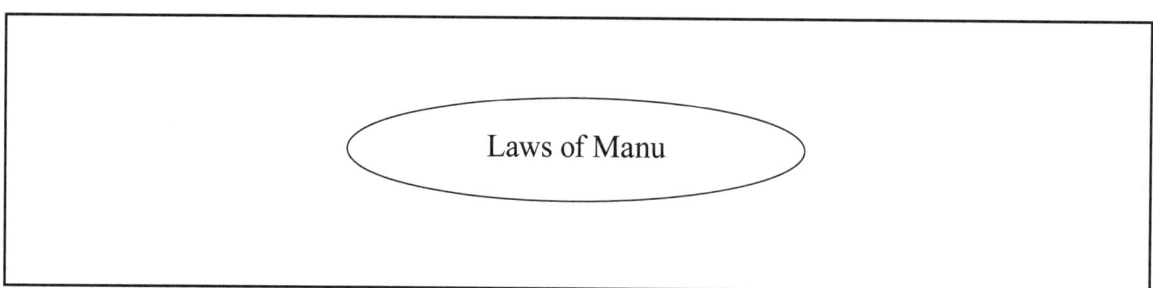

Synthesis

Backward Looking

One Similarity

Second Similarity

Laws of Manu are similar to . . .

Forward Looking

One Similarity

Second Similarity

____

____

____

____

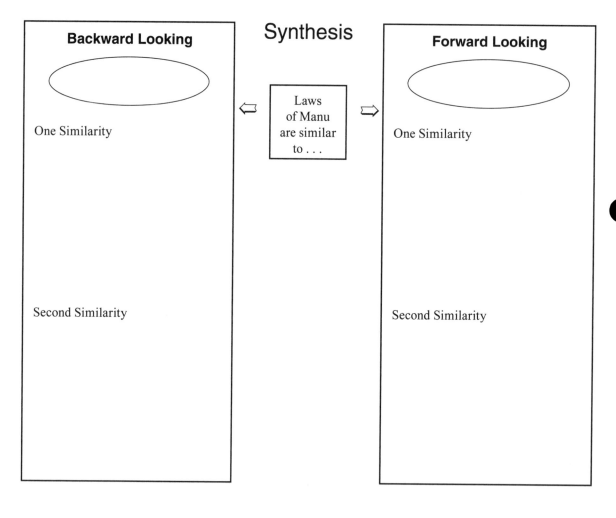

■ NAME: ______________________ ■ Date: __________

Contextualization and Synthesis: Teotihuacan

Contextualization

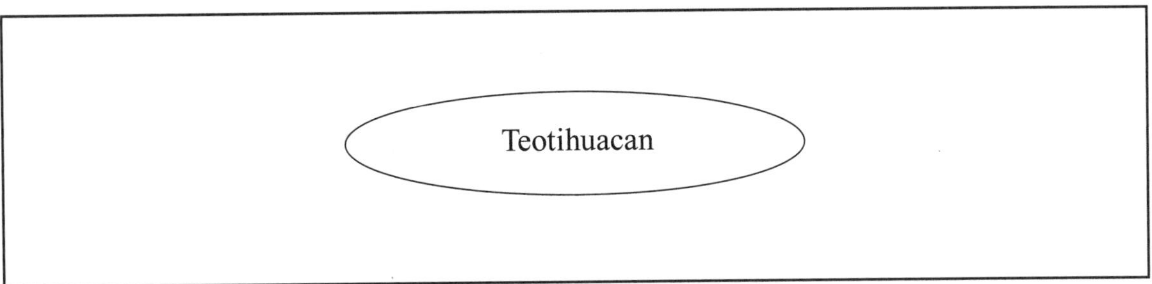

Synthesis

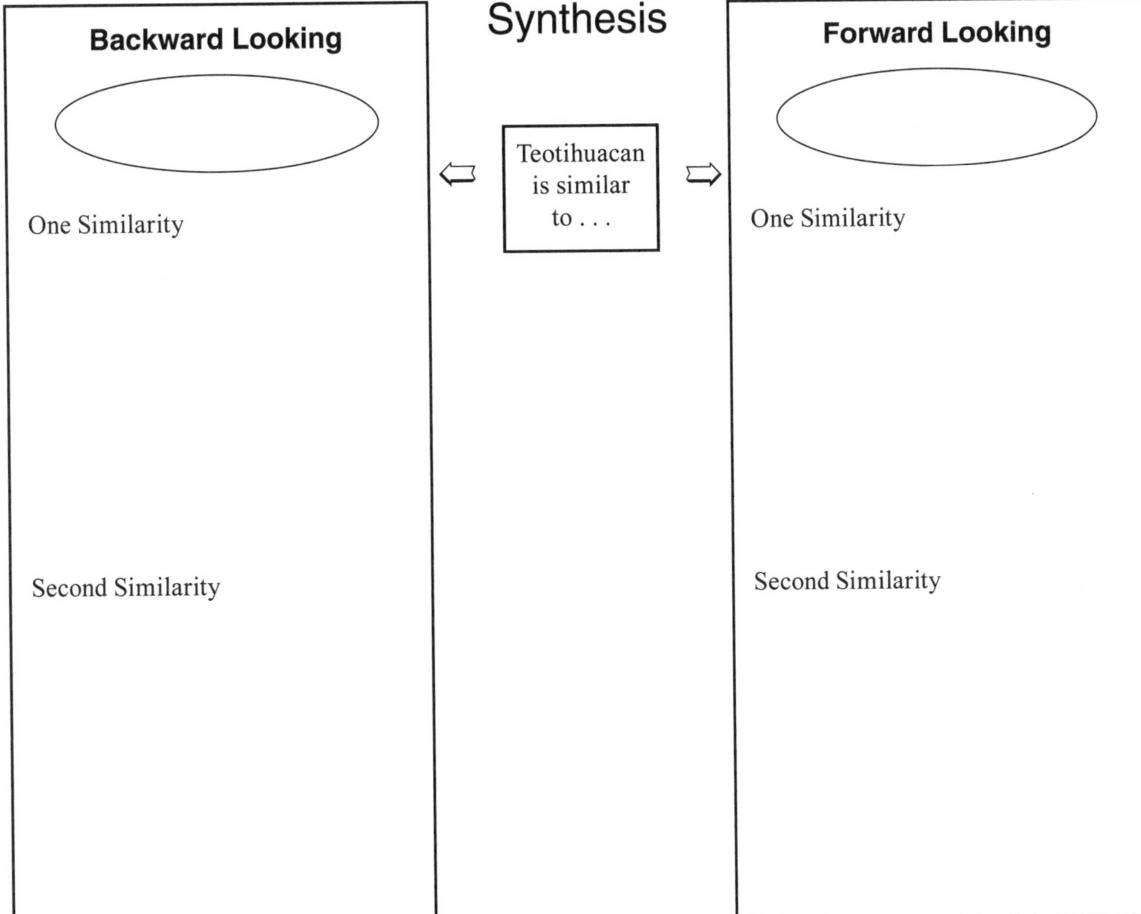

____

____

____

____

■ NAME: ____________________ ■ Date: __________

Contextualization and Synthesis: Muhammad's Flight to Medina

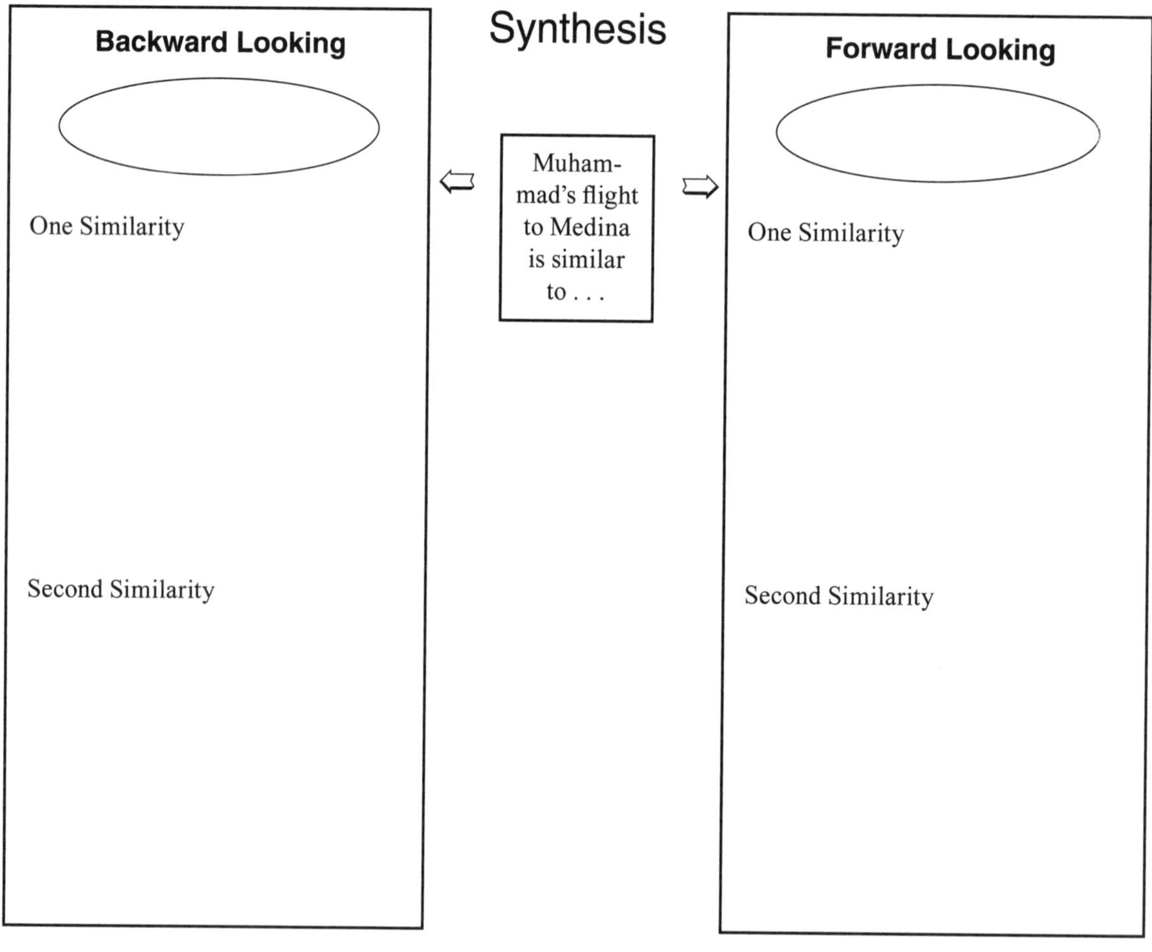

____

____

____

____

■ NAME: ______________________ ■ Date: __________

Contextualization and Synthesis: Sunni-Shi'a Split

Contextualization

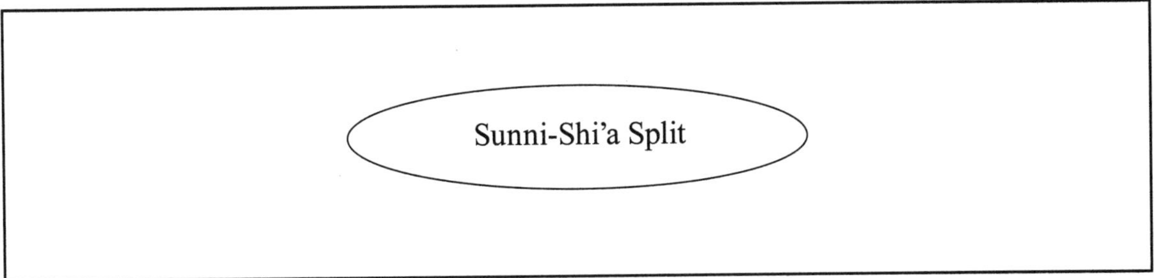

Synthesis

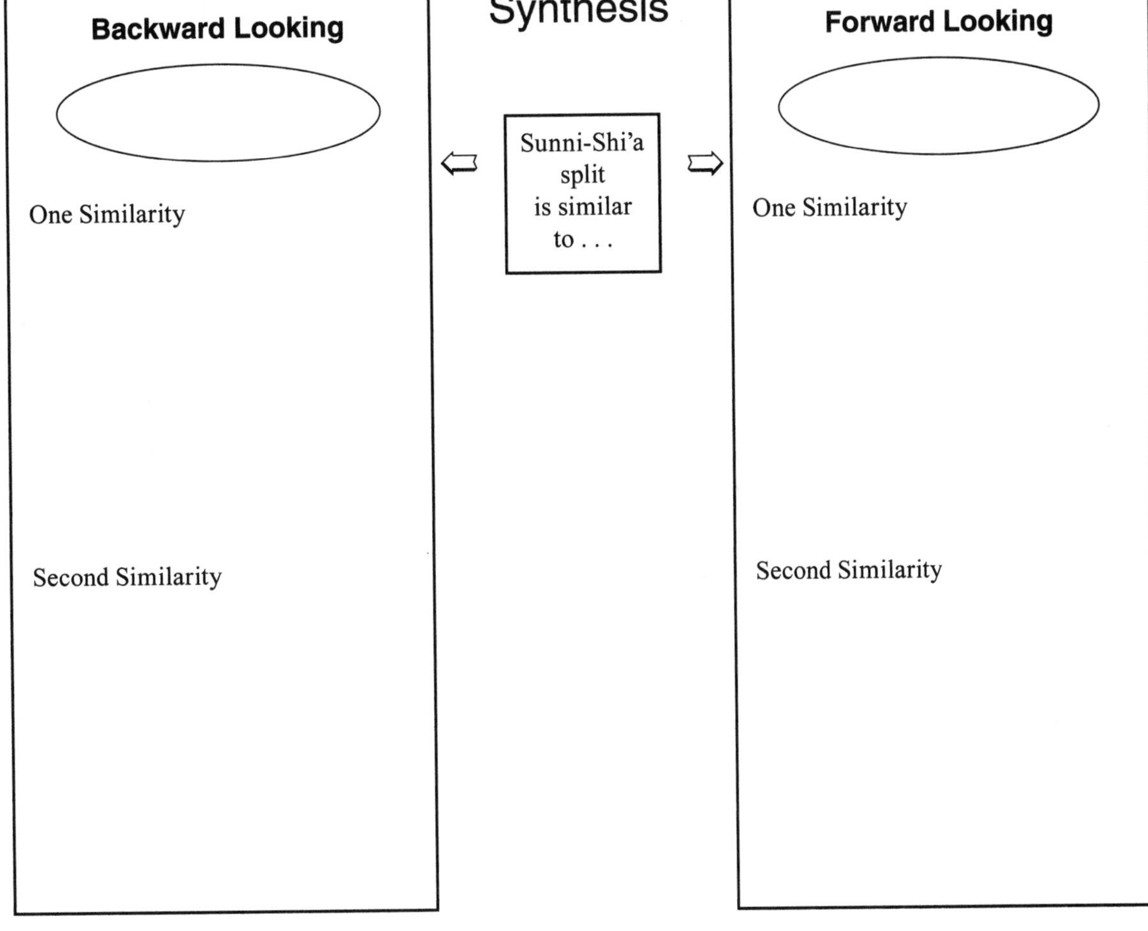

____

____

____

____

■ NAME: ______________________ ■ Date: __________

Contextualization and Synthesis: Zen Buddhism

Contextualization

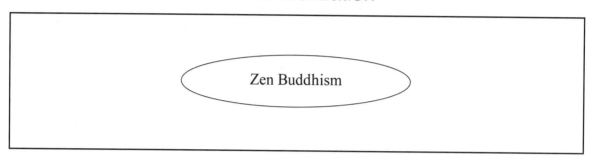

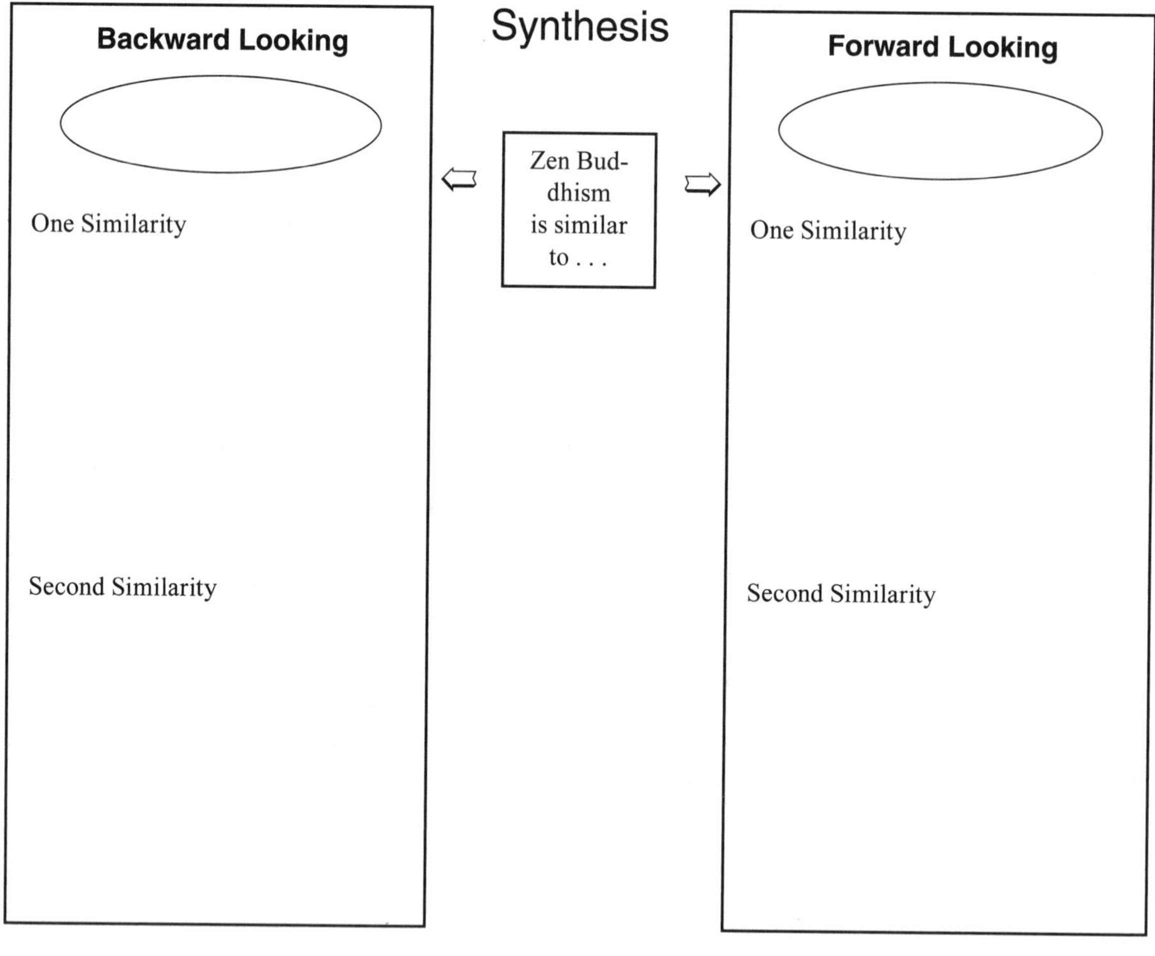

____

____

____

____

■ NAME: ______________________ ■ Date: __________

Contextualization and Synthesis: Sinification of Japan

Contextualization

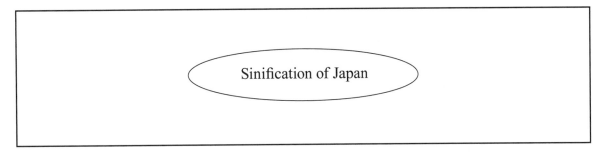

Sinification of Japan

Synthesis

Backward Looking

One Similarity

Second Similarity

Sinification of Japan is similar to . . .

Forward Looking

One Similarity

Second Similarity

■ NAME: ______________________ ■ Date: __________

Contextualization and Synthesis: Kievan Rus'

Contextualization

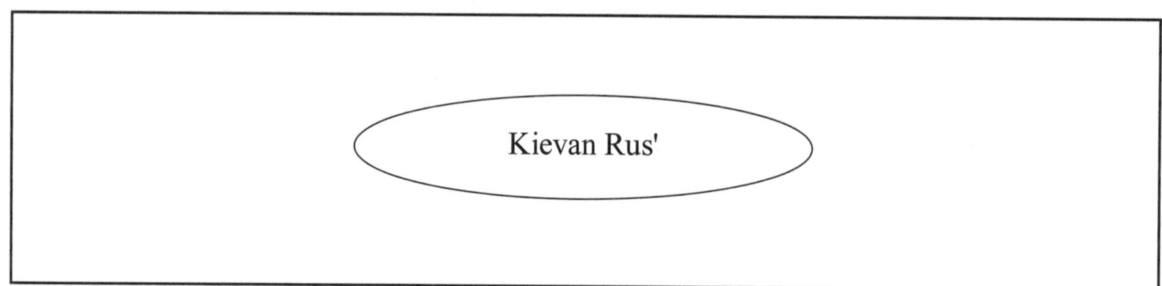

Synthesis

Kievan Rus' is similar to . . .

Backward Looking

One Similarity

Second Similarity

Forward Looking

One Similarity

Second Similarity

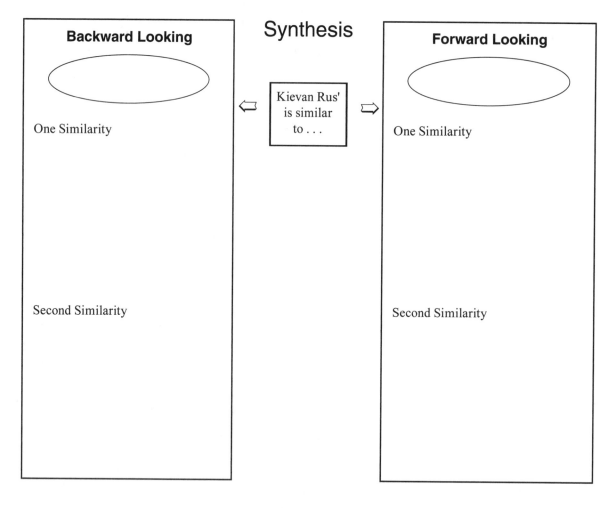

■ NAME: ____________________ ■ Date: __________

Contextualization and Synthesis: Transpacific Silver Trade

Contextualization

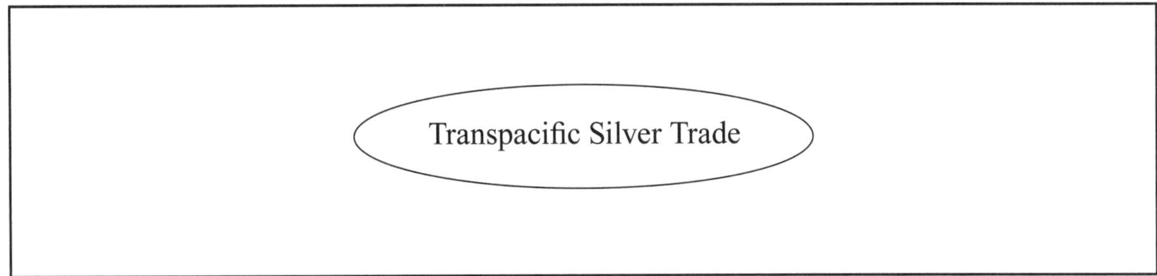

Synthesis

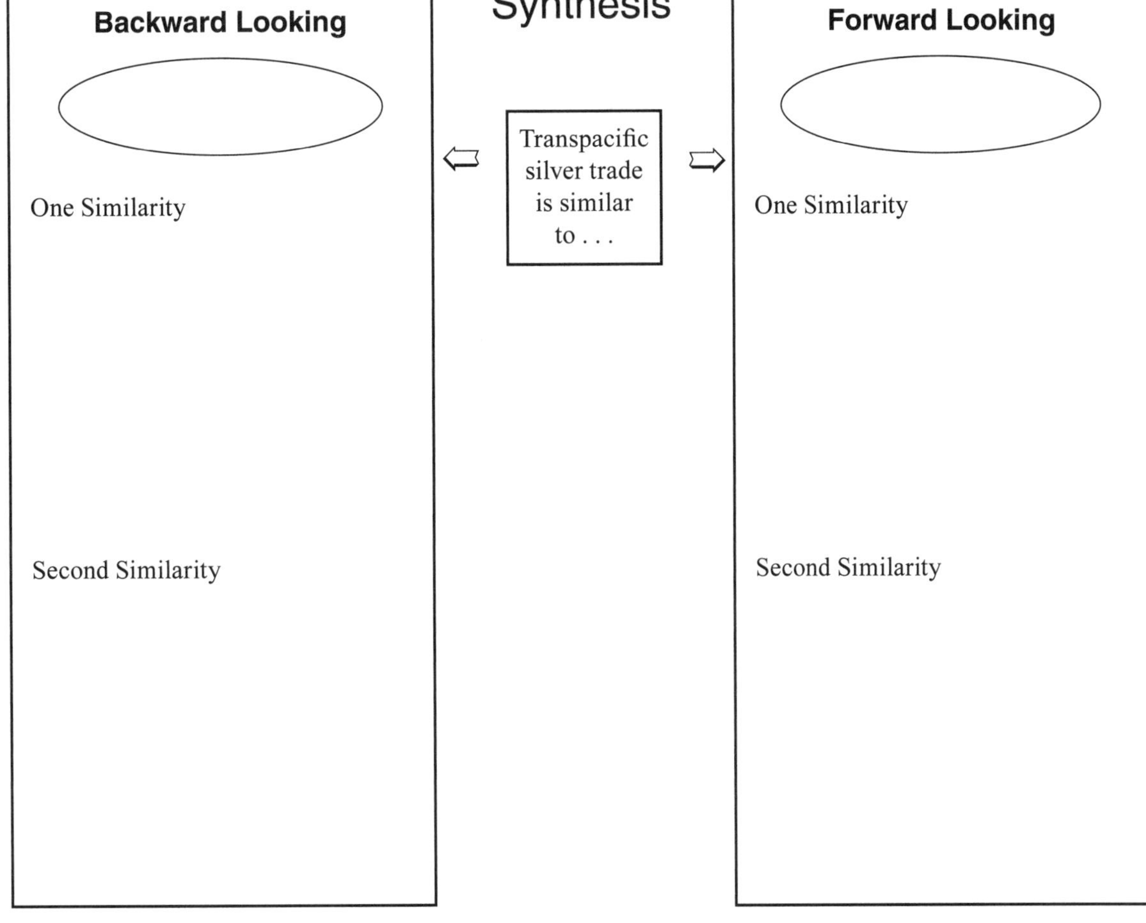

■ NAME: ______________________ ■ Date: __________

Contextualization and Synthesis: Protestant Reformation

Contextualization

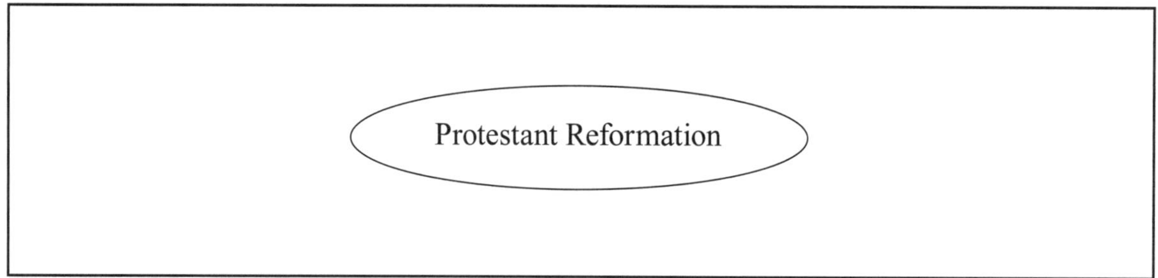

Synthesis

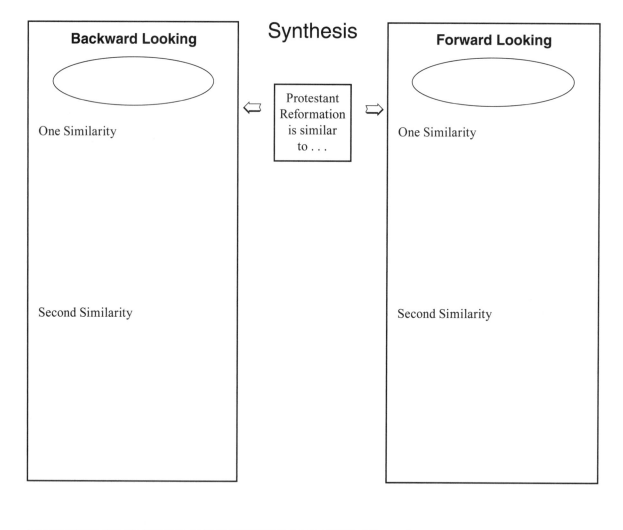

Backward Looking

One Similarity

Second Similarity

Protestant Reformation is similar to . . .

Forward Looking

One Similarity

Second Similarity

____

____

____

____

■ NAME: ______________________ ■ Date: __________

Contextualization and Synthesis: Caribbean Plantation Complex

Contextualization

Caribbean Plantation Complex

Synthesis

Backward Looking

One Similarity

Second Similarity

⇦ Caribbean plantation complex is similar to . . . ⇨

Forward Looking

One Similarity

Second Similarity

____

____

____

____

■ NAME: ______________________ ■ Date: __________

Contextualization and Synthesis: Kingdom of Kongo

Contextualization

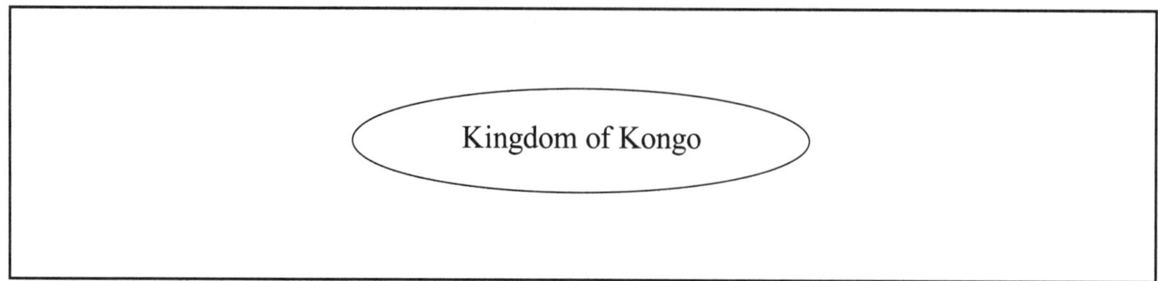

Synthesis

Backward Looking		Forward Looking
One Similarity	⇦ Kingdom of Kongo is similar to . . . ⇨	One Similarity
Second Similarity		Second Similarity

____

____

____

____

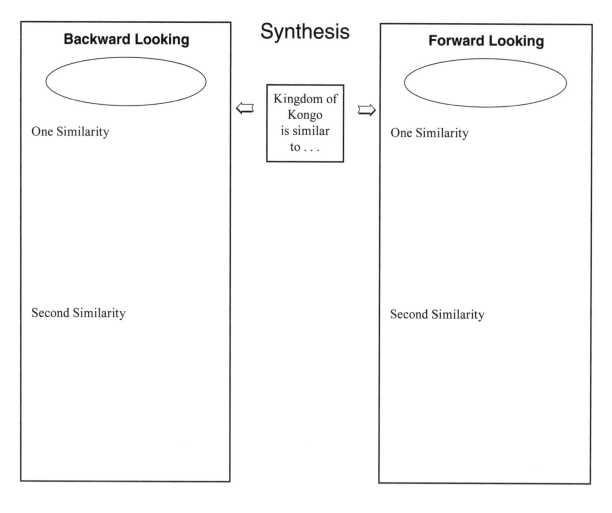

■ NAME: ______________________ ■ Date: __________

Contextualization and Synthesis: Qing China

Contextualization

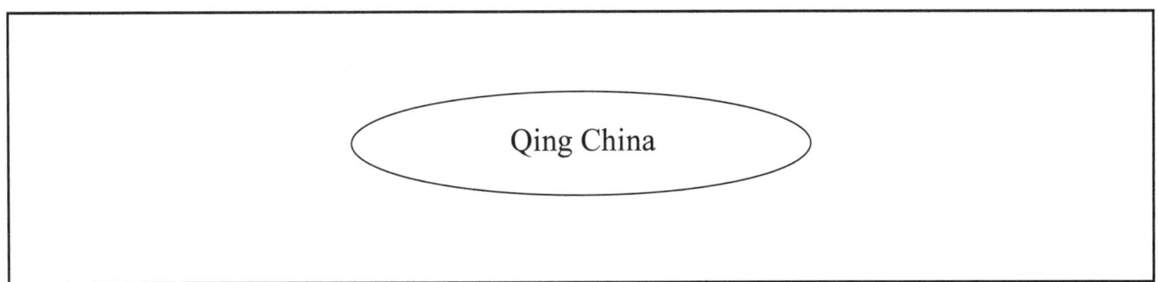

Synthesis

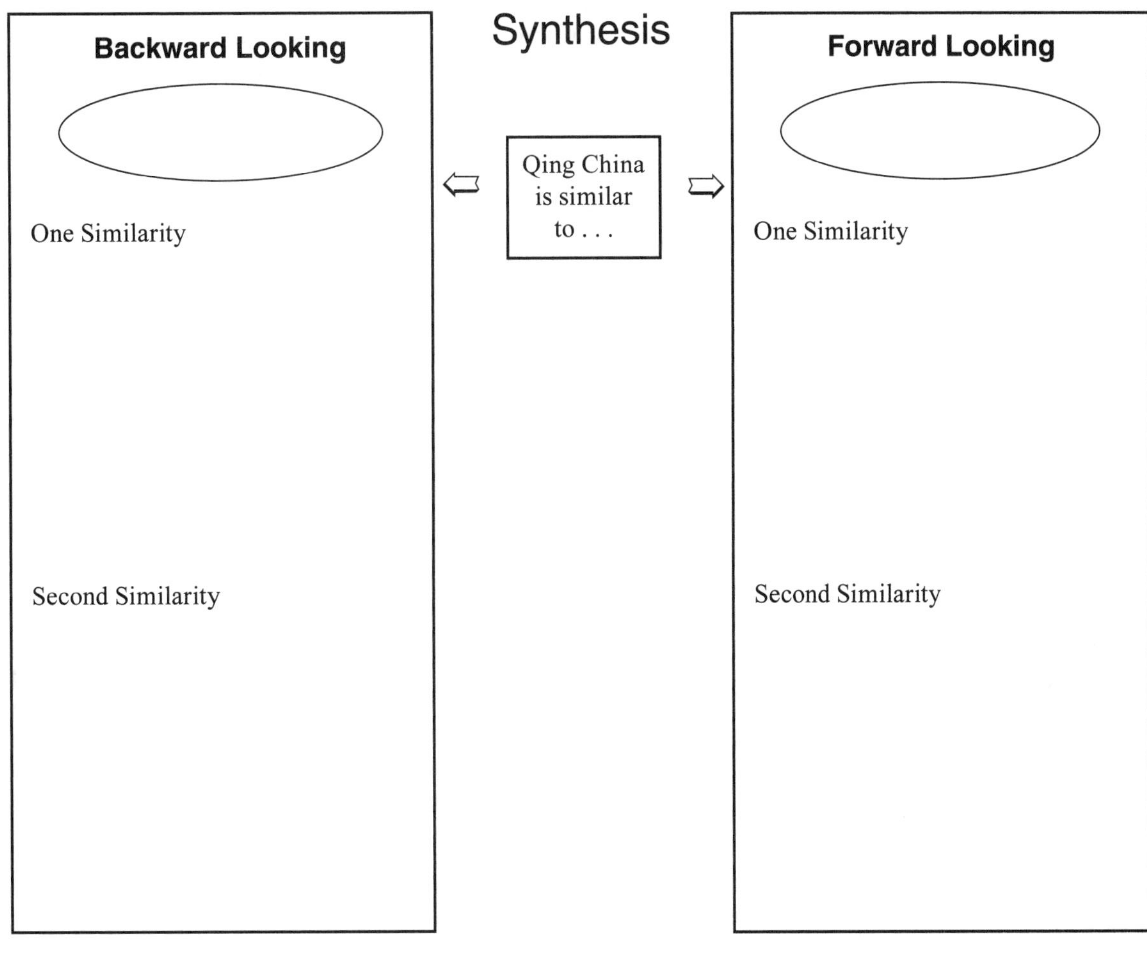

____

____

____

____

■ NAME: ______________________ ■ Date: __________

Contextualization and Synthesis: Russian Expansion

Contextualization

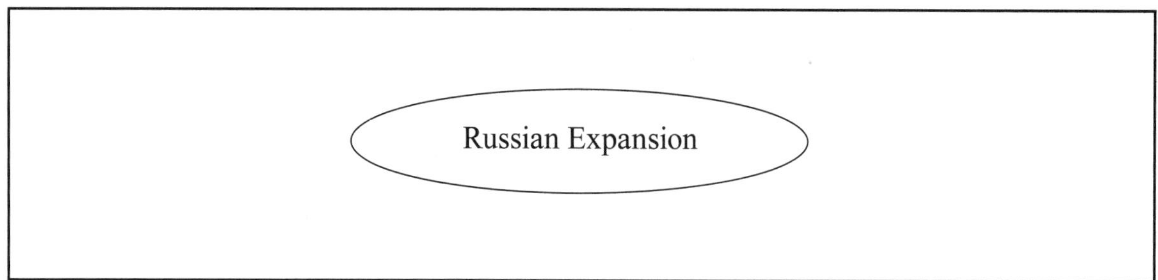

Synthesis

Backward Looking

One Similarity

Second Similarity

Russian expansion is similar to . . .

Forward Looking

One Similarity

Second Similarity

____

____

____

____

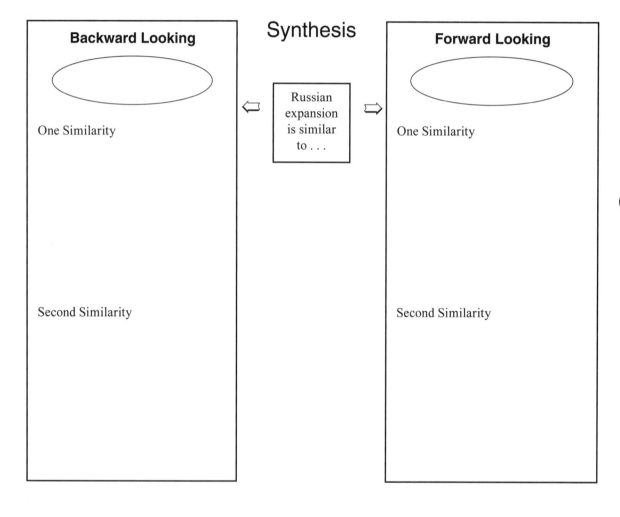

■ NAME: ______________________ ■ Date: __________

Contextualization and Synthesis: Haitian Revolution

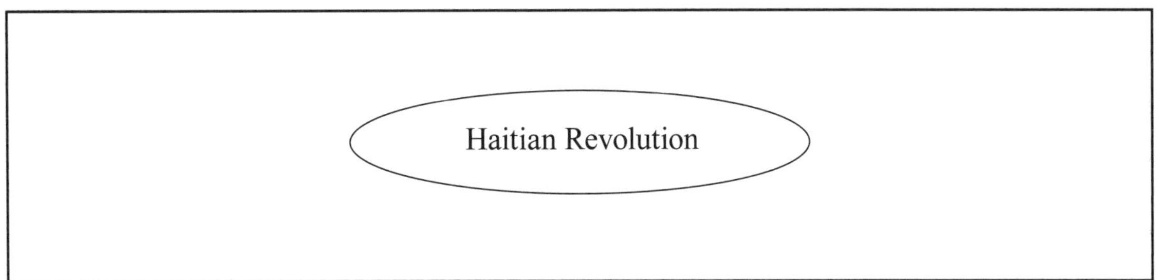

Synthesis

Backward Looking		Forward Looking
⇦	Haitian Revolution is similar to . . .	⇨
One Similarity		One Similarity
Second Similarity		Second Similarity

____

____

____

____

■ NAME: ________________________________ ■ Date: ____________

Contextualization and Synthesis: State-Sponsored Industrialization in Russia

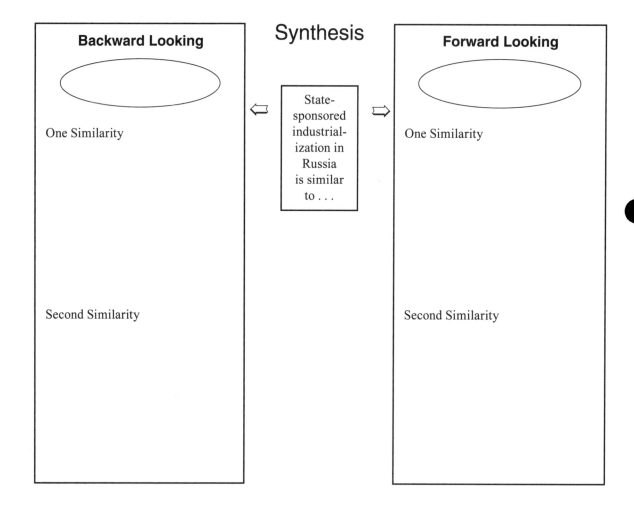

Contextualization

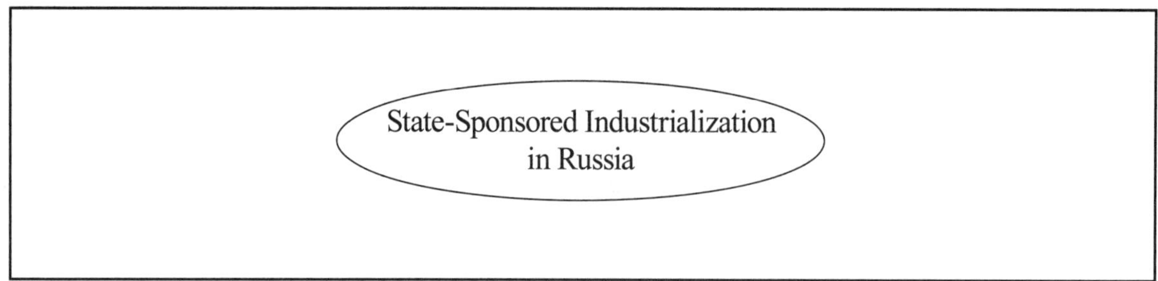

Synthesis

Backward Looking

One Similarity

Second Similarity

⇦ State-sponsored industrialization in Russia is similar to . . . ⇨

Forward Looking

One Similarity

Second Similarity

____

____

____

____

■ NAME: ______________________ ■ Date: __________

Contextualization and Synthesis: British East India Company

Contextualization

British East India Company

Synthesis

Backward Looking

One Similarity

Second Similarity

British East India Company is similar to . . .

Forward Looking

One Similarity

Second Similarity

■ NAME: ______________________ ■ Date: __________

Contextualization and Synthesis: Opium Wars

Contextualization

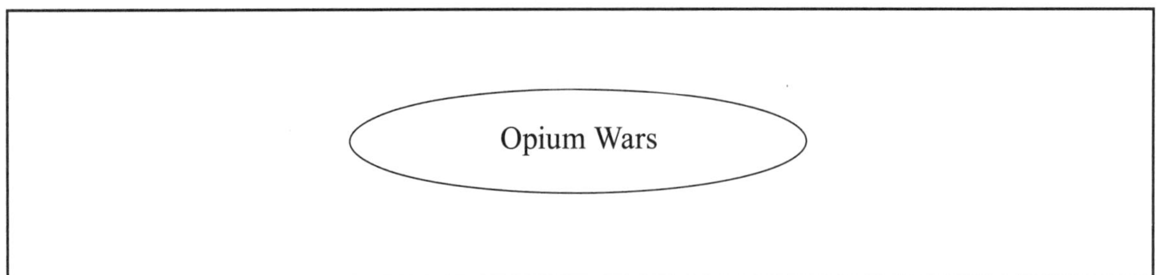

Synthesis

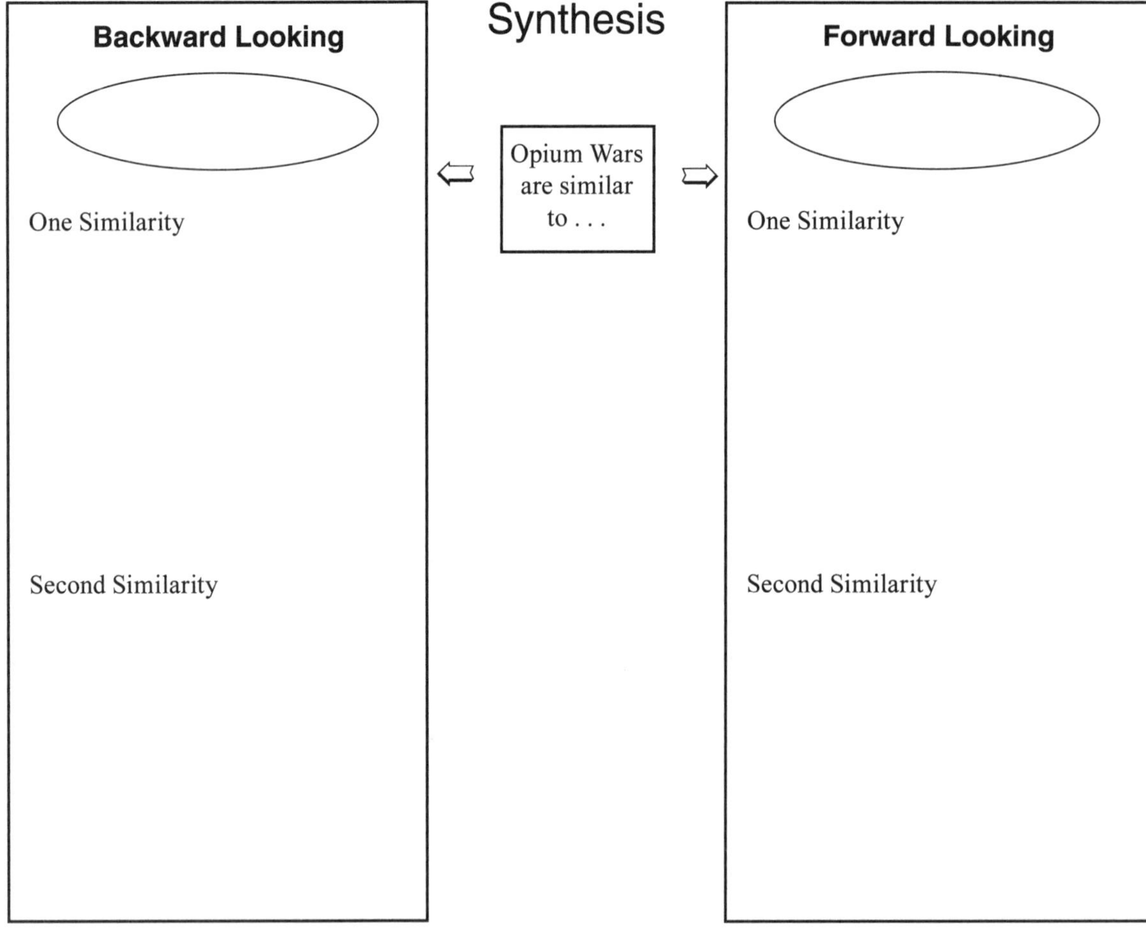

■ NAME: ______________________ ■ Date: __________

Contextualization and Synthesis: Mfecane

Contextualization

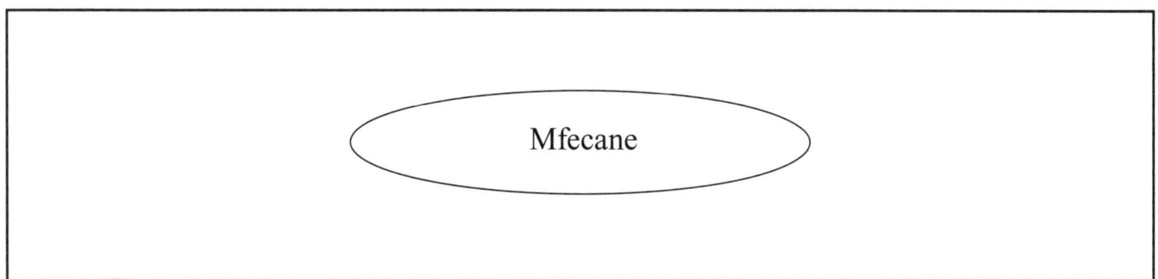

Synthesis

Backward Looking		Forward Looking
One Similarity	Mfecane is similar to . . .	One Similarity
Second Similarity		Second Similarity

____

____

____

____

■ NAME: ______________________ ■ Date: __________

Contextualization and Synthesis: Marxism

Contextualization

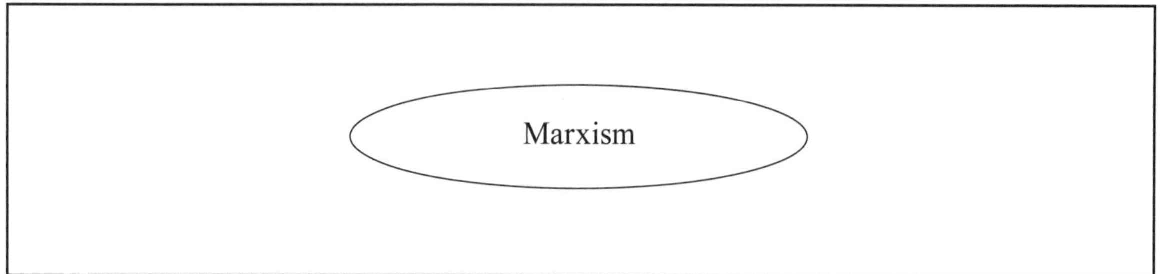

Synthesis

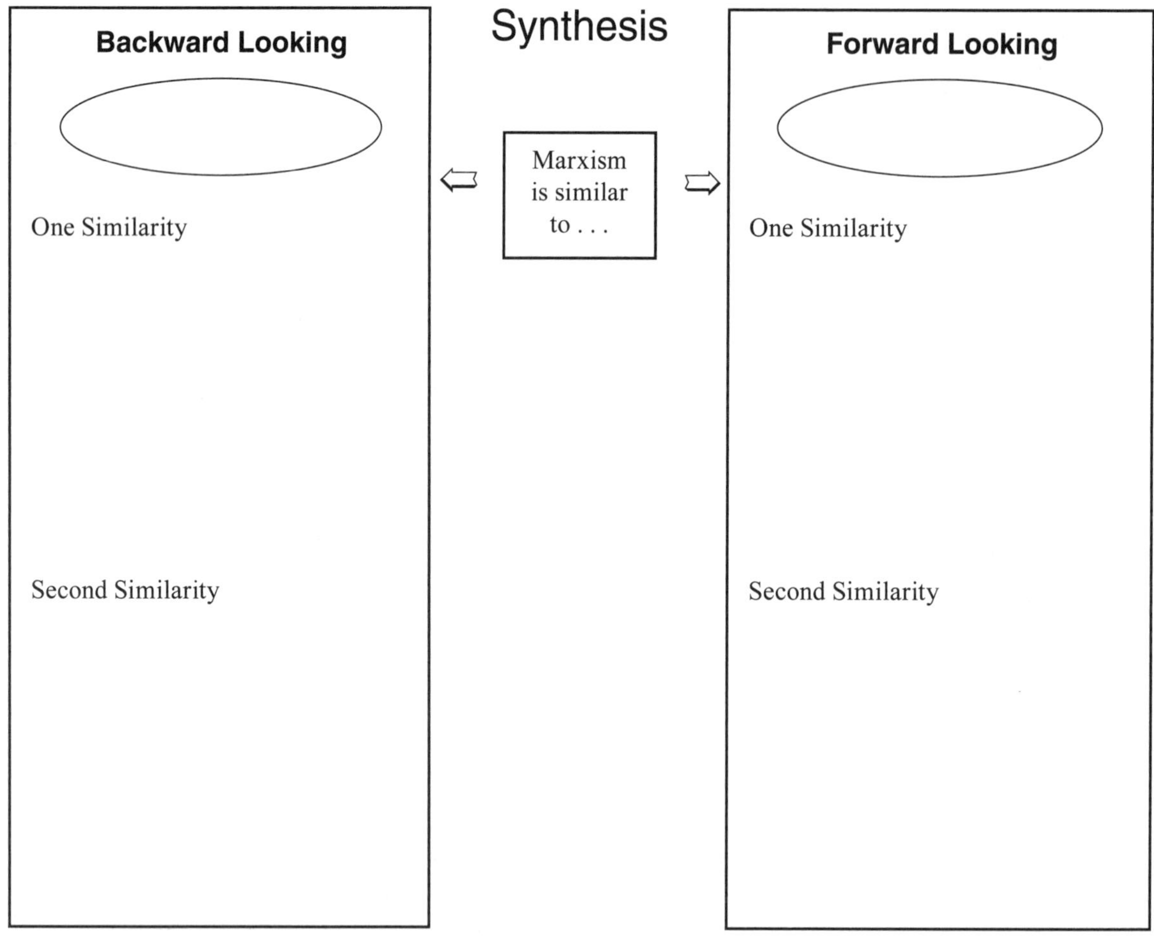

■ NAME: ______________________ ■ Date: __________

Contextualization and Synthesis: American Civil War

Contextualization

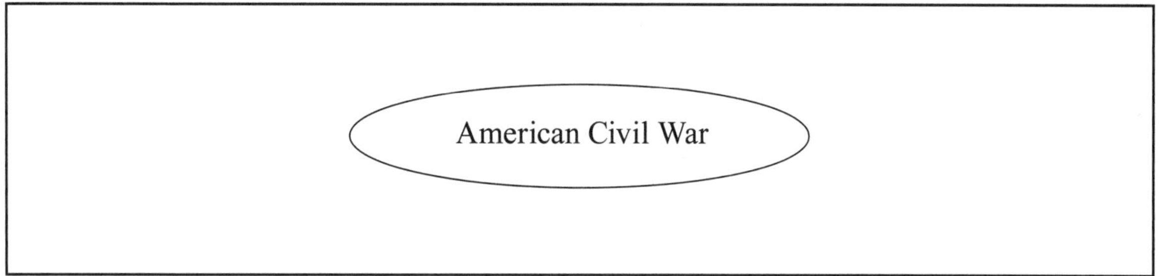

Synthesis

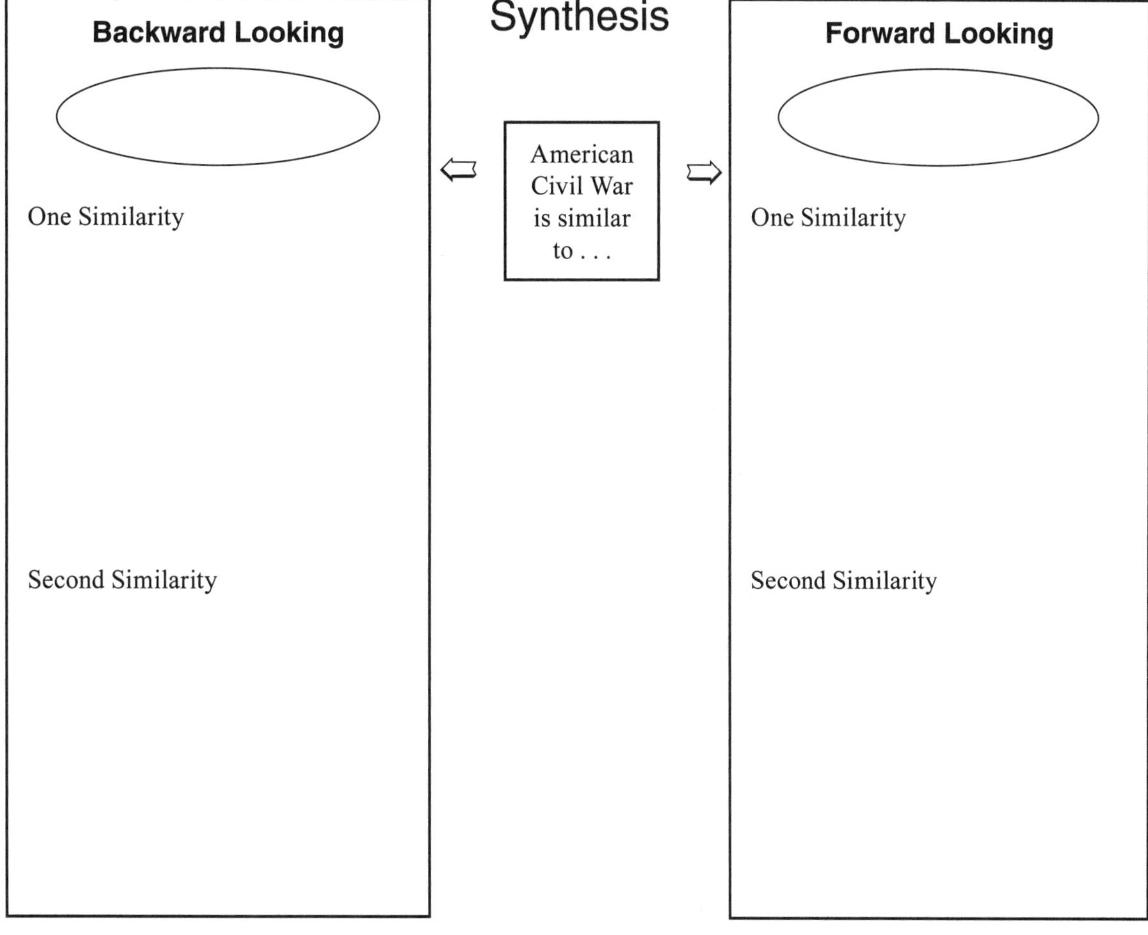

____

____

____

____

■ NAME: ______________________ ■ Date: __________

Contextualization and Synthesis: Women's Suffrage

Contextualization

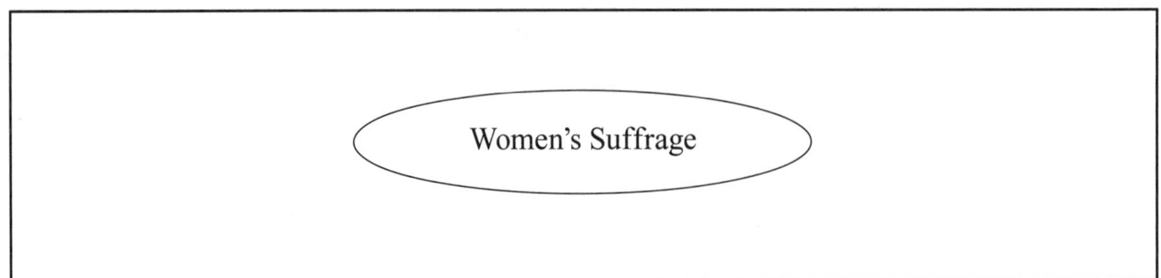

Synthesis

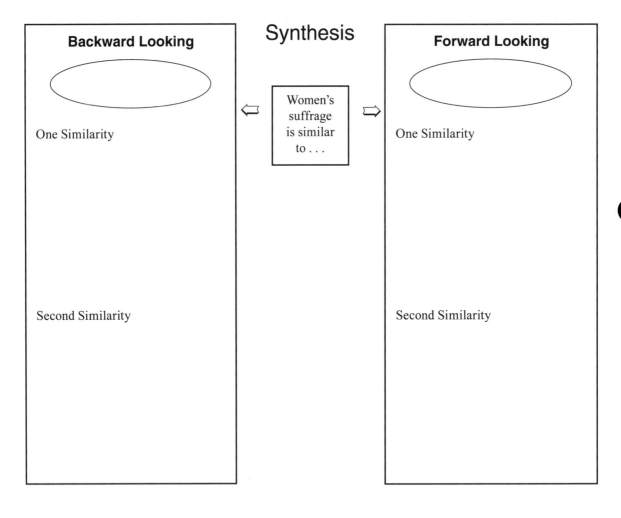

Backward Looking

One Similarity

Second Similarity

Women's suffrage is similar to . . .

Forward Looking

One Similarity

Second Similarity

____

____

____

____

■ NAME: ______________________ ■ Date: __________

Contextualization and Synthesis: Chinese Nationalism

Contextualization

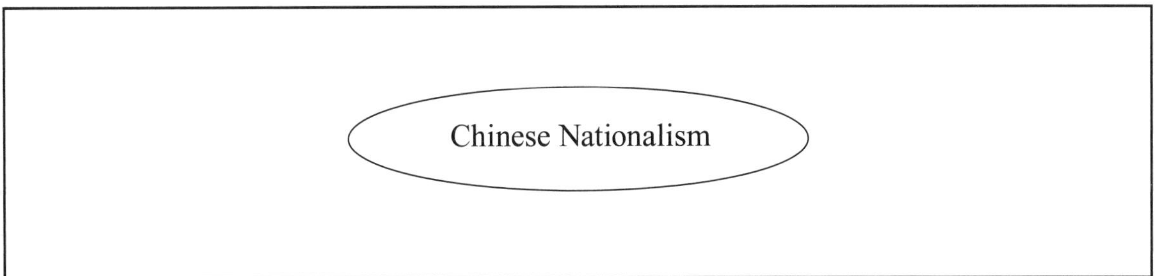

Synthesis

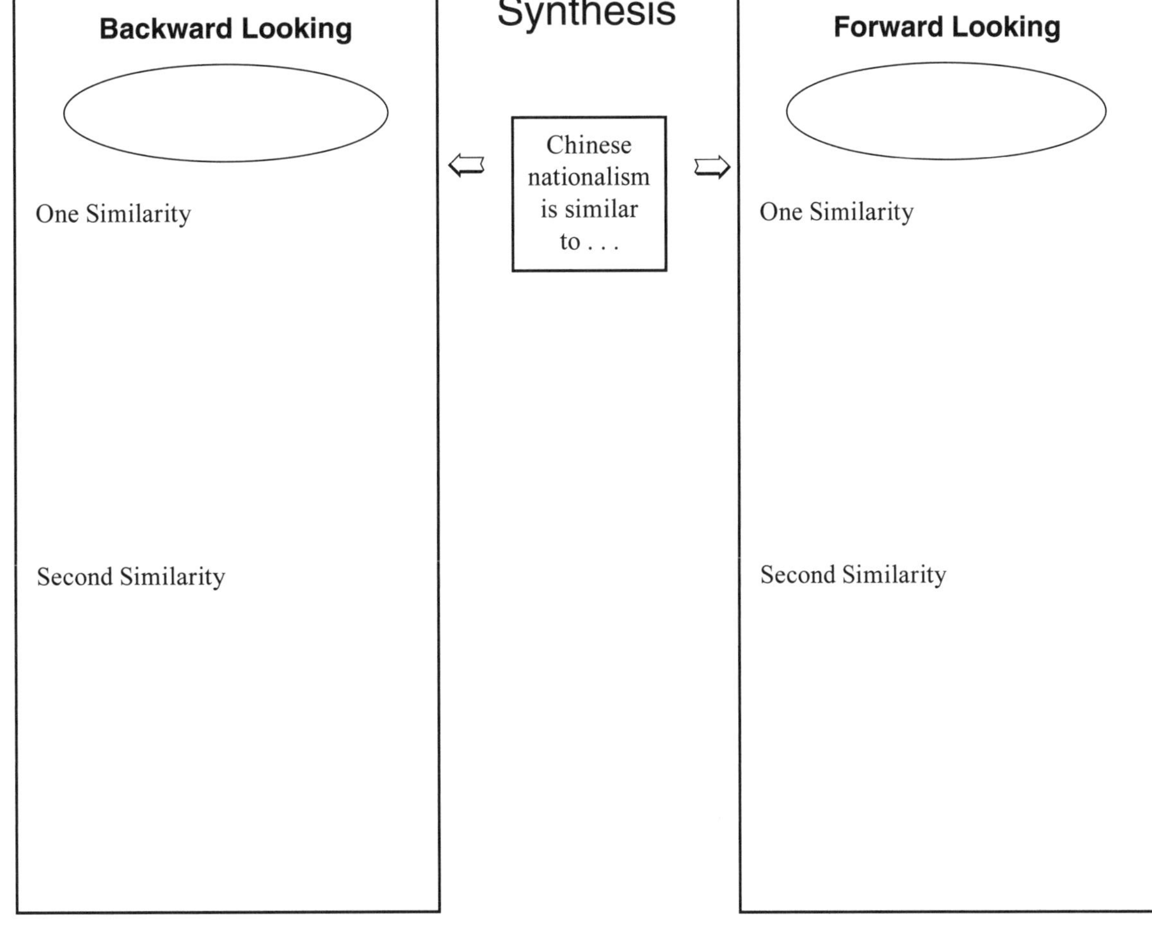

____

____

____

____

■ NAME: ______________________________ ■ Date: ______________

Contextualization and Synthesis: Zionism

Contextualization

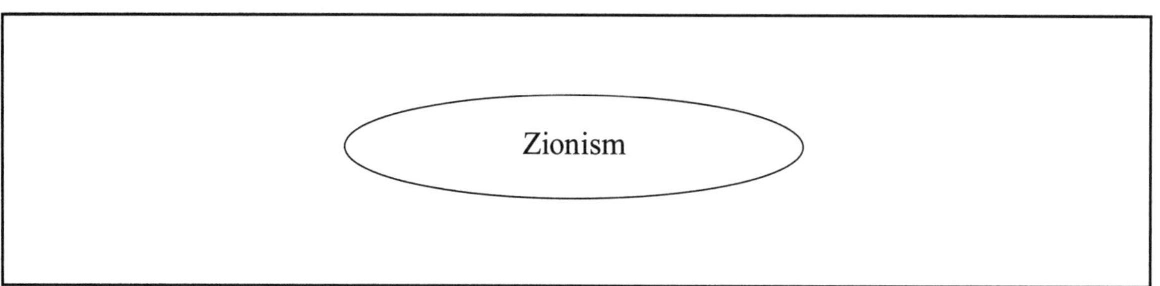

Synthesis

Backward Looking

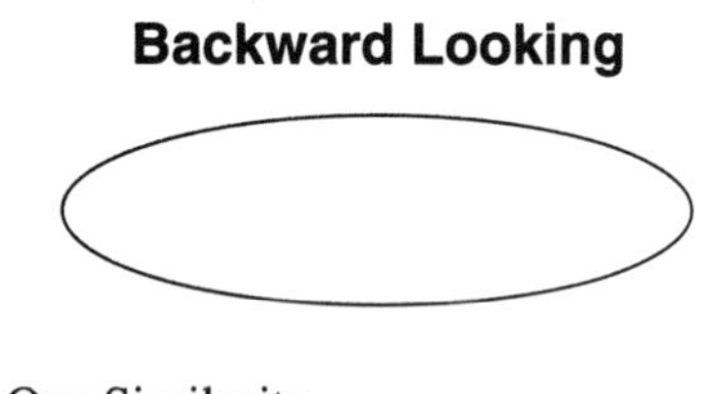

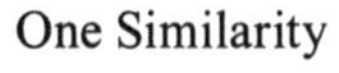

One Similarity

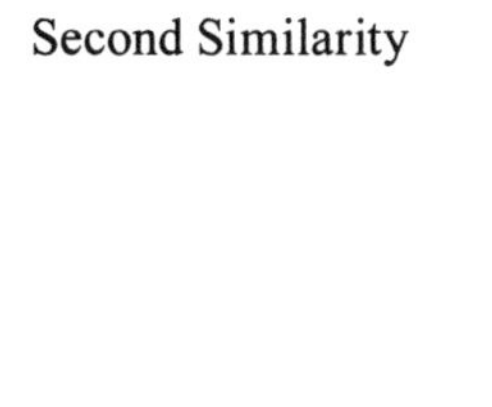

Second Similarity

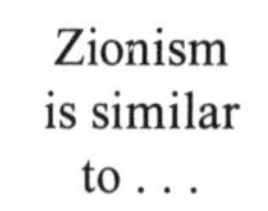

Forward Looking

One Similarity

Second Similarity

____

____

____

____

■ NAME: ______________________ ■ Date: __________

Contextualization and Synthesis: Cuban Revolution

Contextualization

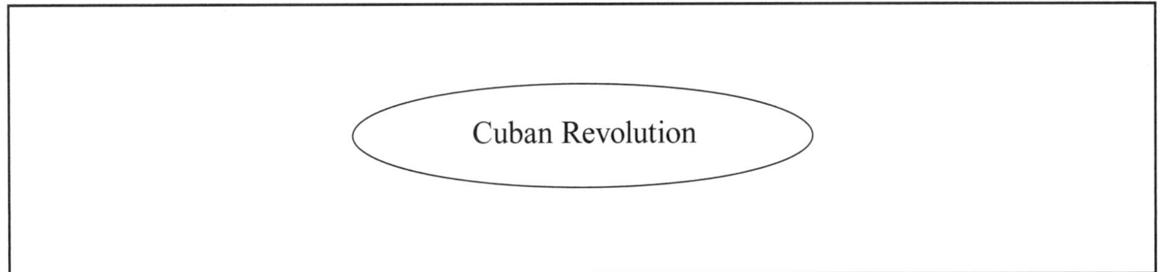

Synthesis

Backward Looking

One Similarity

Second Similarity

Cuban Revolution is similar to . . .

Forward Looking

One Similarity

Second Similarity

____

____

____

____

■ NAME: ______________________ ■ Date: __________

Contextualization and Synthesis: Collapse of the Communist Bloc

Contextualization

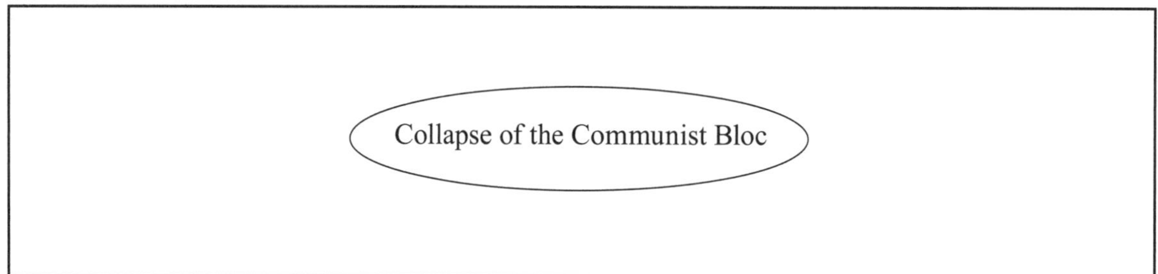

Synthesis

Backward Looking

One Similarity

Second Similarity

Collapse of the Communist bloc is similar to . . .

Forward Looking

One Similarity

Second Similarity

____

____

____

____

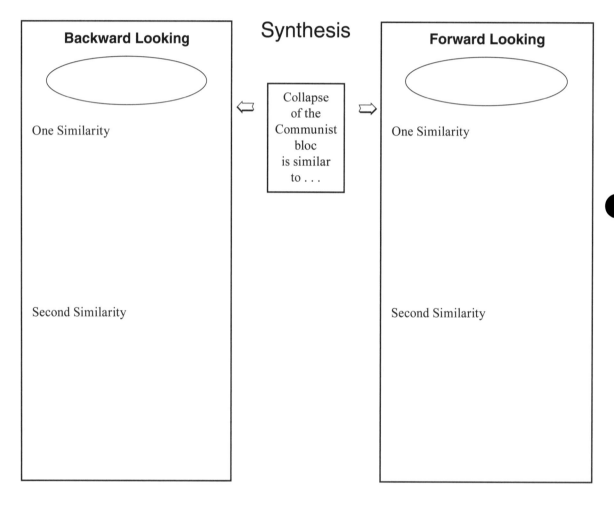

Student Instructions: Turning Points

When we are asked to determine a turning point, we are asked to determine how a single event brought about significant change in history. This is different from looking at continuity and change over time, which normally requires us to consider multiple events and gives us a defined time period. Determining a turning point involves focusing on a single event and determining to what extent that event served as a major turning point in history.

The purpose of these Turning Point activities is to explain the historical context of each of the three events and then determine which event constitutes a turning point in history. These worksheets prompt us to discuss what history was like before and after a particular event, helping us to confirm whether the event is, in fact, a turning point.

■ NAME: ______________________ ■ Date: ________

Turning Point: Early Societies (Example)

Give specific historical details about the three events listed below (e.g., who, what, when, where, why).

Pastoralism:

Pastoralism is when groups of people learned how to domesticate animals, such as cows, horses, pigs, sheep, goats, and camels. The earliest known domesticate was the dog, but soon thereafter came those animals that humans relied on for food and clothing. Domesticated animals were docile enough to be around humans, yet bred quickly enough that they could multiply relatively quickly in a short amount of time. This gave humans a steady diet of meat as well as the hides to use for clothing and shelter.

Farming:

Learning to farm took a considerable period of time. Plants became domesticated slowly, much as animals did. Cultivation began in areas with fertile soil and abundant water and allowed people to slowly transition from being nomadic to becoming settled in one spot. Early farming villages were small, with bands of related people living together and growing grains in small plots.

Urban Living:

Once people learned to domesticate plants and animals and began to settle into farming villages, these villages began attracting more people. City living and the monumental architecture that came with it, successfully attracted so many people that stratified social structures and with it a strong legal system and leadership became necessary.

Select one of the above events you believe to be a turning point in world history, then describe what it was like before and after that event.

The world prior to the event:

Before urbanization, people lived in familial bands and tribes. Whether they hunted and gathered, were pastoral nomads, or lived in small farming villages, their lives were not significantly different. Men and women lived in different spheres but were essentially equal partners.

The world after the event:

Urban living changed the way humans lived. Although many continued to live in small villages and kept hunting and gathering, urban living was the genesis for monumental architecture, social hierarchy, and law codes.

■ NAME: ______________________ ■ Date: __________

Turning Point: Early Societies

Give specific historical details about the three events listed below (e.g., who, what, when, where, why).

Pastoralism:

Farming:

Urban Living:

Select one of the above events you believe to be a turning point in world history, then describe what it was like before and after that event.

The world prior to the event:

The world after the event:

■ NAME: ____________________ ■ Date: __________

Turning Point: Creation of Larger Human Societies

Give specific historical details about the three events listed below (e.g., who, what, when, where, why).

Codification of Religion:

Codification of Laws:

Development of Bureaucracy:

Select one of the above events you believe to be a turning point in world history, then describe what it was like before and after that event.

The world prior to the event:

The world after the event:

■ NAME: ______________________ ■ Date: __________

Turning Point: Emergence of Large Empires before 1400

Give specific historical details about the three events listed below (e.g., who, what, when, where, why).

Innovations in Military Weaponry:

____

____

____

____

Expansion of State Bureaucracy:

____

____

____

____

Desire to Control Interregional Trade:

____

____

____

____

Select one of the above events you believe to be a turning point in world history, then describe what it was like before and after that event.

The world prior to the event:

____

____

____

____

The world after the event:

____

____

____

____

■ NAME: ______________________________ ■ Date: ____________

Turning Point: Fall of Classical Empires

Give specific historical details about the three events listed below (e.g., who, what, when, where, why).

Environmental Damage:

____

____

____

____

Problems on the Borders:

____

____

____

____

Loss of Ideological Unity:

____

____

____

____

Select one of the above events you believe to be a turning point in world history, then describe what it was like before and after that event.

The world prior to the event:

____

____

____

____

The world after the event:

____

____

____

____

■ NAME: ______________________ ■ Date: __________

Turning Point: Spread of Christianity

Give specific historical details about the three events listed below (e.g., who, what, when, where, why).

Conversion of Constantine:

____

____

____

____

Fall of Rome:

____

____

____

____

Justinian's Code:

____

____

____

____

Select one of the above events you believe to be a turning point in world history, then describe what it was like before and after that event.

The world prior to the event:

____

____

____

____

The world after the event:

____

____

____

____

■ NAME: ______________________________ ■ Date: ____________

Turning Point: Emergence of Early Transregional Trade

Give specific historical details about the three events listed below (e.g., who, what, when, where, why).

Domestication of Pack Animals:

____

____

____

____

Demand for Luxury Goods:

____

____

____

____

Technological Innovation (Saddle, Sail, etc.):

____

____

____

____

Select one of the above events you believe to be a turning point in world history, then describe what it was like before and after that event.

The world prior to the event:

____

____

____

____

The world after the event:

____

____

____

____

■ NAME: ______________________________ ■ Date: ____________

Turning Point: Diffusion of Knowledge

Give specific historical details about the three events listed below (e.g., who, what, when, where, why).

Overland Trade:

____

____

____

____

Sea Trade:

____

____

____

____

Religious Missionaries:

____

____

____

____

Select one of the above events you believe to be a turning point in world history, then describe what it was like before and after that event.

The world prior to the event:

____

____

____

____

The world after the event:

____

____

____

____

■ NAME: ______________________ ■ Date: __________

Turning Point: Rise of Dar al-Islam

Give specific historical details about the three events listed below (e.g., who, what, when, where, why).

Collapse of Classical Empires:

Military Prowess of Pastoralists:

Unifying Force of Islam:

Select one of the above events you believe to be a turning point in world history, then describe what it was like before and after that event.

The world prior to the event:

The world after the event:

■ NAME: ______________________ ■ Date: __________

Turning Point: Spread of Buddhism

Give specific historical details about the three events listed below (e.g., who, what, when, where, why).

Trade:

____

____

____

____

Inter-Dynastic Turmoil in China:

____

____

____

____

Imperial Expansion under the Tang:

____

____

____

____

Select one of the above events you believe to be a turning point in world history, then describe what it was like before and after that event.

The world prior to the event:

____

____

____

____

The world after the event:

____

____

____

____

■ NAME: ____________________ ■ Date: __________

Turning Point: Transoceanic Exploration

Give specific historical details about the three events listed below (e.g., who, what, when, where, why).

Zheng He:

Henry the Navigator:

Christopher Columbus:

Select one of the above events you believe to be a turning point in world history, then describe what it was like before and after that event.

The world prior to the event:

The world after the event:

■ NAME: ______________________ ■ Date: __________

Turning Point: European Age of Navigation

Give specific historical details about the three events listed below (e.g., who, what, when, where, why).

Rise of the Ottoman Empire:

____

____

____

____

End of Reconquista:

____

____

____

____

Crusades:

____

____

____

____

Select one of the above events you believe to be a turning point in world history, then describe what it was like before and after that event.

The world prior to the event:

____

____

____

____

The world after the event:

____

____

____

____

■ NAME: ______________________________ ■ Date: __________

Turning Point: Transatlantic Slave Trade

Give specific historical details about the three events listed below (e.g., who, what, when, where, why).

Desire for Sugar:

____

____

____

____

Virgin Soil Diseases:

____

____

____

____

Tropical Diseases:

____

____

____

____

Select one of the above events you believe to be a turning point in world history, then describe what it was like before and after that event.

The world prior to the event:

____

____

____

____

The world after the event:

____

____

____

____

■ NAME: ______________________________ ■ Date: ______________

Turning Point: Increase in Transoceanic Trade

Give specific historical details about the three events listed below (e.g., who, what, when, where, why).

Chinese Demand for Silver:

____

____

____

____

European Demand for Silk:

____

____

____

____

African Demand for Cotton Textiles:

____

____

____

____

Select one of the above events you believe to be a turning point in world history, then describe what it was like before and after that event.

The world prior to the event:

____

____

____

____

The world after the event:

____

____

____

____

■ NAME: ______________________ ■ Date: ____________

Turning Point: Plantation Economies

Give specific historical details about the three events listed below (e.g., who, what, when, where, why).

Mercantilism:

____

____

____

____

Global Demand for Raw Materials:

____

____

____

____

Global Demand for Finished Goods:

____

____

____

____

Select one of the above events you believe to be a turning point in world history, then describe what it was like before and after that event.

The world prior to the event:

____

____

____

____

The world after the event:

____

____

____

____

■ NAME: ____________________ ■ Date: ____________

Turning Point: Migration

Give specific historical details about the three events listed below (e.g., who, what, when, where, why).

Lack of Economic Opportunity at Home:

Demand for Workers in Urban Areas:

Coerced Labor Systems:

Select one of the above events you believe to be a turning point in world history, then describe what it was like before and after that event.

The world prior to the event:

The world after the event:

■ NAME: ______________________ ■ Date: __________

Turning Point: Enlightenment

Give specific historical details about the three events listed below (e.g., who, what, when, where, why).

Scientific Revolution:

____

____

____

____

French Revolution:

____

____

____

____

Locke's *Concerning Human Understanding*:

____

____

____

____

Select one of the above events you believe to be a turning point in world history, then describe what it was like before and after that event.

The world prior to the event:

____

____

____

____

The world after the event:

____

____

____

____

■ NAME: ______________________ ■ Date: __________

Turning Point: Imperial Expansion

Give specific historical details about the three events listed below (e.g., who, what, when, where, why).

Demand for Raw Materials:

Market for Finished Goods:

Development in Military Technology:

Select one of the above events you believe to be a turning point in world history, then describe what it was like before and after that event.

The world prior to the event:

The world after the event:

■ NAME: ______________________ ■ Date: __________

Turning Point: Industrial Production

Give specific historical details about the three events listed below (e.g., who, what, when, where, why).

Improved Agricultural Production:

____

____

____

____

Geographical Distribution of Coal, Iron, and Timber:

____

____

____

____

Access to Foreign Resources:

____

____

____

____

Select one of the above events you believe to be a turning point in world history, then describe what it was like before and after that event.

The world prior to the event:

____

____

____

____

The world after the event:

____

____

____

____

■ NAME: ______________________ ■ Date: __________

Turning Point: Shift In Gender Roles

Give specific historical details about the three events listed below (e.g., who, what, when, where, why).

New Social Classes:

____

____

____

____

Rapid Urbanization:

____

____

____

____

Public Education:

____

____

____

____

Select one of the above events you believe to be a turning point in world history, then describe what it was like before and after that event.

The world prior to the event:

____

____

____

____

The world after the event:

____

____

____

____

■ NAME: ______________________________ ■ Date: ____________

Turning Point: Rise of Capitalism

Give specific historical details about the three events listed below (e.g., who, what, when, where, why).

Protestant Reformation:

Puritan Work Ethic:

Rise in Power of the Merchant Class:

Select one of the above events you believe to be a turning point in world history, then describe what it was like before and after that event.

The world prior to the event:

The world after the event:

■ NAME: ______________________ ■ Date: __________

Turning Point: Nationalism

Give specific historical details about the three events listed below (e.g., who, what, when, where, why).

Nonviolence Movements:

____

____

____

____

Religious Challenges to Imperialism:

____

____

____

____

Transnational Ideologies:

____

____

____

____

Select one of the above events you believe to be a turning point in world history, then describe what it was like before and after that event.

The world prior to the event:

____

____

____

____

The world after the event:

____

____

____

____

Student Instructions: Continuity and Change

When we are asked to identify continuity and change over time, we are asked to identify a series of events over a distinct time period in history. Normally these events are centered on a specific theme with defined start and end dates within that period.

The purpose of these Continuity and Change activities is to investigate a series of events, place them in chronological order, then determine whether there was either more continuity or change during that historical period. There is almost always a significant change within the period under investigation. As with all of the worksheets in this book, there are no right or wrong answers. The worksheets will hopefully provide you with opportunities to articulate arguments for class discussions.

The bottom part of the worksheet asks you to select the three events you think are the most important, then narrow it down to one event, then articulate the reasons why you selected the event in question, and finally, to discuss what world history was like both before and after that event. Discussing what life was like both before and after the event is critical to finishing the task because it demonstrates a sophisticated understanding of the event under investigation.

■ NAME: ______________________ ■ Date: ____________

Continuity and Change: Use of Tools in Afro-Eurasia (6000–1000 BCE) (Example)

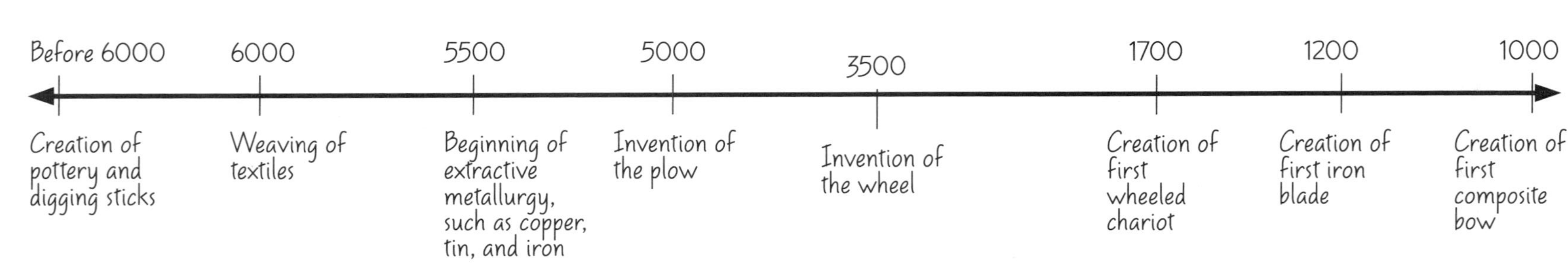

List three key dates/events from the timeline. Circle the most important one.

Plow—5000

Extractive metallurgy—5500 (circled)

Textiles—6000

Characteristics of history before: 5500

Before extractive metallurgy, tools were soft. People could only farm areas that had very soft soils. Weapons were not very effective, as rocks and wooden clubs were more lethal than copper weapons.

Characteristics of history after: 5500

After extractive metallurgy, tools became much harder and could cut through tougher soils. Weapons, a tool for warfare, became more lethal. Civilizations that learned smelting had a tremendous advantage over those that did not, and iron tools became highly valuable trade items.

■ NAME: ______________________ ■ Date: ____________

Continuity and Change: Use of Tools in Afro-Eurasia (6000–1000 BCE)

List three key dates/events from the timeline. Circle the most important one.

____________ ____________ ____________

Characteristics of the history before: ____________

Characteristics of the history after: ____________

■ NAME: ______________________ ■ Date: __________

Continuity and Change: Social Systems (8000 BCE–600 CE)

List three key dates/events from the timeline. Circle the most important one.

__________ __________ __________

Characteristics of history before: __________

Characteristics of history after: __________

■ NAME: ______________________ ■ Date: __________

Continuity and Change: Role of Political Philosophies in Creating the Structure of Qin/Han China

List three key dates/events from the timeline. Circle the most important one.

______________ ______________ ______________

Characteristics of history before: ______________

Characteristics of history after: ______________

■ NAME: ______________________ ■ Date: __________

Continuity and Change: Silk Road Trade (200 BCE–1000 CE)

List three key dates/events from the timeline. Circle the most important one.

Characteristics of history before: ______________

Characteristics of history after: ______________

■ NAME: ______________________ ■ Date: __________

Continuity and Change: Imperial Administrative Institutions in Eurasia (200 BCE–600 CE)

List three key dates/events from the timeline. Circle the most important one.

____________ ____________ ____________

Characteristics of history before: ______________

Characteristics of history after: ______________

■ NAME: ______________________ ■ Date: __________

Continuity and Change: Indian Ocean Trade (400–1600 CE)

List three key dates/events from the timeline. Circle the most important one.

Characteristics of history before:

Characteristics of history after:

■ NAME: ______________________ ■ Date: ________

Continuity and Change: Political Structure of the Arab Caliphates (650–1300 CE)

List three key dates/events from the timeline. Circle the most important one.

Characteristics of history before: ______________

Characteristics of history after: ______________

■ NAME: ______________________ ■ Date: ____________

Continuity and Change: Japan after Its Contact with Tang China (800–1400 CE)

List three key dates/events from the timeline. Circle the most important one.

______________ ______________ ______________

Characteristics of history before: ______________

Characteristics of history after: ______________

■ NAME: ______________________ ■ Date: __________

Continuity and Change: Coerced Labor Forms (600–1600 CE)

List three key dates/events from the timeline. Circle the most important one.

Characteristics of history before: ______________

Characteristics of history after: ______________

■ NAME: ____________ ■ Date: ____________

Continuity and Change: Use of Domesticated Pack Animals in Long-Distance Trade (1400–1900 CE)

List three key dates/events from the timeline. Circle the most important one.

____________ ____________ ____________

Characteristics of history before: ____________

Characteristics of history after: ____________

■ NAME: ______________________________ ■ Date: ____________

Continuity and Change: Forms of Monetization to Facilitate Trade (600–1450 CE)

List three key dates/events from the timeline. Circle the most important one.

______________ ______________ ______________

Characteristics of history before: ______________

Characteristics of history after: ______________

■ NAME: ______________________ ■ Date: __________

Continuity and Change: Interregional Travel (1000–1400 CE)

List three key dates/events from the timeline. Circle the most important one.

__________ __________ __________

Characteristics of history before: __________

Characteristics of history after: __________

■ NAME: ____________________ ■ Date: __________

Continuity and Change: Cultural Traditions in Africa (800–1500 CE)

List three key dates/events from the timeline. Circle the most important one.

Characteristics of history before: ____________

Characteristics of history after: ____________

■ NAME: ______________________ ■ Date: ____________

Continuity and Change: Technical Innovations in Agriculture (1000–1450 CE)

List three key dates/events from the timeline. Circle the most important one.

Characteristics of history before: ____________

Characteristics of history after: ____________

■ NAME: ______________________ ■ Date: __________

Continuity and Change: Gender Roles and Buddhism in East and Southeast Asia (800–1500 CE)

List three key dates/events from the timeline. Circle the most important one.

______________ ______________ ______________

Characteristics of history before: ______________

Characteristics of history after: ______________

■ NAME: ______________________ ■ Date: __________

Continuity and Change: Transoceanic Trade (1450–1700 CE)

List three key dates/events from the timeline. Circle the most important one.

Characteristics of history before: ______________

Characteristics of history after: ______________

■ NAME: ______________________ ■ Date: __________

Continuity and Change: Urbanization (1600–1900 CE)

List three key dates/events from the timeline. Circle the most important one.

______________ ______________ ______________

Characteristics of history before: ______________

Characteristics of history after: ______________

■ NAME: ______________________ ■ Date: __________

Continuity and Change: Military Tactics (1800–1950 CE)

List three key dates/events from the timeline. Circle the most important one.

______________ ______________ ______________

Characteristics of history before: ______________

Characteristics of history after: ______________

■ NAME: ____________________ ■ Date: __________

Continuity and Change: Economically Powerful Regions (1500–1900 CE)

List three key dates/events from the timeline. Circle the most important one.

__________ __________ __________

Characteristics of history before: __________

Characteristics of history after: __________

■ NAME: ______________________ ■ Date: __________

Continuity and Change: Importance of Popular Culture (1750–2010 CE)

List three key dates/events from the timeline. Circle the most important one.

Characteristics of history before: ______________

Characteristics of history after: ______________

Student Instructions: Argumentation

When we are asked to construct a historical argument, we are asked to accumulate evidence and then to determine how it will be applied within the argument. The goal of historical argumentation is to convince an audience of the validity of our arguments.

The purpose of these Argumentation activities is to practice the necessary steps in constructing a valid argument. First, we must accumulate evidence that will support our arguments. Second, we must decide what evidence is compelling enough to side one way or the other on the topic at hand. Third, we must pick a side, and then begin the process of prewriting. If we do not want to pick a side, we have the option of modifying the prompt—that is, agreeing and disagreeing simultaneously. Fourth, we need to establish our thesis statement. The thesis statement is a critical part of the argument. It's a roadmap for our audience: Where are you going and what routes are you going to take to get there?

■ NAME: ______________________ ■ Date: __________

Argumentation: "Trading organizations were more important than the state in promoting long-distance trade." (Example)

Support, modify, or refute this statement with specific historical evidence.

Trading Organizations	State
• Trading companies encouraged trade by creating forms of credit and the use of checks. They also used bills of exchange among members of their organizations to facilitate the exchange of goods and minimize the use of gold and silver, which might attract pirates and robbers. • Trading organizations created banking houses for traders to store their profits. • Trading organizations helped build caravanserais as way points to help facilitate trade and to house traveling merchants.	• Ghana, Mali, and Songhay kings controlled the gold and salt trade across the Sahara. All gold and salt belonged to the king. • States, such as the Muslim caliphates and the Mongol Khanates, helped protect traders in exchange for ability to tax trade. • Road systems, such as the Inca road system, facilitated trade. • State-sponsored infrastructure buildings, such as the canals in Venice and the Grand Canal in China, facilitated trade. • State-minted coins and in some cases paper money also facilitated trade.

Thesis Statement:

Although trade organizations and the state supported trade and commercial activity to a large extent, it was the state that proved to be most important in promoting long-distance trade because of the infrastructure it provided.

■ NAME: ______________________ ■ Date: __________

Argumentation: "Trading organizations were more important than the state in promoting long-distance trade."

Support, modify, or refute this statement with specific historical evidence.

Thesis Statement:

■ NAME: ______________________________ ■ Date: ____________

Argumentation: "Epidemic disease only had negative effects on humankind."

Support, modify, or refute this statement with specific historical evidence.

Thesis Statement:

■ NAME: ______________________ ■ Date: __________

Argumentation: "Religious institutions weakened the power of state structure."

Support, modify, or refute this statement with specific historical evidence.

Thesis Statement:

■ NAME: ______________________ ■ Date: ____________

Argumentation: "Islam was the first transregional religion."

Support, modify, or refute this statement with specific historical evidence.

Thesis Statement:

____

____

____

____

____

____

____

■ NAME: ____________________ ■ Date: __________

Argumentation: "Interregional conflicts led to death and destruction."

Support, modify, or refute this statement with specific historical evidence.

Thesis Statement:

■ NAME: ______________________ ■ Date: __________

Argumentation: "The fate of cities varied greatly over time."

Support, modify, or refute this statement with specific historical evidence.

Thesis Statement:

■ NAME: ______________________________ ■ Date: ______________

Argumentation: "Although there were multiple types of coerced labor, they all netted the same results: increased crop production."

Support, modify, or refute this statement with specific historical evidence.

Thesis Statement:

■ NAME: ______________________ ■ Date: __________

Argumentation: "The terms *peasant* and *serf* are essentially interchangeable."

Support, modify, or refute this statement with specific historical evidence.

Thesis Statement:

■ NAME: ______________________ ■ Date: ____________

Argumentation: "If Zheng He had been allowed to keep sailing, China would have been able to rule the Americas."

Support, modify, or refute this statement with specific historical evidence.

Thesis Statement:

____

____

____

____

____

____

____

■ NAME: ______________________ ■ Date: __________

Argumentation: "Europe only modernized because of the Americas."

Support, modify, or refute this statement with specific historical evidence.

Thesis Statement:

■ NAME: ______________________ ■ Date: __________

Argumentation: "The Byzantine Empire was not significantly different from the Roman Empire."

Support, modify, or refute this statement with specific historical evidence.

Thesis Statement:

____

____

____

____

____

____

____

■ NAME: ______________________ ■ Date: __________

Argumentation: "Maritime empires were different than land empires."

Support, modify, or refute this statement with specific historical evidence.

Thesis Statement:

■ NAME: ______________________ ■ Date: __________

Argumentation: "The Great Dying in America and the Black Death in Europe had similar effects."

Support, modify, or refute this statement with specific historical evidence.

Thesis Statement:

■ **NAME:** ______________________________ ■ **Date:** ____________

Argumentation: "Addictive foods, such as coffee, tobacco, and sugar, allowed for better living conditions."

Support, modify, or refute this statement with specific historical evidence.

Thesis Statement:

■ NAME: ______________________ ■ Date: __________

Argumentation: "After its initial creation shortly after the Neolithic revolution, social hierarchy changed very little until 1750."

Support, modify, or refute this statement with specific historical evidence.

Thesis Statement:

■ **NAME:** ______________________________ ■ **Date:** ____________

Argumentation: "Guns were more effective than other weapons, such as the crossbow and the longbow, in the period from 1450 to 1750."

Support, modify, or refute this statement with specific historical evidence.

Thesis Statement:

■ NAME: ______________________ ■ Date: __________

Argumentation: "The Chinese exam system was an example of meritocracy: induction and promotion solely based on ability."

Support, modify, or refute this statement with specific historical evidence.

Thesis Statement:

■ NAME: ______________________ ■ Date: __________

Argumentation: "Communism was popular in industrializing countries."

Support, modify, or refute this statement with specific historical evidence.

Thesis Statement:

■ NAME: ________________________________ ■ Date: ____________

Argumentation: "After 1810, most Latin American countries were independent."

Support, modify, or refute this statement with specific historical evidence.

Thesis Statement:

■ NAME: ________________________________ ■ Date: ____________

Argumentation: "The major difference between 19th- and early 20th-century empires and previous ones is their size."

Support, modify, or refute this statement with specific historical evidence.

Thesis Statement:

____

____

____

____

____

____

____

■ NAME: ______________________ ■ Date: __________

Argumentation: "Industrialized states were the most successful at implementing social reforms."

Support, modify, or refute this statement with specific historical evidence.

Thesis Statement:

■ NAME: ______________________ ■ Date: __________

Argumentation: "Urbanization raised the standard of living for people."

Support, modify, or refute this statement with specific historical evidence.

Thesis Statement:

■ NAME: ______________________________ ■ Date: ____________

Argumentation: "Colonies were useful mostly because they provided a ready market for manufactured goods."

Support, modify, or refute this statement with specific historical evidence.

Thesis Statement:

■ NAME: ______________________ ■ Date: __________

Argumentation: "Britain's use of favorite minorities changed dynamics within regions."

Support, modify, or refute this statement with specific historical evidence.

Thesis Statement:

■ NAME: ______________________________ ■ Date: ____________

Argumentation: "Women's suffrage ended patriarchy."

Support, modify, or refute this statement with specific historical evidence.

Thesis Statement:

AR26

■ NAME: ______________________ ■ Date: ____________

Argumentation: "Men were the bulk of migrants between 1750 and 1950."

Support, modify, or refute this statement with specific historical evidence.

Thesis Statement:

Student Instructions: Interpretation

When we are asked to make historical interpretations, we are asked to read and interpret excerpts from secondary sources. The difference between primary and secondary sources is the nature of when the excerpts were written. Primary sources are written by the historical figures under investigation. Secondary sources are written by historians about the historical figures under investigation. Sometimes secondary sources can become primary sources if the nature of the writing becomes so important that it lasts well into the future. Historical interpretation can involve either primary or secondary sources, but for the purposes of this workbook, we will strictly stick to secondary sources.

The purpose of these Interpretation activities is to practice reading a variety of small secondary excerpts from important historical scholarship, which is a challenging task. Historians are often products of their environment, thus the language can serve as a deterrent to the reader. If the language employs terms that are no longer part of the vernacular, then the meaning can be lost. Another reason this can be a challenging task is that historians often agree on something but disagree with regard to the importance of the event under investigation. For example, two historians may agree that the rise of the Nazi party in Germany was a bad thing, but they may disagree as to why it was bad. Since this is one of the primary purposes of historiography—that is, the interpretation and writing of historical events—it is important that we effectively engage secondary sources and interpret their different arguments.

Interpretation: Creation of Patriarchy (Example)

A: In Mesopotamian societies the institutionalization of patriarchy created sharply defined boundaries between women of different classes, although the development of the new gender definitions and of the customs associated with them proceeded unevenly. The state, during the process of the establishment of written law codes, increased the property rights of upper-class women, while it circumscribed their sexual rights and finally totally eroded them. The lifelong dependency of women on fathers and husbands became so firmly established in law and custom as to be considered "natural" and god-given. In the case of lower-class women, their labor power served either their families or those who owned their families' services. Their sexual and reproductive capacities were commodified, traded, leased, or sold in the interest of male family members. Women of all classes had traditionally been excluded from military power and were, by the turn of the first millennium BC, excluded from formal education, insofar as it had been institutionalized.—Gerda Lerner, *The Creation of Patriarchy*, 1986

B. What was the real cause of the rise of patriarchy, which became increasingly oppressive to women in the Near East after Sumerian civilization waned? Several reasons suggest themselves. The first is militarism . . . Second, where commercialism held sway at the same time [as militarism] the worst examples of patriarchy were found. The third factor [for increasing patriarchy]: confidence [or more specifically, lack of confidence.] It is the threatened male and the threatened society . . . which created such a restricted role for women.—Barbara S. Lesko, "Women of Egypt and the Ancient Near East," 1987

Specific historical evidence to SUPPORT the interpretation above (not mentioned in passage):

Archaeologists and anthropologists agree that the rise of patriarchy occurred in history in tandem with urban living and the rise of large cities and the later rise of states.

Specific historical evidence to SUPPORT the interpretation above (not mentioned in passage):

With the coming of agriculture, people began to lead a sedentary rather than nomadic life. The large amounts of fields and people needed to cultivate the crops also left civilizations vulnerable to attack. Because men worked to defend cities, they gained a measure of power that women could not enjoy since they did not go into combat.

Specific historical evidence to REFUTE the interpretation above (not mentioned in passage):

Erosion of women's rights occurred as land became more valuable and the measure of wealth. Under nomadism and even in early agricultural villages, the property of men and women were roughly equal in value. Once land became the premier commodity, however, women's property lost relative value. This meant that it became important that only heirs inherited property, thus causing women's reproductive rights to be severely controlled. This required women to be under the almost-constant vigilance of men.

■ NAME: ______________________________ ■ Date: ____________

Interpretation: Creation of Patriarchy

A: In Mesopotamian societies the institutionalization of patriarchy created sharply defined boundaries between women of different classes, although the development of the new gender definitions and of the customs associated with them proceeded unevenly. The state, during the process of the establishment of written law codes, increased the property rights of upper-class women, while it circumscribed their sexual rights and finally totally eroded them. The lifelong dependency of women on fathers and husbands became so firmly established in law and custom as to be considered "natural" and god-given. In the case of lower-class women, their labor power served either their families or those who owned their families' services. Their sexual and reproductive capacities were commodified, traded, leased, or sold in the interest of male family members. Women of all classes had traditionally been excluded from military power and were, by the turn of the first millennium BC, excluded from formal education, insofar as it had been institutionalized.—Gerda Lerner, *The Creation of Patriarchy*, 1986

B. What was the real cause of the rise of patriarchy, which became increasingly oppressive to women in the Near East after Sumerian civilization waned? Several reasons suggest themselves. The first is militarism . . . Second, where commercialism held sway at the same time [as militarism] the worst examples of patriarchy were found. The third factor [for increasing patriarchy]: confidence [or more specifically, lack of confidence.] It is the threatened male and the threatened society . . . which created such a restricted role for women.—Barbara S. Lesko, "Women of Egypt and the Ancient Near East," 1987

Specific historical evidence to SUPPORT the interpretation above (not mentioned in passage):

____

____

____

____

____

Specific historical evidence to SUPPORT the interpretation above (not mentioned in passage):

____

____

____

____

____

Specific historical evidence to REFUTE the interpretation above (not mentioned in passage):

■ NAME: ______________________________ ■ Date: ____________

Interpretation: Indus Valley Civilizations

A: What seems clear is that between 1500 and 100 BC, Aryan tribes conquered the remaining pre-Aryans *dasas* through the Indus Valley and the Punjab, moving as far east as the plains of Delhi. When they first reached India, the Aryans were still pastoral nomads; hence no trace has been found of their villages or huts. By the end of this half-millennium, however, no doubt because of much they learned about urban civilization from the *dasas* they enslaved, Aryan cities began to rise on those plains around Delhi, whose first capital was named for Lord Indra (*Indraprastha*).—Stanley Wolpert, *India,* 1991

B: The decline of the cities [of Mohenjo-Daro and Harappa] was once ascribed to invading Aryans. However, there is little archaeological evidence for the type of massive invasion that would have led to the collapse of a well-established political and economic system, resulting in a displacement of culture, although the denial of an invasion does not preclude the possibility of migrants bringing the Indo-Aryan language into India. The argument supporting an invasion was based on the subsequent culture of the Vedic corpus, using a language—Indo-Aryan—that has affinities with central Asian Indo-European, particularly with Old Iranian. That this language gained currency in northern India was thought to be the result of a conquest of the local population by Indo-Aryan speakers, the evidence being drawn from the hostility of the *arya* toward the *dasa* in the *Rig-Veda.* The reference to Indra attaching the *pur*, enclosed settlements of the *dasas*, was erroneously read as referring to the cities of the Indus civilization. However, there are alternative explanations for the introduction of Indo-Aryan into India and its gradual spread across northern India. These explanations have more to do with the historical context of urban decline the coexistence of differing cultures or languages, and the filtering of Indo-Aryan speaker into north India through small-scale migrations, than with the overly simplistic theory of an invasion as a historical explanation.—Romila Thapar, *Early India*, 2004

Specific historical evidence to SUPPORT the interpretation above (not mentioned in passage):

____

____

____

____

____

Specific historical evidence to SUPPORT the interpretation above (not mentioned in passage):

____

____

____

____

____

Specific historical evidence to REFUTE the interpretation above (not mentioned in passage):

■ NAME: ______________________________ ■ Date: ____________

Interpretation: Patriotism in Sparta

A: Had it not been for the Spartans' remarkably successful organization of their society into a well-oiled military machine, and their diplomatic development of a rudimentary multi-state Greek alliance well before the Persians came to Greece, there would have been no core of leadership around which the Greek resistance could coalesce. Had it not been for the Spartans' suicidal but heroic stand at Thermopylae, which showed that the Persians could be resisted, it is unlikely that the small, wavering, and uncohesive force of loyalist Greeks would have had the nerve to imagine that they one day might win.—Paul Cartledge, "To Die For," 2002

B: All were killed. No Spartan survived the final day of the Battle of Thermopylae. Deserted by their allies, even the Thespaseans, who had stood by the longest, the survivors of the three-hundred-man contingent sent by Sparta to face the massive invading army of Xerxes stood firm and fought. Each knew his fate: death on this day in battle. No one lived to give an account of the slaughter and desperate valor of the final hours.—Byron Farwell, "The Spartan Way," 1999

Specific historical evidence to SUPPORT the interpretation above (not mentioned in passage):

____

____

____

____

____

Specific historical evidence to SUPPORT the interpretation above (not mentioned in passage):

____

____

____

____

____

Specific historical evidence to REFUTE the interpretation above (not mentioned in passage):

____

____

____

____

____

■ NAME: ______________________________ ■ Date: ____________

Interpretation: Alexander the Great

A: When his forces were assembled at Susa, Alexander announced to them that all exiles, except those under a curse and those exiled from Thebes, were to be recalled and reinstated . . . The wording was as follows: "Alexander to the exiles from the Greek cities . . . We shall be responsible for your return . . . we have written to Antipater about this, in order that he may compel any states which are unwilling to restore you" . . . The purpose of Alexander was twofold: to resettle the floating population of exiles (we may call them refugees today), which caused instability and often led to mercenary service; and to reconcile the parties which had fought one another and caused the vicious circle of revolutionary faction.—N.G.L. Hammond, *The Genius of Alexander the Great*, 1997

B: Alexander's autocratic nature and its adverse impact on his army has been illustrated many times, but it extended beyond the men with him to the Greeks back on the mainland. One example is his Exiles Decree of 324, which ordered all exiles to return to their native cities (excluding those under a religious curse and the Thebans). If any city was unwilling, then Antipater was authorized to use force against it. The context was no doubt to send home the large bands of mercenaries now wandering the empire and which posed no small military or political danger. The decree was technically illegal since it clearly flouted the autonomy of the Greek state, not to mention the principles of the League of Corinth, but Alexander cared little about polis autonomy or the feelings of the Greeks.—Ian Worthington, "How 'Great' Was Alexander?" 1999

Specific historical evidence to SUPPORT the interpretation above (not mentioned in passage):

____

____

____

____

____

Specific historical evidence to SUPPORT the interpretation above (not mentioned in passage):

____

____

____

____

____

Specific historical evidence to REFUTE the interpretation above (not mentioned in passage):

■ NAME: ______________________________ ■ Date: ____________

Interpretation: The Fall of Rome

A: There is no good case for claiming that the enemies of the Late Roman Empire were simply more formidable than those of earlier periods. This also makes it harder to argue that the Roman Empire had to adapt in the third century to face new and more dangerous threats, most of all the Sassanid 'superpower.' Does this mean that it was the sheer quantity rather than the scale of individual threats that was the problem? There certainly do seem to have been more major wars in the third and subsequent centuries than in the early Principate. In particular, raiding by barbarian groups in Europe is much more prominent in our sources. Such predatory attacks, often on a small scale, were not new. In the past they had always increased in scale and frequency whenever the frontier defenses were perceived to be weak. An impression of vulnerability encouraged attacks and this makes it hard to judge whether an increase in raids and invasions was the consequence of a rise in barbarian numbers and strength or a result of Roman weakness. It is clear that all of Rome's enemies, including the Persians, exploited the empire's frequent internal disputes and civil wars.—Adrian Goldsworthy, *How Rome Fell: Death of a Superpower*, 2009

B: The Western [Roman] Empire was poorer and less populous, and its social and economic structure more unhealthy. It was thus less able to withstand the tremendous strains imposed by its defensive effort, and the internal weaknesses which it developed undoubtedly contributed to its final collapse in the fifth century. But the major cause of its fall was that it was more exposed to barbarian onslaughts which in persistence and sheer weight of numbers far exceeded anything which the empire had previously had to face. The Eastern [Byzantine] Empire, owing to its greater wealth and population and sounder economy was better able to carry the burden of defense, but its resources were overstrained and it developed the same weaknesses as the West, if perhaps in a less acute form. Despite these weaknesses, it managed in the sixth century not only to hold its own against the Persians in the East but to reconquer parts of the West, and even when, in the seventh century, it was overrun by the onslaughts of the Persian and the Arabs and the Slaves it succeeded despite heavy territorial losses in rallying and holding its own. The internal weaknesses of the empire cannot have been a major factor in its decline.— H. M. Jones, *The Later Roman Empire*, Volume II, 1964

Specific historical evidence to SUPPORT the interpretation above (not mentioned in passage):

____

____

____

____

____

Specific historical evidence to SUPPORT the interpretation above (not mentioned in passage):

Specific historical evidence to REFUTE the interpretation above (not mentioned in passage):

■ NAME: ______________________________ ■ Date: ____________

Interpretation: Early Christians and the Role of Women

A: Paul's letters offer some important glimpses into the inner workings of ancient Christian churches. These groups did not own church buildings but met in homes, no doubt due in part to the fact that Christianity was not legal in the Roman world of its day and in part because of the enormous expense to such fledgling societies. Such homes were a domain in which women played key roles. It is not surprising then to see women taking leadership roles in house churches. Paul tells of women who were leaders of such house churches (Apphia in Philemon2; Prisca in I Corinthians 16:19). This practice is confirmed by other texts that also mention women who headed churches in their homes such as Lydia of Thyatira (Acts 16:15) and Nympha of Laodicea (Colossians 4:15). Women held offices and played significant roles in group worship. Paul, for example, greets a deacon named Phoebe (Romans 16:1) and assumes that women are praying and prophesying during worship (I Corinthians 11). As prophets, women's roles would have included not only ecstatic public speech, but preaching, teaching, leading prayer, and perhaps even performing the eucharist meal.—Karen L. King "Women in Ancient Christianity: The New Discoveries," 1998

B: In both the first and second centuries, the radical hospitality and table culture of the house churches, following the examples of Jesus, was an invitation to scandal: Uncovered women, eating and talking with men- teaching men! They could be nothing else but prostitutes and courtesans. Celibate women- in particular- were thought of as sexual deviants and outlaws, because of their defiance of the enforced convention. They rebelled against the state which imposed strict marriage and childbearing requirements on women, backed up by severe punishments written into the Roman law codes. The very existence of Christian women who deliberately chose a life of celibacy posed an embarrassment to the honor of the law-abiding, paternalistic Roman household.—Lisa Bellan-Boyer, "Conspicuous in Their Absence: Women in Early Christianity," 2003

Specific historical evidence to SUPPORT the interpretation above (not mentioned in passage):

____

____

____

____

____

Specific historical evidence to SUPPORT the interpretation above (not mentioned in passage):

____

____

____

____

____

Specific historical evidence to REFUTE the interpretation above (not mentioned in passage):

■ NAME: ______________________________ ■ Date: ____________

Interpretation: Maya Civilization

A: The war between Kaan and Mutal [two Mayan city-states] lasted more than a century and consumed much of the Maya heartland. Kaan's strategy was to surround Mutal and its subordinate city-states with a ring of enemies. By conquest, negation and marriage alliance, Kaan succeeded in encircling its enemy—but not in winning the war. . . . Kaan's loss marks the onset of the Maya collapse. Kaan never recovered from its defeat; Mutal lasted another century before it, too, sank into oblivion. Between 800 and 830 A.D, most of the main dynasties fell; cities winked out throughout the Maya heartland.—Charles Mann, *1491: New Revelations of the Americas before Columbus*, 2005

B: In a pattern of cyclical inevitability that the Maya themselves would have understood, any civilization tends to accumulate imbalances and tensions within the very system that has created its success. The Maya were no exception, for centuries of growth produced intolerable strains which in the end proved socially and politically explosive . . . The picture that emerges is of the environment progressively degraded, of Maya agriculture reaching the very limits of its capacity and being unable to feed populations adequately.—David Drew, *The Lost Chronicles of the Maya Kings*, 1999

Specific historical evidence to SUPPORT the interpretation above (not mentioned in passage):

____

____

____

____

____

Specific historical evidence to SUPPORT the interpretation above (not mentioned in passage):

____

____

____

____

____

Specific historical evidence to REFUTE the interpretation above (not mentioned in passage):

____

____

____

____

____

NAME: ____________________ Date: __________

Interpretation: The University System

A: Europe was in its medieval period when the Muslims wrote a colorful chapter in history of education . . . The Muslims assimilated through their educational system the best of classical cultures and improved them. Among the assimilated fields were philosophy and Hellenistic medical, mathematical, and technological sciences; Hindu mathematics, medicine, and literature; Persian religions, literature, and sciences; and Syrian commentaries on Hellenistic science and philosophy. By applying the classical sciences to practical pursuits, the Muslims developed the empirical-experimental method. Later the method was adopted in Europe . . . They introduced the sciences and philosophy of the Greeks, Persians, and Hindus to Western Christian schoolmen . . . Throughout the twelfth and part of the thirteenth centuries, Muslim works on science, philosophy, and other fields were translated into Latin, particularly from Spain, and enriched the curriculum of the West, especially in northwestern Europe.—Mehdi Nakosteen, *History of Islamic Origins of Western Education, AD 800–1350*, 1964

B: The University is a European institution; indeed, it is the European institution par excellence. As a community of teacher and taught, accorded certain rights, such as administrative autonomy and the determination and realization of curricula and of the objectives of research as well as the award of publicly recognized degrees, it is a creation of medieval Europe, which was the Europe of Paper Christianity . . . Moreover, the university is a European institution because it has, in its social role, performed certain functions of all European societies. It has developed and transmitted scientific and scholarly knowledge and the methods of cultivating that knowledge with has arisen and formed part of the common European intellectual tradition. It has at the same time formed an academic elite, the ethos of which rests on common European values and which transcends all national boundaries.—Hilde de Ridder-Symoens, ed. *A History if the University in Europe*, Volume 1, 1992

Specific historical evidence to SUPPORT the interpretation above (not mentioned in passage):

____

____

____

____

____

Specific historical evidence to SUPPORT the interpretation above (not mentioned in passage):

____

____

____

____

____

Specific historical evidence to REFUTE the interpretation above (not mentioned in passage):

■ NAME: ________________ ■ Date: ________

Interpretation: Zheng He

A: In 1405, China's progressive attitude toward exploitation of the sea culminated in a series of naval expeditions into the South China Sea and the Indian Ocean . . . But China's prominence as the world's largest naval and maritime power was short-lived. The last of seven expeditions ended in 1433; never again were naval expeditions attempted by emperors. As a result, it is tempting to dismiss these voyages as a temporary aberration of the Chinese emperor who sponsored them. To do so, however, would be to ignore the ineluctable influence of the maritime spirit on China, particularly the growing awareness of the potential of sea power to expand and control the tribute system. At the same time, the subsequent cessation of the voyages clearly highlights the equally strong force of continentalism among member of the imperial court as they attempted to steer China away from maritime pursuits. —Bruce Swanson, *Eighth Voyage of the Dragon: A History of China's Quest for Sea Power*, 1982

B: The disappearance of the great Chinese fleet from a great India port symbolized one of history's biggest lost opportunities—Asia's failure to dominate the second half of this millennium. So how did this happen? . . . While Zheng He was crossing the Indian Ocean, the Confucian scholar—officials who dominated the upper echelons of the Chinese Government were at political war with the eunuchs, a group they regarded as corrupt and immoral. The eunuch's role at court involved looking after the concubines, but they also served as palace administrators, often doling out contracts in exchange for kickbacks. Partly as a result of their legendary greed, they promoted commerce. Unlike the scholars—who owed their position to their mastery of 2,000 year old texts—the eunuchs, lacking any roots in a classical past, were sometimes outward-looking and progressive. Indeed, one can argue that it was the virtuous, incorruptible scholars who in the mid-15th century set China on its disastrous course.—Nicholas D. Kristof, "1492: The Prequel," 1999

Specific historical evidence to SUPPORT the interpretation above (not mentioned in passage):

____

____

____

____

____

Specific historical evidence to SUPPORT the interpretation above (not mentioned in passage):

____

____

____

____

____

Specific historical evidence to REFUTE the interpretation above (not mentioned in passage):

■ NAME: ______________________________ ■ Date: ____________

Interpretation: Columbus's Voyage

A: [Christopher Columbus] and the culture he represented have been castigated for initiating the modern cultural dominance of Europe and every subsequent world evil: colonialism, slavery, cultural imperialism, environmental damage, and religious bigotry. There is a kernel of truth to these charges, but obviously to equate a single individual or a complex entity like culture with what are currently judged to be the negative dimension of the emergence of an interconnected human world is to do great historical injustice to both individuals and ideas.—Robert Royal, *First Things*, 1999

B: Christopher Columbus, with the authorization of a letter from the Spanish monarchs to the emperor of China, had discovered this paradise through a geographical error that changed the course of history. On the eve of his arrival, he wrote in his shipboard diary that they were met on the beach by natives as naked as the day they were born, handsome, gentle, and so innocent they traded all they had for strings of colored beads and tin trinkets. But his heart almost burst from his chest when he discovered that their nose rings were made of gold, and their bracelets, necklaces, earrings, and ankles; that they had gold bells to play with and some sheathed their private parts in gold. Those splendid ornaments, and not their human values, condemned the natives to their roles as protagonists in the second Genesis which began that day. Many of them died not knowing where the invaders had come from. Many of the invaders died not knowing where they were. Five centuries later the descendants of both still do not know who we are.—Gabriel Garcia Marquez, "For a Country within Reach of the Children," *America's Magazine*, Volume 49, Number 6, 1997

Specific historical evidence to SUPPORT the interpretation above (not mentioned in passage):

____

____

____

____

____

Specific historical evidence to SUPPORT the interpretation above (not mentioned in passage):

____

____

____

____

____

Specific historical evidence to REFUTE the interpretation above (not mentioned in passage):

■ NAME: ______________________________ ■ Date: ____________

Interpretation: The Beginning of the Enlightenment

A: In the eighteenth century, attention became focused, perhaps for the first time ever, on the future rather than the past and the drive to create a better future generated a belief in progress. The achievements of scientists like Isaac Newton and philosophers like John Locke bred new faith in man's right and power to achieve knowledge of himself and the natural world, and encouraged practical action in such fields as overseas exploration, technology, manufactures, social science and legal reform. Philosophers became committed to the ending of religious strife, bigotry, ignorance, prejudice and poverty, and the creation of polite new social environments and lifestyles.—Roy Porter, "Matrix of Modernity," 2001

B: Definition of the Enlightenment used to be a straightforward matter. It was a group of French philosophers, the *philosophes*, who along with a few curious foreign visitors gathered in Paris in the middle decades of the eighteenth century to talk and to write about ways of improving the world. While the subjects they discussed were many and varied, they shared and expounded a common set of values, prominent among which were reasons, humanity, liberty and tolerance. The Enlightenment, in other words, existed in a certain time and place, was identified with a group of men, and was characterized by specific ideas . . . The intensive discussion of ideas of human betterment, and their critical application to the existing social and political order, a discussion which took place almost everywhere in the European world in the mid- and late-eighteenth century, did not occur in eighteenth-century England.—John Robertson, "The Enlightenment," 1997

Specific historical evidence to SUPPORT the interpretation above (not mentioned in passage):

____

____

____

____

____

Specific historical evidence to SUPPORT the interpretation above (not mentioned in passage):

____

____

____

____

____

Specific historical evidence to REFUTE the interpretation above (not mentioned in passage):

■ NAME: ______________________ ■ Date: __________

Interpretation: French Revolution

A: The France we see during the last days of the eighteenth century, at the moment of the Coup D'état on the 18th Brumaire, is not the France that existed before 1789. Would it have been possible for the old France, wretchedly poor and with a third of her population suffering yearly from dearth, to have maintained the Napoleonic Wars, coming so soon after the terrible wars of the Republic between 1792 and 1799, when all Europe was attacking her? The fact is, that a new France had been constituted since 1792–1793. Scarcity still prevailed in many of the departments, and its full horrors were felt especially after the coup d'état of Thermidor, when the maximum price for all foodstuffs was abolished. There were still some departments which did not produce enough wheat to feed themselves, and as the war went on, and all means of transport were requisitioned for its supplies, there was scarcity in those departments. But everything tends to prove that France was even then producing much more of the necessaries of life of every kind than in 1789.—Peter Kropotkin, *The Great French Revolution, 1789–1793*, 1971

B: The French naturally see their revolution as the great founding act of modern political culture. In their view, it provided the model for the process of revolution; it explored the principles central to modern political concepts; its institutional experiments left a framework for others to build on. As liberal and democratic thought and practice emerged in continental Europe—especially in the German, Italian and Spanish lands occupied under Napoleon—it was the revolution that informed them . . . The revolution's high ideals of a regenerated man in a regenerated society culminated in the guillotine and the substitution of the state for the sovereignty of the nation. This tragedy also was not without import for the next 200 years.—*Economist* staff writer, "The French Revolution: Bliss Was It in that Dawn?," *Economist*, 1988

Specific historical evidence to SUPPORT the interpretation above (not mentioned in passage):

____

____

____

____

____

Specific historical evidence to SUPPORT the interpretation above (not mentioned in passage):

____

____

____

____

____

Specific historical evidence to REFUTE the interpretation above (not mentioned in passage):

■ NAME: ______________________ ■ Date: __________

Interpretation: Irish Potato Famine

A: The response of the British government to the [Irish Potato] Famine was inadequate in terms of humanitarian criteria, and increasingly after 1847, systematically and deliberately so. The localized shortages that followed the blight of 1845 were adequately dealt with but, as shortages became more widespread, the government retrenched. With the short-lived exception of the soup kitchens, access to relief—or even more importantly, access to food—became more restricted. That the response illustrated a view of Ireland and its people as distant and marginal is hard to deny . . . There was no shortage of resources to avoid the tragedy of a Famine. Within Ireland itself there were substantial resources of food which, had the political will existed, could have been diverted, even as a short-term measure, to supply a starving people. Instead, the government pursued the objective of economic, social and agrarian reform as a long-term aim, although the price paid for this ultimately elusive goal was privation, disease, emigration, mortality and an enduring legacy of disenchantment.—Christine Kinealy, *This Great Calamity: The Irish Famine 1845–52*, 1995

B: The [Irish Potato] Famine might be seen as the great convincer. It demonstrated to all the folly of agrarian practices that denied a postage-stamp-size piece of land as enough just because it brought forth potatoes. Irish agriculture was going to have to become much more diversified, and though potatoes would remain a central dish on the Irish family's table, that same farm family would also have to produce a cash crop as well as butter, eggs, and other dairy products for markets. The Famine also demonstrated to Irish parents that no one prospered if they cut up their holdings into equal portions for all their sons. An inheritance came to be the entire holding or nothing. Similarly, the Famine also convinced Irish men and women that early marriage was reckless marriage; that non-marriage was an option too. As the Irish changed their marriage patterns, they basically adapted the behavior to the more economically stable elements in the society, convinced that the devastation and destruction of the late 1840s had in part been caused by irrational, carefree marriage and family practices that failed to treat conjugal life as a fundamentally economic enterprise.—Hasia R. Diner, *Erin's Daughters in America: Irish Immigrant Women in the Nineteenth Century*, 1983

Specific historical evidence to SUPPORT the interpretation above (not mentioned in passage):

____

____

____

____

____

Specific historical evidence to SUPPORT the interpretation above (not mentioned in passage):

Specific historical evidence to REFUTE the interpretation above (not mentioned in passage):

Interpretation: Capitalism and Confucianism

A: Classical capitalism that first set the West on its course towards economic prosperity. The fundamental tenets of classical capitalism are perfectly compatible with the key elements of Chinese philosophy. Indeed, many historians of ideas have traced the origins of classical capitalism all the way back to Chinese thought . . . Economic harmony will be attained if the opposing forces in the economy are kept in a balance, if no one economic system is allowed to dominate the others. Thus, only a competitive economic system is consistent with the Chinese idea of harmony. A system consisting of monopolies, state of private, lacks the checks and balances necessary for harmony. Such a system may be stable in the sense of producing a technical equilibrium with predictable an non-fluctuating outputs and prices, but it is not harmonious and is contrary to the order of nature, contrary to the tao.—T. Nuyin, "Chinese Philosophy and Western Capitalism," 1999

B: Confucius saw commerce as a pursuit of low status, an attitude that would persist in China except for the small entrepreneurial class that emerged around the European Enclaves in the late nineteenth century. These entrepreneurs became the "overseas Chinese," the foundation of expatriate communities in Hong Kong, Singapore, Vietnam, and elsewhere after the communist victory in 1949.—Jack Scarborough, "Comparing Chinese and Western Cultural Roots: Why 'East Is East and . . . ,'" 1998

Specific historical evidence to SUPPORT the interpretation above (not mentioned in passage):

______

______

______

______

______

Specific historical evidence to SUPPORT the interpretation above (not mentioned in passage):

______

______

______

______

______

Specific historical evidence to REFUTE the interpretation above (not mentioned in passage):

■ NAME: ______________________ ■ Date: ____________

Interpretation: Japanese Modernism

A: The Japanese mode of modern revolution was not unique. Rather, it contrasted with earlier Western revolutions and resembled some later ones. This sort of elite-led revolution took place in Japan because of particular features of the samurai class, both weaknesses and strengths. On the negative side, change was possible because the samurai were not securely landed elite. They were essentially salaried employees of their lords. Although this status was hereditary, it was less rooted in property than a European-style feudal estate, a Chinese gentry holding, or a Korean aristocratic status. The samurai had less to lose than elites in such societies. They were hard-pressed to protect their privilege as hereditary government employees once the new rulers decided to revoke it. Some did protest the actions of their former comrades bitterly, but others were either unable or unwilling to resist. On the positive side, many of the activists in the restoration movement had already developed a commitment to serving and building a realm that went beyond the narrow confines of a single domain. This emerging national consciousness offered a compelling reason for many to accept programs of far-reaching change.—Andrew Gordon, *A Modern History of Japan: From Tokugawa Times to the Present*, 2003

B: History offers many different examples of the kind of motivating force that is capable of overcoming inertia and the bonds of tradition: imperial ambition, religious faith, the pursuit of social justice, the aspirations of a newly emergent class. For Japan, in the nineteenth century, nationalism had this function. Again and again there are phrases that put policy of every kind—economic and political, as well as diplomatic—into the context of the "national" interest, justifying proposals on the grounds that they would "restore our national strength" or "make the imperial dignity resound beyond the seas." What is more, most of the major political crises centered on the question of Japan's relations with the outside world. Throughout, Japanese opinion was moving from a consciousness of foreign threat to an awareness of national identity, expressed in demands for unity and independence.— W. G. Beasley, *Meiji Restoration*, 1972

Specific historical evidence to SUPPORT the interpretation above (not mentioned in passage):

____

____

____

____

____

Specific historical evidence to SUPPORT the interpretation above (not mentioned in passage):

____

____

____

____

____

Specific historical evidence to REFUTE the interpretation above (not mentioned in passage):

■ NAME: ______________________ ■ Date: ____________

Interpretation: The Scramble for Africa

A: It is admitted by all businessmen that the growth of the powers of production in their country exceeds the growth in consumption, that more goods can be produced than can be sold at a profit, and that more capital exists than can find remunerative investment. It is this economic condition of affairs that forms the taproot of Imperialism. If the consuming public in this country raised its standard of consumption to keep pace with every rise of productive powers, there could be no excess of goods or capital clamorous to use Imperialism in order to find markets: foreign trade would indeed exist, but there would be no difficulty in exchanging a small surplus of our manufactures for the food and raw material we annually absorbed, and all the savings that we made could find employment, if we chose, in home industries.— J.A. Hobson, *Imperialism: A Study*, 1965

B: The Scramble for Africa seems to have emerged from a combination of exaggerated hope and overheated anxiety. The economic conditions of the day, the trough between the first industrial revolution of coal, cotton and iron, and the second of electricity, copper and steel; the appearance of new industrial states protecting themselves with tariffs; the decline in some commodity prices; and the heightened commercial competition everywhere produced all the alarms associated with the transition from one economic system to another. At the same time there were many publicists concerned to argue that Africa was a tropical treasure house, capable of producing plantation corps, base and precious metals, as well as other valuable commodities like rubber and ivory . . . The growth in the palm oil trade, the buoyant prices of rubber and ivory, the discovery of diamonds and then of gold, all seemed to confirm this view. Africa could solve some of the problems of the age. A state which missed out on these opportunities might be imperiled in the future. These hopes and anxieties took some time to foment fully, but by the mid-1880s they were ready to blow the lid off the politicians' restraint.—John M. McKenzie, *Partition of Africa, 1880–1900 and European Imperialism in the Nineteenth Century*, 1983

Specific historical evidence to SUPPORT the interpretation above (not mentioned in passage):

____

____

____

____

____

Specific historical evidence to SUPPORT the interpretation above (not mentioned in passage):

____

____

____

____

____

Specific historical evidence to REFUTE the interpretation above (not mentioned in passage):

■ **NAME:** ______________________________ ■ **Date:** ____________

Interpretation: Boxer Rebellion

A: A wide range of sources, including gazetteers, diaries, official memorials, oral history accounts, and the reports of foreigners, indicate a direct link between the spread and intensification of the Boxer movement, beginning in late 1899, and growing popular nervousness, anxiety, unemployment and hunger occasioned by drought . . . . I do not at all want to suggest that the expansion of the Boxer movement in the spring and summer of 1900 was due to drought alone. Within a given area, the official stance towards the Boxers, pro or con, played a role of perhaps equivalent weight. Nevertheless, drought—and the range of emotions associated with it—was a factor of crucial importance. It is significant, in this connection, that in a number of instances when rain fell to interrupt the drought and possibly bring it to an end, Boxers dropped everything and returned to their fields. Esherick observes that when "a substantial penetrating rain" fell in early April along the Zhili-Shandong border, peasants went home to plant their spring crops, "quieting things down considerably." After being defeated by the foreign forces in Tianjin during a torrential downpour on July 4, fleeing Boxers are reported to have said to one another: "It's raining. We can return home and till the soil. What use is it for us to suffer like this?" The following day, accordingly, most of them dispersed.—Paul A. Cohen, *History in Three Keys: The Boxers as Event, Experience, and Myth*, 1997

B: The Boxers' opposition to the foreign powers and especially to Christianity struck a chord with many Chinese and drew widespread support. China's defeat by Japan in the war over Korea in 1894 was a turning point in perceptions of the foreign threat. The country's perception of itself as the Middle Kingdom, a central realm of civilization surrounded by tributary states, and by savages and barbarians beyond that, had been affirmed by Korea which had conducted an elaborate tributary relationship with China. The loss of Korea, moreover, brought with it humiliating defeat by the Japanese, hitherto often dismissively referred to as 'dwarf pirates.' In the Treaty of Shimonoseki, which concluded the war, China not only agreed to Korean independence but ceded Taiwan to Japan and gave the Japanese the same treaty rights as those of Westerners . . . The news was carried across the country and was talked about by the farmers in Chiqiao village, all of whom opposed the treaty. Li Hongzhang, who had been the chief negotiator on the Chinese side, became extremely unpopular . . . It is important to remember that, though often condemned as ignorant, superstition and xenophobic, the Boxers were acting in an environment where China's changing international situation was widely known and resented.—Henrietta Harrison, "Justice on Behalf of Heaven: The Boxer Movement," *History Today*, 2000

Specific historical evidence to SUPPORT the interpretation above (not mentioned in passage):

____

____

____

____

____

Specific historical evidence to SUPPORT the interpretation above (not mentioned in passage):

Specific historical evidence to REFUTE the interpretation above (not mentioned in passage):

■ NAME: ______________________________ ■ Date: ____________

Interpretation: World War I

A: It was the men gathered at the Imperial Palace in Berlin who pushed Europe over the brink. These men during the week prior to August 1 had, together with the "hawks" in Vienna, deliberately exacerbated the crisis, although they were in the best position to de-escalate and defuse it . . . The Kaiser and his advisors encouraged Vienna to launch a limited war in the Balkans. Their expectations that the war would remain limited turned out to be completely wrong. The Kaiser and his entourage, who under the Reich Constitution at that brief moment held the fate of millions in their hands, were not prepared to beat a retreat and to avoid a world war. The consequences of that total war and the turmoil caused in all spheres of life were enormous. The world had been turned upside down.—Volker R., *Berghahn Imperial Germany, 1871–1914: Economy, Society, Culture, and Politics*, 1994

B: Accounts of the outbreak of World War One often communicate a sense that Britain was propelled into the conflict by force of circumstance, that it was, in some way, an accidental belligerent or a bystander 'dragged' into war by forces beyond its control . . . This, however is not the case for on Monday, 3 August, 1914, London witnessed an uncharacteristic public clamor for intervention that decisively pushed Britain into war . . . There can be little doubt that it was news that Germany intended the invasion of neutral Belgium, guaranteed by Britain under the treaty of 1839, that tilted the balance in favor of a British intervention, changed the public mood from indifference to war fever and propelled the nation towards action.—Christopher Ray, "Britain and the Origins of World War I," *History Review*, 1998

Specific historical evidence to SUPPORT the interpretation above (not mentioned in passage):

____

____

____

____

____

Specific historical evidence to SUPPORT the interpretation above (not mentioned in passage):

____

____

____

____

____

Specific historical evidence to REFUTE the interpretation above (not mentioned in passage):

■ **NAME:** ______________________________ ■ **Date:** ______________

Interpretation: Russian Revolution and Women

A: Russian society before 1917 was a world of patriarchal power, deferential ritual, clear authority patterns, and visible hierarchy with stratified social classes or estates . . . In a series of decrees, codes, electoral laws, and land reforms, the Bolsheviks proclaimed an across-the-board equality of the sexes- the first regime in history ever to do so. All institutions of learning were opened to women and girls. Women attained equal status in marriage- including the right to change or retain their own names- divorce, family and inheritance and equal rights in litigation and the ownership of property . . . Taken together, these measures offered a structure for equality between the sexes unprecedented in history.—Richard Stites, "Women and the Revolutionary Process in Russia," 1987

B: [Are] women and men the same or different? Could a *baba*, generally defined as an ignorant peasant woman, become a comrade, a full-fledged human and citizen? For practical and historical reasons, women, who were less literate than men and who were charged with all household and childcare duties, in addition to whatever work they might have outside the home, could not be reached by Communist activists as easily as men. Many women could not or would not attend meetings with men, nor would they speak out with men present. But the Communists needed to appeal to women in order to mobilize their support. And if the backward *baba* was not made to support the new regime, then she might hinder the revolution and even become a source of counterrevolution (defined in practice as any opposition to Bolshevik policy). And as women would be raising the next generation, it was critical that they understood and supported the new order. The specter of the *baba* who would harm the revolution if not won over became the justification for focusing activism on women separately.—Lesley A. Rimmel, "The Baba and the Comrade: Gender and Politics in Revolutionary Russia," *Women's Review of Books*, 1998

Specific historical evidence to SUPPORT the interpretation above (not mentioned in passage):

____

____

____

____

____

Specific historical evidence to SUPPORT the interpretation above (not mentioned in passage):

____

____

____

____

____

Specific historical evidence to REFUTE the interpretation above (not mentioned in passage):

■ NAME: ______________________________ ■ Date: ____________

Interpretation: Rwandan Genocide

A: Mobilizing thousands of Rwandans to slaughter tens of thousands of others required effective organization. Far from the "failed state" syndrome that appears to plague some parts of Africa, Rwanda was too successful as a state. Extremists used its administrative apparatus, its military, and its party organizations to carry out a "cottage-industry" genocide that reached out to all levels of the population and produced between five hundred thousand and one million victims. Those with state power used their authority to force action from those reluctant to kill. They also offered attractive incentives to people who are very poor, giving license to loot, and promising them the land and businesses of the victims. In some cases, local officials even decided ahead of time the disposition of the most attractive items of movable property. Everyone knew who had a refrigerator, a plush sofa, a radio, and assailants were guaranteed their rewards before attacking. But even with the powerful levers of threat and bribe, officials could not have succeeded so well had people not been prepared to hate and fear the Tutsi. Extremists were ready to use slaughter to hold on to political power constructed an ideology of genocide from a faulty history that had long been accepted by both Hutu and Tutsi. Like the identity cards that had guaranteed privileges to the Tutsi during the colonial period and then served to identify them as victims for the genocide, the history that had once legitimated their rule was ultimately turned against them to justify their massacre.—Alison Des Forges, "The Ideology of Genocide," *Issue: A Journal of Opinion*, 1995

B: Seen in the broader context of 20th-century genocides, the Rwanda tragedy underscores the universality—one might say the normality—of African phenomena. The logic that set in motion the infernal machine of the Rwanda killings is no less "rational" than that which presided over the extermination of millions of human beings in Hitler's Germany or Pol Pot's Cambodia. The Rwanda genocide is neither reducible to a tribal meltdown rooted in atavistic hatreds nor to a spontaneous outburst of blind fury set off by the shooting down of the presidential plane of April 6 . . . However widespread, both views are travesties of reality. What they mask is the political manipulation that lies behind the systematic massacre of civilian populations. Planned annihilation, not the sudden eruption of long-simmering hatreds, is the key to the tragedy of Rwanda.—Rene Lemarchand, "Rwanda: the Rationality of Genocide," *Issue: A Journal of Opinion*, 1995

Specific historical evidence to SUPPORT the interpretation above (not mentioned in passage):

____

____

____

____

____

Specific historical evidence to SUPPORT the interpretation above (not mentioned in passage):

Specific historical evidence to REFUTE the interpretation above (not mentioned in passage):

Student Instructions: Chronological Reasoning

When we are asked to use chronological reasoning, we place a variety of events into historical order. Although it might not seem important to know historical dates, the reality is that dates help us to conceptualize important trends. Understanding when and why things occurred is critical to understanding history. It would be impossible to practice many, if not all, of this workbook's historical thinking skills without the proper chronology of content.

The purpose of the Chronological Reasoning activities is not only to practice placing a number of historical events in the correct order but also to understand how and why things occurred based on that order. This practice will help reinforce your knowledge of the given historical period and will encourage you to think about how these events relate to each other.

■ NAME: ______________________ ■ Date: __________

Chronological Reasoning: The Very Early Years (Example)

Beginning of agricultural revolution in SW Asia	Millet cultivation develops in Huang He River Valley
Pastoralism begins in Inner Asia	Rice cultivation develops in Yangtze
Homo sapiens emerge in Africa and migrate	Maize cultivation begins in central Mexico
Cave art develops in Europe	Neanderthals evident in Europe
Beginning of Ice Age across the Northern Hemisphere	Agricultural settlements using SW Asian domesticants emerge

1ST EVENT Homo sapiens emerge in Africa and migrate

2ND EVENT Beginning of Ice Age across the Northern Hemisphere

3RD EVENT Neanderthals evident in Europe

4TH EVENT Cave art develops in Europe

5TH EVENT Pastoralism begins in Inner Asia

6TH EVENT Beginning of agricultural revolution in SW Asia

7TH EVENT Millet cultivation develops in Huang He River Valley

8TH EVENT Agricultural settlements using SW Asian domesticants emerge

9TH EVENT Rice cultivation develops in Yangtze

10TH EVENT Maize cultivation begins in central Mexico

■ NAME: ______________________ ■ Date: __________

Chronological Reasoning: The Very Early Years

Beginning of agricultural revolution in SW Asia	Maize cultivation begins in central Mexico
Agricultural settlements using SW Asian domesticants emerge	Rice cultivation develops in Yangtze
Homo sapiens emerge in Africa and migrate	Millet cultivation develops in Huang He River Valley
Neanderthals evident in Europe	Pastoralism begins in Inner Asia
Cave art develops in Europe	Beginning of Ice Age across the Northern Hemisphere

1ST EVENT ______________________

2ND EVENT ______________________

3RD EVENT ______________________

4TH EVENT ______________________

5TH EVENT ______________________

6TH EVENT ______________________

7TH EVENT ______________________

8TH EVENT ______________________

9TH EVENT ______________________

10TH EVENT ______________________

■ NAME: ______________________ ■ Date: __________

Chronological Reasoning: Neolithic Period

Minoan culture	Earliest Sumerian cities in southern Mesopotamia appear
Vedic migrations into India	Development of chariot technology
Beginning of Austronesian migrations	Shang state emerges
Sargon's Akkadian territorial state	First writing appears
Cities begin to appear in the Indus Valley	
First dynasty emerges in Egypt	

1ST EVENT ______________________

2ND EVENT ______________________

3RD EVENT ______________________

4TH EVENT ______________________

5TH EVENT ______________________

6TH EVENT ______________________

7TH EVENT ______________________

8TH EVENT ______________________

9TH EVENT ______________________

10TH EVENT ______________________

■ NAME: ______________________ ■ Date: __________

Chronological Reasoning: Early Empires

Chavin culture flourishes in Central Andes of South America	Eastern Zhou Dynasty
Olmec culture emerges and diffuses throughout Mesoamerica	Siddhartha Gautama develops Buddhist principles
Early iron smelting in the Nok culture	Phoenician settlements and trade networks emerge
Plato, Socrates, and Aristotle teach in Athens	Confucius
	Warring states period
	Peloponnesian wars

1ST EVENT ______________________

2ND EVENT ______________________

3RD EVENT ______________________

4TH EVENT ______________________

5TH EVENT ______________________

6TH EVENT ______________________

7TH EVENT ______________________

8TH EVENT ______________________

9TH EVENT ______________________

10TH EVENT ______________________

■ NAME: ____________________ ■ Date: __________

Chronological Reasoning: Early Classical Period

Roman–Carthaginian war	Emergence of Hellenistic kingdoms
Roman expansion in the Italian peninsula begins	Han expands into the Silk Road
Establishment of the Kushan Empire	Emergence of the Han
Conquests of Alexander the Great	Unification of China under the Qin
Mauryan Empire	
Transformation of Buddhism begins	

1ST EVENT ____________________

2ND EVENT ____________________

3RD EVENT ____________________

4TH EVENT ____________________

5TH EVENT ____________________

6TH EVENT ____________________

7TH EVENT ____________________

8TH EVENT ____________________

9TH EVENT ____________________

10TH EVENT ____________________

■ NAME: ____________________ ■ Date: ____________

Chronological Reasoning: Classical Period

Christianity expands to broader Roman Empire	Wang Mang usurps the Han throne
Roman Empire reaches its maximum size under Trajan	Yellow Turban Rebellion
Popular Rebellion against the Han	Parthian Empire
Jesus preaches in Judea	Sassanian Empire supplants Parthian
Roman Empire begins	Augustus reigns as first emperor

1ST EVENT ____________________

2ND EVENT ____________________

3RD EVENT ____________________

4TH EVENT ____________________

5TH EVENT ____________________

6TH EVENT ____________________

7TH EVENT ____________________

8TH EVENT ____________________

9TH EVENT ____________________

10TH EVENT ____________________

■ NAME: ______________________ ■ Date: __________

Chronological Reasoning: Rise of Universal Religions

Xuanzang, Chinese Buddhist pilgrim, visits south Asia	Daoism reforms and gains popularity in East Asia
Emperor Constantine patronizes Christianity in the Roman Empire	Gupta Dynasty begins ruling much of northern India
Nestorian Christianity begins to spread along the Silk Road	Talmud produced in the Levant
Mayan culture reaches its zenith	Transformation of Vedic religions to Hinduism begins
Teotihuacan dominates Mexico valley	Buddhism spreads in Chinese society

1ST EVENT ______________________

2ND EVENT ______________________

3RD EVENT ______________________

4TH EVENT ______________________

5TH EVENT ______________________

6TH EVENT ______________________

7TH EVENT ______________________

8TH EVENT ______________________

9TH EVENT ______________________

10TH EVENT ______________________

■ NAME: ______________________ ■ Date: ____________

Chronological Reasoning: Islam

Abbasid Caliphate	Trans-Saharan trade routes established
Fatimid Caliphate	Islam spreads to Swahili Coast
Ibn Sina publishes *The Canon of Medicine*	Flight to Medina
Umayyad Caliphate	Sunni-Shi'a split
Birth of Muhammad	
Battle of Badr	

1ST EVENT ______________________

2ND EVENT ______________________

3RD EVENT ______________________

4TH EVENT ______________________

5TH EVENT ______________________

6TH EVENT ______________________

7TH EVENT ______________________

8TH EVENT ______________________

9TH EVENT ______________________

10TH EVENT ______________________

■ NAME: ______________________ ■ Date: __________

Chronological Reasoning: Post-Classical Period

Rise of Christian monasticism	Reign of Empress Wu
Great Zimbabwe	Black Death begins in China
Mongols conquer Southern Song Dynasty	Crusades
Toltec Empire begins	
Kingdom of Mali emerges	
Taika reforms in Japan	
Beginning of the Koryo Dynasty	

1ST EVENT ______________________

____

2ND EVENT ______________________

____

3RD EVENT ______________________

____

4TH EVENT ______________________

____

5TH EVENT ______________________

____

6TH EVENT ______________________

____

7TH EVENT ______________________

____

8TH EVENT ______________________

____

9TH EVENT ______________________

____

10TH EVENT ______________________

■ NAME: ____________________ ■ Date: __________

Chronological Reasoning: Hemispheres Unite

Christians complete the Reconquista of Granada	Ming Dynasty falls to Qing
First permanent Portuguese settlement in Macao	Romanov Dynasty established in Russia
Battle of Lepanto	Tokugawa Shogunate founded
Luther posts 95 Theses	Columbus discovers the Americas
Transatlantic slave trade	Consolidation of the Mughal Empire

1ST EVENT ____________________

2ND EVENT ____________________

3RD EVENT ____________________

4TH EVENT ____________________

5TH EVENT ____________________

6TH EVENT ____________________

7TH EVENT ____________________

8TH EVENT ____________________

9TH EVENT ____________________

10TH EVENT ____________________

■ NAME: ______________________ ■ Date: __________

Chronological Reasoning: Early Modern World

Eli Whitney invents the cotton gin	Castas System in New Spain
Matteo Ricci brings cartography to China	James Watt develops the steam engine
John Locke's essay *Concerning Human Understanding*	Chinese expansion under the Qianlong Emperor
Adam Smith's *Wealth of Nations* published	Haitian Revolution
Movement for native learning begins in Japan	End of British involvement in the transatlantic slave trade

1ST EVENT ______________________

2ND EVENT ______________________

3RD EVENT ______________________

4TH EVENT ______________________

5TH EVENT ______________________

6TH EVENT ______________________

7TH EVENT ______________________

8TH EVENT ______________________

9TH EVENT ______________________

10TH EVENT ______________________

■ NAME: ______________________ ■ Date: ____________

Chronological Reasoning: 19th Century

Indian Revolt of 1857
Shaka creates Zulu empire
Raj begins in India
Opening of the Suez Canal
Commodore Perry reforms Japan
Spanish-American War
Russia constructs trans-Siberian railway
Meiji era in Japan
French occupation of Vietnam, Cambodia, and Laos
Taiping Rebellion

1ST EVENT ______________________

2ND EVENT ______________________

3RD EVENT ______________________

4TH EVENT ______________________

5TH EVENT ______________________

6TH EVENT ______________________

7TH EVENT ______________________

8TH EVENT ______________________

9TH EVENT ______________________

10TH EVENT ______________________

■ NAME: ______________________ ■ Date: __________

Chronological Reasoning: Between the 19th and 20th Centuries

Muslim League established	Maji Maji Rebellion
Sino-Japanese war	Indian National Congress established
Chinese Republican Revolution	Boer War
Social welfare laws passed in Germany	Women vote in national elections of Finland for the first time
Russo-Japanese war	
Mexican Revolution	

1ST EVENT ______________________

2ND EVENT ______________________

3RD EVENT ______________________

4TH EVENT ______________________

5TH EVENT ______________________

6TH EVENT ______________________

7TH EVENT ______________________

8TH EVENT ______________________

9TH EVENT ______________________

10TH EVENT ______________________

■ NAME: ______________________ ■ Date: __________

Chronological Reasoning: Early 20th Century

United States enters WWI	Hitler becomes chancellor of Germany
Great Depression begins	Muslim Brotherhood established in Egypt
Great War begins	May Fourth Movement in China
Treaty of Versailles ends WWI	
Japan annexes Manchuria	
Dissolution of the Ottoman Empire	
Bolshevik Revolution	

1ST EVENT ______________________

2ND EVENT ______________________

3RD EVENT ______________________

4TH EVENT ______________________

5TH EVENT ______________________

6TH EVENT ______________________

7TH EVENT ______________________

8TH EVENT ______________________

9TH EVENT ______________________

10TH EVENT ______________________

■ NAME: ______________________ ■ Date: __________

Chronological Reasoning: Beginning of the Cold War

Cuban Missile Crisis	Warsaw Pact formed
Sputnik launched	Algerian War
NATO formed	United States enters WWII
Nationalists fight communists in China	
Pakistan and India gain independence	
Marshall Plan	
Prague Spring	

1ST EVENT ______________________

2ND EVENT ______________________

3RD EVENT ______________________

4TH EVENT ______________________

5TH EVENT ______________________

6TH EVENT ______________________

7TH EVENT ______________________

8TH EVENT ______________________

9TH EVENT ______________________

10TH EVENT ______________________

■ NAME: ______________________ ■ Date: ____________

Chronological Reasoning: New World Order

Khomeini establishes theocratic state in Iran	Germany reunited
NAFTA negotiated	Soviet War in Afghanistan
Eastern European communist regimes toppled	United States' War on Terror begins
Tiananmen Square demonstrations	Free elections in South Africa
Chernobyl nuclear disaster	Dissolution of the Soviet Union

1ST EVENT ______________________

2ND EVENT ______________________

3RD EVENT ______________________

4TH EVENT ______________________

5TH EVENT ______________________

6TH EVENT ______________________

7TH EVENT ______________________

8TH EVENT ______________________

9TH EVENT ______________________

10TH EVENT ______________________